ULTIMATE
PERFORMANCE
CARS
Fast. Faster. Fastest.

ULTIMATE PERFORMANCE CARS

Fast. Faster. Fastest.

General Editor
RICHARD GUNN

MOTORBOOKS
INTERNATIONAL

This edition published in 2005 by
Motorbooks International,
an imprint of MBI Publishing Company,
Galtier Plaza, Suite 200,
380 Jackson Street,
St. Paul, MN 55101-3885
USA

The information in this book is true and complete to the best of our knowledge.
All recommendations are made without any guarantee on the part of the author
or Publisher, who also disclaim any liability incurred in connection with the use
of this data or specific details.

We recognize that some words, model names and designations, for example,
mentioned herein are the property of the trademark holder. We use them for
identification purposes only. This is not an official publication.

Motorbooks International titles are also available at discounts in bulk quantity for
industrial or sales-promotional use. For details write to Special Sales Manager at
Motorbooks International Wholesalers & Distributors, Galtier Plaza, Suite 200,
380 Jackson Street, St. Paul, MN 55101-3885, USA.

ISBN: 0-7603-2203-1

Produced by:
Amber Books Ltd
Bradley's Close
74–77 White Lion Street
London N1 9PF
United Kingdom
www.amberbooks.co.uk

Printed in Singapore

Contents

Introduction 6

AC 12
Aston Martin 16
Audi 24
Bentley 28
Bizzarini 32
BMW 36
Bugatti 48
Buick 52
Callaway 56
Chevrolet 60
De Tomaso 76
Dodge 84
Ferrari 92
Ford 112
Honda 132
Iso 136
Jaguar 140
Jensen 160
Lamborghini 164
Lancia 176
Lotus 188
Maserati 192
Mazda 208
McLaren 212
Mercedes 216
Mercury 224
MG 228
Mitsubishi 232
Nissan 240
Oldsmobile 248
Plymouth 252
Pontiac 260
Porsche 268
Renault 284
Subaru 292
Sunbeam 296
Toyota 300
TVR 304
Vector 312

Glossary of Technical Terms 316
Index 318

Introduction

In theory, of course, all cars are created for one purpose: to carry people from A to B. However, if that were the only reason cars were built, then everything on our roads would be more or less the same, and all cars would be the most innocuous, blandest machines for getting that job done effectively and safely. And wouldn't the world be a far more boring place?

Thankfully, as one quick glance through the pages of this book will prove, not all cars are created

Below: In the 1950s there was little to touch the Mercedes-Benz 300SL for both performance and style, even if its price tag was way beyond most pockets.

equal. A tantalizing few stand out from the crowd so distinctly that there is only one word that can be used to describe them. That word is "ultimate," and this book is a tribute to the automotive greats from around the world that truly deserve this accolade.

Inside this volume you will find some of the most fantastic four-wheeled creations of all time, gathered together to illustrate just how awesome some of the world's ultimate performance cars can be, both in terms of what they do, and how good they look doing it. These wonder machines are as diverse as they are exciting, hailing from America, Europe, and Japan, and built for the road, the rally course, and the race circuit. The styles vary

considerably, and more than four decades separate the earliest and latest cars. Yet all are members of a very exclusive club—one that many aspire to, but few are good enough to join.

It hasn't been an easy task selecting the models featured in this book, as anybody who lives and breathes fast cars will appreciate. Since the first days of the automobile, when those early pioneers bolted primitive internal combustion engines onto basic frames and attached wheels, somebody somewhere has always wanted to go just that little bit faster. That meant thousands of potential vehicles had to be considered for inclusion, all of which could lay claim to being performance machines. For example, to motoring enthusiasts in 1898, the first world speed record of 39.24 mph was

Above: The Ford Mustang brought affordable performance to the masses. Hertz hired out these specially commissioned GT350H models—all of which came in Raven Black with gold stripes—and often found they'd been used for weekend racing!

a feat of engineering which could hardly be believed. To those who witnessed Henry Ford's record-breaking 91.37 mph in his 999 racer of 1904, it must have seemed like an extraordinary achievement. Today these figures pale into insignificance beside the performance of even the humblest family runabout. However, looking back from the first decade of the 21st century, with over a hundred years of motoring now behind us, there are some landmark performers that not only impressed at the time, but continue to astonish even now.

Above: Many sports cars are pretty to look at, but the Jaguar E-type was a cut above the rest. Its 150 mph performance put it among the elite of 1960s performance machines.

Birth of the Performance Car

The 1950s saw the birth of the kind of performance car that can still be appreciated today. With the end of World War II, and a new-found prosperity and optimism flooding through America and Europe, cars started to become more affordable and consequently more available to those who previously couldn't have considered owning one before. But alongside this development in the lower reaches of the market, there was also increased progress at the top end. The newly established Ferrari was forging its reputation, while older marques with sporting heritage started to apply racing technology to road cars. Representative of this era are the Jaguar D-type and the Maserati Birdcage. Ostensibly, both of these were race cars, but both occasionally found

themselves on the roads, driven by the privileged few who could afford the high prices that their raw speeds dictated. The most remarkable of the track-bred cars that made the leap from circuit to street was the groundbreaking Mercedes-Benz 300SL. Its distinctive sleek and sensual design, with "gull wing" doors that lifted upwards instead of outwards, were enough to make it stand out in a crowd, but it was the 300SL's epic performance that made it one of the true greats. Mercedes-Benz claimed that a 300SL could manage 165 mph, and although 130 mph to 150 mph were more realistic figures, nobody could deny that its performance was blistering for its day. Even by current standards, a 183 cu in engine that can propel a car to 60 mph in around eight seconds demands respect, but in 1954 such feats were almost science fiction. The 300SL has been dubbed the first supercar, the stuff of motoring legend, and a template for many of the high-performance machines that would follow it.

The Golden Age of Muscle

It was in the 1960s that performance took off in a big way. This was the golden era of the muscle car in the United States, typified by the hotter versions of the Ford Mustang and its various V8 contemporaries and rivals. Power was everything—especially with fuel being so cheap—and the more cubic inches an owner had under the hood, the more respect could be commanded on the street.

The need for speed was driving the elite of European manufacturers as well. Although the V8 engine would never generate quite the same admiration as it did in the United States, Europe still realised that if you wanted a car that was a cut above its contemporaries, you needed more than just the usual four cylinders. Britain seemed to prefer six, with Jaguar's legendary XK straight-six engine appearing in the sublime road-going sculpture that was the E-type, while Aston Martin captured the attention of the world with its DB4, 5, and 6 range. Being driven by James Bond didn't do Aston Martin any harm of course, but the cars were so charismatic in their own right that they deserved all the adulation they received even without 007's help.

Italy's real love affair was with the V12. Ferrari led the way in 12-cylinder style and sophistication, at least up until the middle of the decade. But 1966 saw the introduction of the only other car to possibly rival the Mercedes-Benz 300SL for the trophy of the world's first supercar… and although it was Italian, it wasn't from the prancing horse's stable. The Lamborghini Miura, intended to show Ferrari a thing or two about how to blend beauty

Below: The Porsche 911 has an instantly recognizable shape which marks it out as a member of a rare breed. Today's 911s still bear a strong resemblance to the originals of 1963, even if the technology under the hood has advanced tremendously.

Above: Designed by a Formula 1 team, the McLaren F1 was stunning in every way. It was more than capable of tearing up racing tracks as well as the open road.

Right: The subtle approach to supercars: take one V10 truck engine, wrap a lightweight skin around it and call it a Dodge Viper. The result is one of the most exhilarating cars ever built.

with speed, was the first production sports car to have its engine mid-mounted. Putting the V12 behind the seats, instead of at the front or the rear, created a perfectly balanced car with handling that had to be experienced to be believed. Which was just as well, because with a top speed of 180mph, and a 0–60mph time of 5.5 seconds, the Lamborghini Miura still needed a skilled driver at the wheel despite its inherent agility.

The Decade of Porsche

The honeymoon for high-performance cars was over by the 1970s, however. Fuel crisis followed fuel crisis, with the economic recession causing problems for the car industry as a whole. It was those who specialized in performance machines who suffered

the most, however. Ferrari, having been taken over by Fiat in 1969, weathered the storm better than most, but companies like Maserati, Lamborghini, and Aston Martin stumbled through several owners in their search for financial security. Only one supercar maker seemed to find its feet during the decade, and that was Porsche. Along with fellow German marque BMW, Porsche pioneered the use of turbocharging in road cars, and nowhere was this application more exciting than in the 911 Turbo. The 911 may have been introduced in the 1960s, but it came of age in the 1970s when turbocharging boosted it from merely extraordinary to simply mind-blowing. In the United States, manufacturers became embroiled in battles against emissions regulations and safety campaigners seeking to emasculate the all-American muscle car. U.S. cars may still have had V8 engines, but a lot of their thunder had been stolen.

Rise of the East

Some of the fun started to come back in the 1980s, as advanced technology began to be applied to engines, making them more efficient yet also more capable too. The decade also saw the first international performance cars emerging from the Far East. Honda took on Italy with the Honda NSX—the first true Japanese supercar—and Mitsubishi joined the party with its Mitsubishi 3000GT. Both Europe and America hit back with some flamboyant inventions in the 1990s. The outrageous Dodge Viper was a compelling reminder that brute strength is always a breathtaking prospect in a sports car, while Ferrari's 1990s creations may have been more subtle in style, but they were just as exhilarating in content. And then there was the McLaren F1, designed by a world-beating Formula 1 team, and perhaps the closest thing to a Grand Prix car for the road there has ever been. With a top speed of 231 mph and the ability to leap from standing to 60 mph in just 3.2 seconds, the McLaren remains the ultimate of ultimate performance cars.

Whether or not the McLaren F1 will ever be equaled or surpassed remains to be seen. Certainly some amazing cars have already marked the opening of the 21st century, despite fresh attempts to condemn such speed machines as extravagant and dangerous. Whatever the future holds, the past half century has produced a rich legacy of extreme performance cars that stir the passions and move the hearts as well as the heads of those who appreciate pure automotive exhilaration. Many of the best of them are in this book. The ultimate performance cars featured here may not have necessarily made the world a better place, but they've certainly made it a lot more exciting.

AC **COBRA 289**

Carroll Shelby had the brilliant idea to crossbreed an AC Ace body and chassis with a Ford V8 engine and the immortal Cobra was born. AC built its chassis in Britain, then shipped it out to California for engine fitting.

"...simply shattering."

"One look at the performance figures for the 289 Cobra tells the story. No other road car in the early 1960s could reach 60 mph so quickly. In a straight line, it is simply shattering, but you have to watch your speed because the Cobra's chassis is hardly sophisticated. Living up to its name, it will snake through bends but it requires the utmost respect and takes skill to pilot properly. The controls are pretty heavy, except for the delightful short-throw gearshift."

Standard interior features include a tachometer and leather bucket seats.

Milestones

1961 Carroll Shelby approaches the Hurlock brothers at AC with the idea to install a V8 engine into their Ace. They jump at the chance.

The AC Ace has more subtle lines than its muscular-looking Cobra offspring.

1962 Production begins at Thames Ditton and Shelby installs 260-cubic inch Ford engines in the U.S.

1963 A larger 289-cubic inch V8 is installed and rack-and-pinion steering replaces worm-and-sector system.

A small number of homologation Cobra 289s were built to qualify the car for sports car racing.

1965 As the monster MKIII Cobra 427 is launched, the 289 model continues into its last year.

1968 Cobra production comes to an end.

UNDER THE SKIN

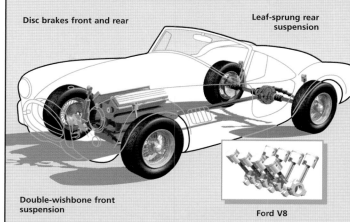

Disc brakes front and rear

Leaf-sprung rear suspension

Double-wishbone front suspension

Ford V8

Tubular chassis

The Cobra's chassis is hardly what one would call sophisticated. It is a slightly strengthened version of the AC Ace chassis and as such, consists of two large tubes joined together with an all-independent suspension, double A-arms and transverse leaf springs. Unlike the Ace, however, the Cobra has four-wheel disc brakes.

THE POWER PACK

Small-block, big bang

The whole point about the Cobra is its engine—an outsized but lightweight Ford V8 shoehorned into a featherweight home. Carroll Shelby had the idea and completed the engine installation in Venice, California. He chose the Ford small-block V8 engine, as Ford was committing itself to a new Total Performance program and was happy to supply engines. Initially the 260-cubic inch V8 was fitted, but only the first 75 cars had this unit. Then Shelby went up to the 289-cubic inch V8 that had a nominal output of 271 bhp, but many were tuned to make more than 300 bhp. It didn't end there, as the Cobra later got Ford's 427 and 428 units.

289 Cobra

While the later wide-bodied 427 steals the limelight with its superior power, in many ways the narrow-arch 289 is purer to Shelby's concept. It is still outrageously fast and there is something fascinating about a beast that can barely be tamed.

The evocative lines of the 289 Cobra continue to draw gasps of admiration.

AC **COBRA 289**

The AC Cobra is the most legendary U.S. sports car ever manufactured. American muscle combined with a lightweight British sports car body to produce a fast machine. On the track it was almost unbeatable.

Ford V8

Ford agreed to supply Carroll Shelby with its V8 engines for use in the Cobra. Cast into the aluminum valve covers were 'Cobra' and 'Powered by Ford.' The 289 small-block engine produced a very healthy 271 bhp but was light enough not to upset the handling.

Manual transmission

Mated to the Ford V8 engine was a Borg-Warner four-speed manual transmission. A Salisbury final drive and limited-slip differential were also standard.

Sports body

The only body option offered for the Cobra was an open sports style shell with a removable soft-top. The coupe option of the earlier Aceca was not carried over.

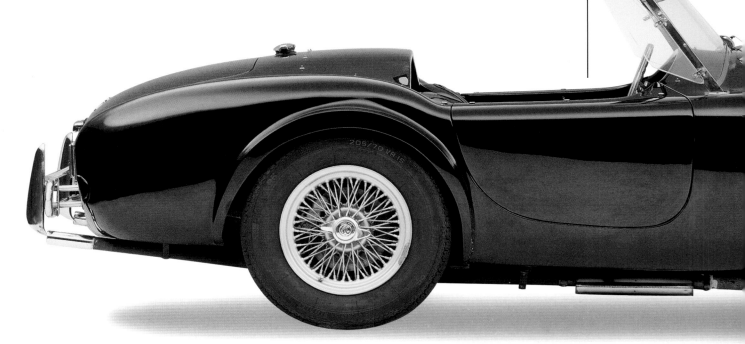

AC chassis

John Tojeiro and John Cooper had built various racing chassis in the early 1950s and the design was adapted to sit under the AC Ace. With surprisingly little modification, this large-diameter twin-tube ladder frame was carried over for the Cobra.

Disc brakes

While the old Ace was equipped with drum brakes, the extra performance of the V8 engine led to the sensible fitment of four-wheel disc brakes.

Wire wheels

72-spoke wire wheels with knock off hubs were standard on all 289 Cobras.

Specifications

1963 Shelby Cobra 289

ENGINE

Type: V8

Construction: Cast-iron cylinder block and cylinder heads

Valve gear: Two valves per cylinder operated by single camshaft with pushrods and rockers

Bore and stroke: 4.00 in. x 2.87 in.

Displacement: 289 c.i.

Compression ratio: 10.5:1

Induction system: Single Holley four-barrel carburetor

Maximum power: 271 bhp at 5,750 rpm

Max torque: 285 lb-ft at 4,500 rpm

Top speed: 140 mph

0–60 mph: 5.5 sec

TRANSMISSION

Four-speed close ratio manual

BODY/CHASSIS

Separate chassis with two-door body in aluminum

SPECIAL FEATURES

The soft-top has a slightly clumsy look to it when up.

The discrete badge just above the cooling vent is the only real clue to the Ford engine.

RUNNING GEAR

Steering: Rack-and-pinion

Front suspension: Wishbones with transverse leaf spring and shocks

Rear suspension: Wishbones with transverse leaf spring and shocks

Brakes: Discs (front and rear)

Wheels: Wire 15-in. dia.

Tires: 6.5 x 15 or 6.7 x 15

DIMENSIONS

Length: 151.5 in.   **Width:** 63.0 in.

Height: 48.0 in.   **Wheelbase:** 90.0 in.

Track: 51.5 in. (front), 52.5 in. (rear)

Weight: 2,020 lbs.

Aston Martin **DB4**

The DB4 was the first in a famous line of Aston Martins. An all-new car, it took the company into the 1960s with a modern performance machine. It was an instant classic and is highly desirable today.

"...a fine grand tourer."

"Stepping inside the DB4, the cabin reeks of class. This is obviously a driver's delight. In standard DB4 tune, the big straight-six is superbly tractable and very torquey. The DB4 GT is definitely more sporty in nature and requires more gear shifts to get the best from it. The ride is excellent for such a sporty car. It is easy to imagine why the DB4 was considered such a fine grand tourer as it effortlessly eats up the miles."

A large-diameter wooden steering wheel dominates the instrument panel.

Milestones

1958 Aston Martin
launches a successor to the DB Mk III. The DB4 is all new, built in Britain but with styling by Touring of Milan. The engine is also new—a 3.7-liter straight six giving a healthy 240 bhp.

A convertible version of the DB4 was also available.

1959 A short-chassis two seater
is built. The DB4 GT has a twin-plug version of the engine that produces 302 bhp.

The rarest and most valuable DB4 variant is the DB4 GT Zagato.

1961 An open-top version,
the Drophead Coupe, is launched.

1962 A high-output engine
giving 266 bhp is part of the Vantage package.

1963 The DB5 replaces
the DB4. Just over 1,200 DB4s have been built.

UNDER THE SKIN

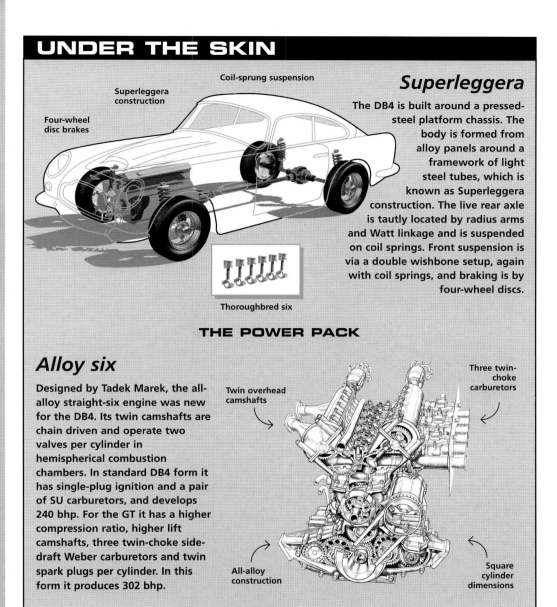

Coil-sprung suspension

Superleggera construction

Four-wheel disc brakes

Thoroughbred six

Superleggera

The DB4 is built around a pressed-steel platform chassis. The body is formed from alloy panels around a framework of light steel tubes, which is known as Superleggera construction. The live rear axle is tautly located by radius arms and Watt linkage and is suspended on coil springs. Front suspension is via a double wishbone setup, again with coil springs, and braking is by four-wheel discs.

THE POWER PACK

Alloy six

Designed by Tadek Marek, the all-alloy straight-six engine was new for the DB4. Its twin camshafts are chain driven and operate two valves per cylinder in hemispherical combustion chambers. In standard DB4 form it has single-plug ignition and a pair of SU carburetors, and develops 240 bhp. For the GT it has a higher compression ratio, higher lift camshafts, three twin-choke side-draft Weber carburetors and twin spark plugs per cylinder. In this form it produces 302 bhp.

Twin overhead camshafts

Three twin-choke carburetors

All-alloy construction

Square cylinder dimensions

Chop job

Launched in 1959, the DB4 GT was intended mainly for competition. With 5 inches chopped out of the wheelbase it is a strict two-seater. It has faired-in headlights, a limited-slip differential and a twin-plug head that boosts power to 320 bhp.

A GT model is worth twice as much as a standard DB4.

Aston Martin **DB4**

The DB4 to DB6 series is perhaps the most famous to roll off Aston Martin's Newport Pagnell production line. The classic Touring styling lasted for more than 12 years and still looks great today.

All-new engine

Unlike the previous model—the Aston Martin DB Mk III—which used the old Lagonda twin-cam engine, the DB4 had a completely new engine. The twin-overhead-camshaft straight six displaces 3.7 liters and produces 240 bhp in standard form and 302 bhp in the DB4 GT.

Short wheelbase

The wheelbase of the GT model is 5 inches shorter than that of the standard DB4. This makes the car lighter and more nimble.

Limited-slip differential

The live rear axle features a Salisbury Powr-lok limited-slip differential to help put all the power onto the road.

Superleggera construction

Styling house Touring was renowned for its use of Superleggera construction, which gives the DB4 a light but rigid bodyshell.

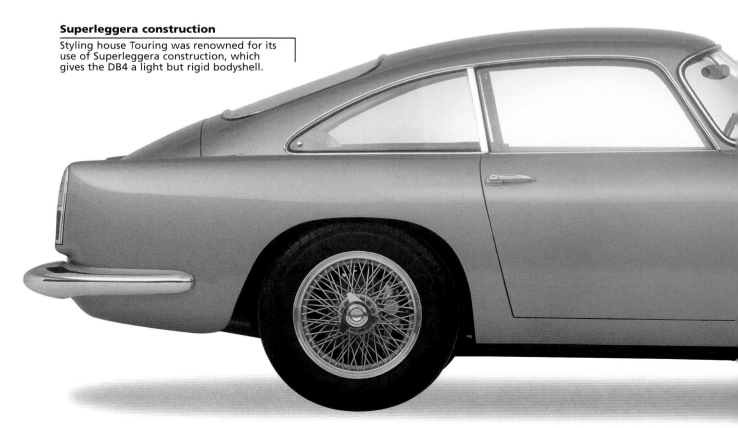

Italian styling

The DB4 was styled by Italian styling house Touring of Milan. This styling lasted, with subtle tweaks, until the demise of the DB6 in 1970.

Strong steel chassis

The DB4 uses a pressed-steel chassis with strong welded box sections. It was introduced for the DB4 and is completely different from the chassis of the DB Mk III.

Specifications

1962 Aston Martin DB4 GT

ENGINE

Type: In-line six-cylinder

Construction: Cast-iron block and head

Valve gear: Two valves per cylinder operated by twin overhead camshafts

Bore and stroke: 3.62 in. x 3.62 in.

Displacement: 3,670 cc

Compression ratio: 9.0:1

Induction system: Three twin-choke Weber carburetors

Maximum power: 302 bhp at 6,000 rpm

Maximum torque: 240 lb-ft at 5,000 rpm

Top speed: 149 mph

0–60 mph: 6.4 sec.

TRANSMISSION

Four-speed manual

BODY/CHASSIS

Steel chassis with alloy over steel tube two-door coupe body

SPECIAL FEATURES

Unlike the standard cars, the DB4 GT has faired-in headlights. A small number of Vantage-engined DB4s also feature these lights.

Hot air from the engine bay exits through vents in the fenders.

RUNNING GEAR

Steering: Rack-and-pinion

Front suspension: Double wishbones with coil springs, telescopic shock absorbers and anti-roll bar

Rear suspension: Live axle with coil springs, radius arms, Watt linkage and lever-arm shock absorbers

Brakes: Discs (front and rear)

Wheels: Wire, 16-in. dia.

Tires: 6.00 x 16 in.

DIMENSIONS

Length: 179.0 in.   **Width:** 55.5 in.

Height: 51.0 in.   **Wheelbase:** 93.0 in.

Track: 54.4 in. (front), 54.5 in. (rear)

Weight: 2,800 lbs.

Aston Martin ZAGATO

When Aston Martin wanted a car to make an instant impact and revitalize its ageing models it turned to Zagato—the master stylists from Milan. The brief was to build a supercar capable of reaching over 180 mph, that had dramatic looks and handling to match.

"...a genuine 180 mph."

"Cruise at 100 mph, floor the throttle and the performance envelope opens up. Beyond 3,000 rpm the Zagato comes into its own, hurling the heavyweight to a genuine 180 mph. The Zagato is quick off the line too, reaching 60 mph in less than 5 seconds. Yet, despite this, it's very easy to drive, with fine visibility and superb seats. The chassis is set up for mild understeer, but the independent suspension keeps the tires firmly planted at all times."

Even inside, the Zagato has very distinctive sharp-edge styling.

Milestones

1984 Aston Martin
Chairman Victor Gauntlett meets Gianni Zagato at the Geneva Motor Show and discusses plans for a car that will lift Aston's image and remind the world about Zagato design. Styling sketches are soon produced and orders worth almost $7 million are taken by Aston Martin just on the car's appearance.

A small number of Aston Martin GTs were bodied by Zagato.

1986 The Zagato
goes into limited production with the intention of building just 50 coupes. The rolling chassis are sent to Zagato's Milan factory for body and trim.

The handsome Virage replaced the Zagato in 1989.

1987 Aston Martin
displays the Zagato Volante convertible at the Geneva Show.

1989 Production
stops, with 50 coupes and 25 convertibles built.

UNDER THE SKIN

Nothing new

Although outwardly different, the Zagato has a V8 Vantage floorpan, shortened by 16 inches. It also uses the V8s double wishbone front suspension coupled to a de Dion rear end which allows the huge rear vented discs to be mounted inboard next to the final drive. The transmission, however, is mounted behind the engine, rather than at the rear axle, resulting in a noticeably front-heavy weight distribution.

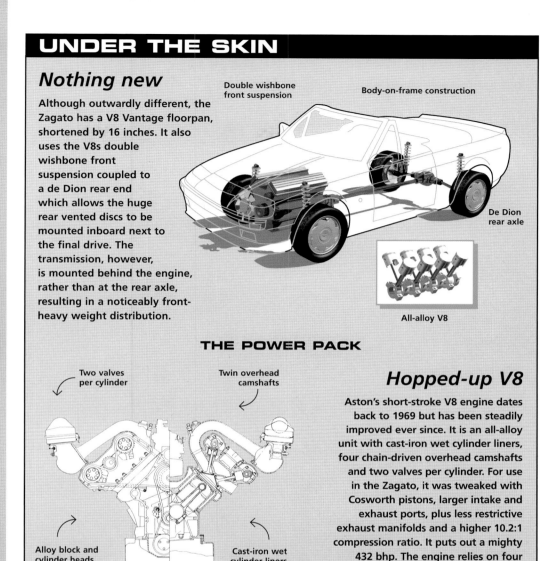

Double wishbone front suspension

Body-on-frame construction

De Dion rear axle

All-alloy V8

THE POWER PACK

Two valves per cylinder

Twin overhead camshafts

Alloy block and cylinder heads

Cast-iron wet cylinder liners

Hopped-up V8

Aston's short-stroke V8 engine dates back to 1969 but has been steadily improved ever since. It is an all-alloy unit with cast-iron wet cylinder liners, four chain-driven overhead camshafts and two valves per cylinder. For use in the Zagato, it was tweaked with Cosworth pistons, larger intake and exhaust ports, plus less restrictive exhaust manifolds and a higher 10.2:1 compression ratio. It puts out a mighty 432 bhp. The engine relies on four Weber carburetors for feeding the fuel.

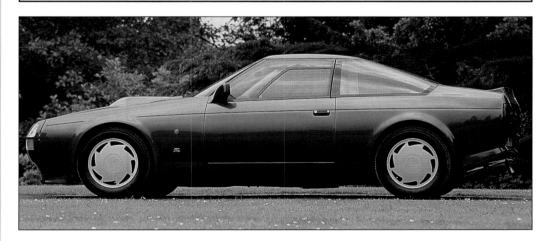

Going topless

The Zagato Volante is even rarer than the coupe, and at the time of its introduction was the fastest convertible on the road. Launched in 1987, only 25 had been built by the time production ceased in 1989. Not surprisingly, they are highly sought after.

Aston Martin made twice as many Zagato coupes as it did Volante convertibles.

Aston Martin ZAGATO

Zagato had the reputation of styling cars unlike any other. Here it went for a short car with tall wheels and a blunt aggressive look which radiated power, performance and exclusivity.

V8 engine

At the time the Zagato had the most powerful version of the aluminum Aston Martin quad-cam V8 engine. Revisions to the camshaft, cylinder head ports and carburetors helped to increase power to 432 bhp from its 5.3 liters. This output was more impressive than the peak torque as the engine was tuned for outright power.

ZF transmission

Aston used the tough German ZF five-speed manual transmission. It featured a dog leg first gear with the rest of the gears in the normal 'H' pattern.

De Dion axle

De Dion axles were popular with Aston Martin. They served the purpose of keeping the rear wheels upright at all times with none of the camber changes.

Short rear overhang

Zagato made its design look more compact than the existing Vantage by chopping 12 inches from the rear, reducing the size of the trunk. Extra luggage could be placed behind the front seats.

Lancia seats

With Zagato in charge of all interior trim, it chose Lancia Delta S4 front seats. These were trimmed in top-quality leather like all Aston Martin seats.

Foam bumpers

One way in which Zagato lightened the Aston was by discarding the steel bumpers and designing deformable foam-filled replacements mounted on hydraulic rams.

In-board discs

In theory, with a de Dion axle the logical place to mount the brakes is inboard next to the final drive, and that's where Aston put them.

Alloy body

Zagato was the master craftsmen in aluminum bodywork and made all the panels for the car, mounted on a modified form of the existing folded and welded sheet-metal substructure. All the panels were formed over a full-size wooden template.

Specifications

1987 Aston Martin Zagato

ENGINE

Type: V8

Construction: Alloy block and heads

Valve gear: Two valves per cylinder operated by four chain-driven overhead camshafts

Bore and stroke: 3.93 in. x 3.35 in.

Displacement: 5,340 cc

Compression ratio: 10.2:1

Induction system: Four downdraft Weber IDF carburetors

Maximum power: 432 bhp at 6,200 rpm

Maximum torque: 395 lb-ft at 5,100 rpm

Top speed: 183 mph

0–60 mph: 4.8 sec

TRANSMISSION

TorqueFlite 727 five-speed automatic

BODY/CHASSIS

Steel substructure with alloy two-door coupe body

SPECIAL FEATURES

Volantes are distinguished from Zagato coupes by their head-light covers.

With its shortened tail and convertible top, the Volante's trunk space is limited.

RUNNING GEAR

Steering: Rack-and-pinion

Front suspension: Double wishbones with coil springs, Koni shock absorbers and anti-roll bar

Rear suspension: Rigid de Dion axle with trailing arms, Watt linkage, coil springs and Koni shock absorbers

Brakes: Vented discs, 11.5-in. dia. (front), 10.4-in. dia. (rear)

Wheels: Alloy, 8 x 16 in.

Tires: Goodyear Eagle, 255/50 VR16

DIMENSIONS

Length: 173.5 in. **Width:** 73.5 in.

Height: 51.1 in. **Wheelbase:** 103.2 in.

Track: 60.1 in. (front), 60.8 in. (rear)

Weight: 3,630 lbs.

Audi **RS2**

BMW has its M series, Mercedes its E500, but the magic digits for Audi were RS2. This station wagon was the ultimate wolf in sheep's clothing: an ultra high-performance car with turbocharging and four-wheel drive.

"...staggering station wagon."

"The RS2 was built with two strictly met objectives—high performance and practicality. With 315 bhp, its turbocharged 2.2-liter will dispense with a Ferrari Testarossa and leave a Porsche 911 floundering. On the practical side, this staggering station wagon is also able to take the family on a long distance road trip in perfect comfort. The all-wheel drive provides plenty of grip, and there's totally neutral handling. Not bad for a fully functional station wagon."

Bucket seats and white-faced gauges hint at the RS2's rocket-like performance.

Milestones

1992 The S2 Avant is launched: a 230-bhp turbocharged version of Audi's station wagon.

The performance S2 Avant boasted 230 bhp.

1993 An even more powerful and desirable RS2 model is launched at the Frankfurt Motor Show.

In 1999 Audi's latest performance wagon was the S4 Quattro Avant with a 265-bhp turbocharged V6.

1995 As the Audi A4 Avant becomes available and Audi presents a more rational model range, the RS2 is dropped along with other models in the old-style lineup.

UNDER THE SKIN

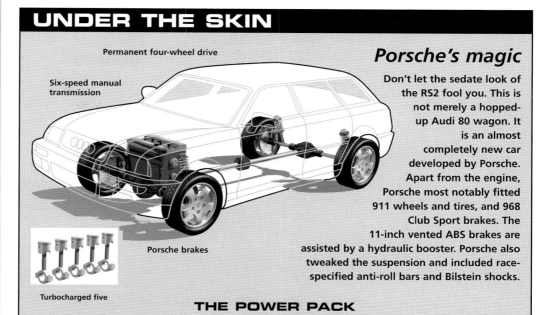

Permanent four-wheel drive

Six-speed manual transmission

Porsche brakes

Turbocharged five

Porsche's magic

Don't let the sedate look of the RS2 fool you. This is not merely a hopped-up Audi 80 wagon. It is an almost completely new car developed by Porsche. Apart from the engine, Porsche most notably fitted 911 wheels and tires, and 968 Club Sport brakes. The 11-inch vented ABS brakes are assisted by a hydraulic booster. Porsche also tweaked the suspension and included race-specified anti-roll bars and Bilstein shocks.

THE POWER PACK

Totally turbo

Audi pioneered the use of five-cylinder inline engines as early as 1978 as a successful halfway house between four- and six-cylinder units. In the RS2, that format reached its ultimate conclusion. Audi had used turbochargers before, of course, but none like the KKK's competition turbo capable of building 16 psi of boost. The modifications from the 230-bhp S2 engine include a larger intercooler, high-flow air filter, new injectors, Porsche 911 fuel pump and high-lift camshafts. Add in a low-pressure exhaust manifold and Audi was understandably happy about the figures: 315 bhp and 302 lb-ft.

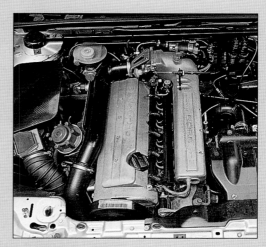

Fastest ever

As the fastest car ever made by Audi, the RS2 has an enviable reputation. In the long term, it might even eclipse the legendary Quattro as the Audi to own. Certainly, the few examples produced are highly prized by enthusiasts and rarely come up for sale—a good indication that collectors like them too much to part with them.

A Porsche heritage and serious performance guarantee exclusivity.

Audi **RS2**

Speedier and more capable than the legendary short-wheelbase Quattro Sport, the RS2 is the fastest car Audi has made. The Porsche effect is evident everywhere.

Sports interior

Audi did not forget about upgrading the cabin on its wicked wagon. Black-on-white gauges, Recaro seats and Kevlar or wood trim were added to the normal-issue Audi 80 interior. Standard equipment on the RS2 includes a power roof, power windows, CD changer and air conditioning.

Six-speed transmission

To make the most of its awesome power, Audi specified a six-speed manual transmission tweaked by Porsche. Its ratios are chosen to keep the power band around 3,000 rpm.

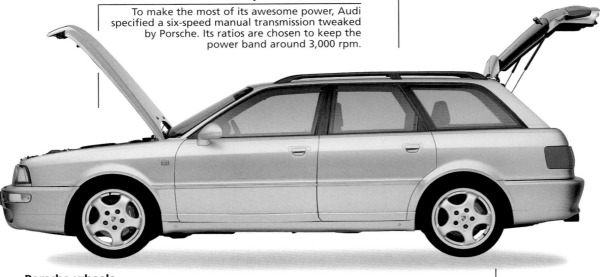

Porsche wheels

The elegance of the five-spoke alloy wheels should come as no surprise, as they were taken straight from the Porsche 911. They are fitted with ultra-low-profile Dunlop tires.

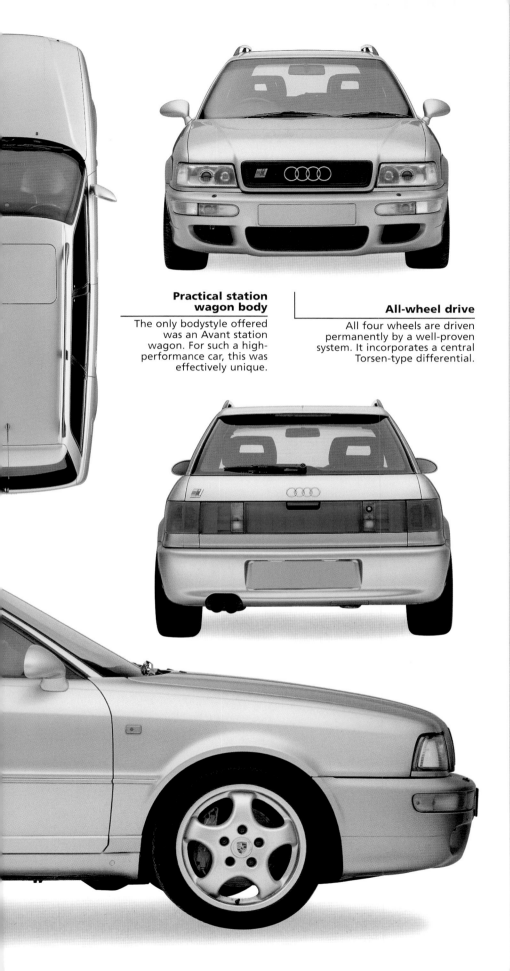

Practical station wagon body

The only bodystyle offered was an Avant station wagon. For such a high-performance car, this was effectively unique.

All-wheel drive

All four wheels are driven permanently by a well-proven system. It incorporates a central Torsen-type differential.

Specifications

1994 Audi RS2

ENGINE

Type: Inline five-cylinder

Construction: Cast-iron block and aluminum head

Valve gear: Four valves per cylinder operated by twin overhead camshafts

Bore and stroke: 3.19 in. x 3.40 in.

Displacement: 2,226 cc

Compression ratio: 9.0:1

Induction system: Sequential fuel injection

Maximum power: 315 bhp at 6,500 rpm

Maximum torque: 302 lb-ft at 3,000 rpm

Top speed: 158 mph

0–60 mph: 4.8 sec

TRANSMISSION

Six-speed manual

BODY/CHASSIS

Unitary monocoque construction with steel five-door station wagon body

SPECIAL FEATURES

The rear lights extend around onto the tailgate.

The larger, red brake calipers come from the Porsche parts bin and are from the 968 model.

RUNNING GEAR

Steering: Rack-and-pinion

Front suspension: Struts with coil springs, shock absorbers and anti-roll bar

Rear suspension: Struts with torsion beam axle, coil springs, shock absorbers and anti-roll bar

Brakes: Vented discs (front and rear)

Wheels: Alloy, 17-in. dia.

Tires: 245/40 ZR17

DIMENSIONS

Length: 177.5 in.   **Width:** 66.7 in.

Height: 54.6 in.   **Wheelbase:** 100.4 in.

Track: 57.0 in. (front), 57.9 in. (rear)

Weight: 3,510 lbs.

Bentley TURBO R/T

W. O. Bentley would have approved of the Turbo R/T, a big, powerful, and fast sedan with the appeal of the fabled sports and luxury cars he built during the 1920s.

"...Appearence is deceiving"

"Appearances can be deceiving, as the Turbo R/T demonstrates. With its chubby exterior you would expect it to be more of a land yacht than a sports car, yet it performs magnificently. The chassis is agile thanks to very stiff springs and electronic shocks. Its massive turbocharged V8 gives simply awesome results. It's hard to believe that this incredible hulk will hit 60 mph from a rest in just 6.7 seconds."

The interior has all the class and luxury of an old-fashioned gentleman's club, with wood and leather everywhere.

Milestones

1965 The first 'modern' Bentley,
the T1, is launched. It is the company's first monocoque car.

Bentley's original Turbo R was based on the 1985 Rolls Royce.

1980 The new Mulsanne is launched.
It uses the Rolls-Royce Silver Spirit bodyshell.

1982 Bentley turbocharges the
Mulsanne, giving an enormous (but undisclosed) power output.

The Turbo R/T uses the engine from the elegant Continental T.

1985 The Turbo R is launched.
It produces 320 bhp and 457 lb-ft of torque.

1997 Bentley introduces the Turbo R/T,
which uses a 400-bhp version of the Continental T engine.

UNDER THE SKIN

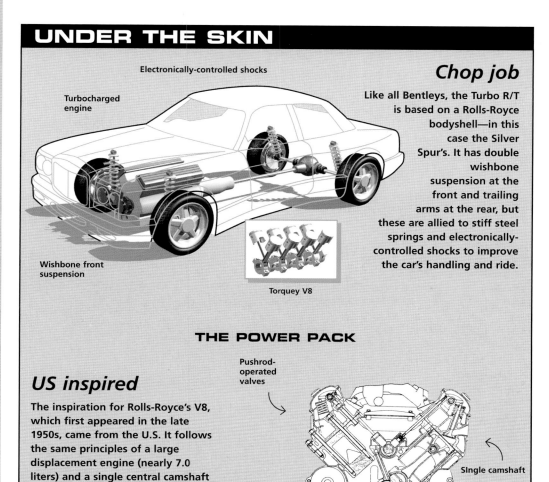

Electronically-controlled shocks

Turbocharged engine

Wishbone front suspension

Torquey V8

Chop job

Like all Bentleys, the Turbo R/T is based on a Rolls-Royce bodyshell—in this case the Silver Spur's. It has double wishbone suspension at the front and trailing arms at the rear, but these are allied to stiff steel springs and electronically-controlled shocks to improve the car's handling and ride.

THE POWER PACK

US inspired

The inspiration for Rolls-Royce's V8, which first appeared in the late 1950s, came from the U.S. It follows the same principles of a large displacement engine (nearly 7.0 liters) and a single central camshaft and two valves per cylinder. Unlike most traditional large American V8s it is made of alloy and not cast iron, with wet liners. In the Turbo R/T it is fitted with a Garrett turbocharger to give masses of power output and impressive torque at just 2,000 rpm.

Pushrod-operated valves

Single camshaft

Alloy construction

Wet cylinder liners

Throwback

Although W.O. Bentley was always opposed to forced induction engines, the turbocharged Bentleys—the Turbo R and Turbo R/T—have recaptured the spirit of the company's sportier cars of the 1930s. There are few modern cars that can boast such a high power output.

Bentley's Turbo R/T is big on performance and, of course, style.

Bentley **TURBO R/T**

The Bentley Turbo R/T is an enormous car with a huge power output and almost excessive luxury. Unsurprisingly, it has an enormous price tag to match.

Electronic shocks

The key to the Bentley's great poise is its electronic shocks. Each shock is adjusted in microseconds to cope with the changes in road surface and speed or cornering forces.

Turbo V8 engine

The naturally aspirated Rolls/Bentley V8 produces enough power, but to increase the output to 400 bhp the engine is now turbocharged. More important for performance is the increase in torque that turbocharging produces.

Four-speed automatic

The four-speed automatic transmission has adaptive changes—it learns the driver's style whether relaxed or enthusiastic, and varies the shift points accordingly.

Alloy wheels

To carry the Bentley's great weight and handle the performance, the Turbo R/T needs large wheels and is fitted with handsome and wide five-spoke alloys.

Semi-trailing arm rear suspension

Semi-trailing arm rear suspension has been used on Rolls-Royces and Bentleys for many years. It's retained on the the Turbo R/T, but with much of the compliance engineered out.

Connolly leather interior

The interior is covered in Connolly leather, including the seats, steering wheel, gear selector, door panels and windshield pillars.

Specifications

1998 Bentley Turbo R/T

ENGINE

Type: V8

Construction: Alloy block and heads

Valve gear: Two valves per cylinder operated by single camshafts via pushrods

Bore and stroke: 4.09 in. x 3.89 in.

Displacement: 6,750 cc

Compression ratio: 8.0:1

Induction system: Zytec EMS3 controlled electronic fuel injection with Garrett T04B turbocharger

Maximum power: 400 bhp at 4,000 rpm

Maximum torque: 490 lb-ft at 2,000 rpm

Top speed: 152 mph

0–60 mph: 6.7 sec

TRANSMISSION

Four-speed automatic

BODY/CHASSIS

Monocoque four-door saloon

SPECIAL FEATURES

The sportier Bentleys have mesh radiator grills rather than the chrome ones used on Rolls-Royces.

Before tire technology caught up, the Turbo had to have an electronically-limited top speed.

RUNNING GEAR

Steering: Rack-and-pinion

Front suspension: Double wishbones with coil springs, electronically-controlled shocks and anti-roll bar

Rear suspension: Semi-trailing arms, coil springs, electronically-controlled shocks and anti-roll bar

Brakes: Vented discs (front), solid discs (rear); ABS standard

Wheels: Alloy, 8.5 x 18 in.

Tires: 265/45 ZR18

DIMENSIONS

Length: 212.4 in.   **Width:** 83.1 in.

Height: 58.5 in.   **Wheelbase:** 124.5 in.

Track: 61 in. (front and rear)

Weight: 5,450 lbs.

Bizzarrini GT STRADA

Giotto Bizzarrini—the designer of the Ferrari 250 GTO—left Ferrari to do his own thing. Racing was his passion but he also built some road cars, of which the GT Strada 5300 is the most fearsome. Its Chevy V8 engine, dramatic body and stripped-out cabin testify to that.

"...an untamed steed."

"Since it measures just 43 inches from floor to roof, your first problem is getting in. Once you're there, you can enjoy the V8 engine's gorgeous rasp—few Chevy small-blocks sound quite this loud or urgent. The GT Strada shoots off the line at a tremendous pace and has an uncanny ability to go around corners; the handling balance is one of the best of any 1960s car. This is an untamed steed that really wants to be let loose on the race track."

The compact cabin has the ambience of a race car simply decked out for road use.

Milestones

1963 At the Turin Motor Show, Bizzarrini presents his Iso Grifo A3C competition coupe as the racing version of the Iso Grifo. It is almost identical, but lighter and lower.

Giotto Bizzarrini was involved in the design of the Ferrari 250 GTO.

1964 The A3C comes 14th in the 24 Hours of Le Mans and wins its class.

1965 The production roadgoing version—the GT Strada 5300—arrives.

The GT Strada 5300 was built like a race car.

1967 A smaller Opel GT-engined model, called the Europa, is launched. Only a small number are sold.

1969 Bizzarrini ends its days as a car manufacturer.

UNDER THE SKIN

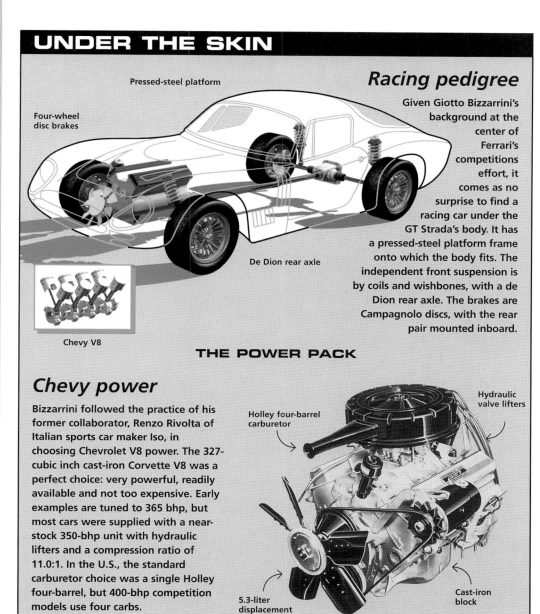

Pressed-steel platform

Four-wheel disc brakes

De Dion rear axle

Chevy V8

Racing pedigree

Given Giotto Bizzarrini's background at the center of Ferrari's competitions effort, it comes as no surprise to find a racing car under the GT Strada's body. It has a pressed-steel platform frame onto which the body fits. The independent front suspension is by coils and wishbones, with a de Dion rear axle. The brakes are Campagnolo discs, with the rear pair mounted inboard.

THE POWER PACK

Chevy power

Bizzarrini followed the practice of his former collaborator, Renzo Rivolta of Italian sports car maker Iso, in choosing Chevrolet V8 power. The 327-cubic inch cast-iron Corvette V8 was a perfect choice: very powerful, readily available and not too expensive. Early examples are tuned to 365 bhp, but most cars were supplied with a near-stock 350-bhp unit with hydraulic lifters and a compression ratio of 11.0:1. In the U.S., the standard carburetor choice was a single Holley four-barrel, but 400-bhp competition models use four carbs.

Holley four-barrel carburetor

Hydraulic valve lifters

5.3-liter displacement

Cast-iron block

GT purity

Unless you can locate one of Bizzarrini's ultra-rare racers, the GT Strada 5300 is the ultimate car bearing Giotto Bizzarrini's name.
In many ways it is a purer and more focused GT car than most 1960s Ferraris, and as a classic it is an interesting choice.

The Bizzarrini makes an interesting alternative to mainstream supercars.

Bizzarrini **GT STRADA** 🇮🇹

Evolved as the racing version of the Iso Grifo, the Strada's dramatic body, racing chassis and powerful engine made an intoxicating brew. For a while in the 1960s, Bizzarrini looked like a major force in the supercar stakes.

Corvette V8

The 327-cubic inch Corvette V8 engine was a logical choice for Bizzarrini, who had worked around this powerplant in the Iso Grifo (which he engineered). It was offered in near-standard specification.

Cast-alloy wheels

The evocative Campagnolo magnesium alloy wheels with knock-off center spinners look extremely purposeful. For competition use, it could be ordered with even wider rims (7 inches front and 9 inches rear).

Three fuel tanks

The GT Strada is a thirsty car, so to prevent constant fuel stops no less than three fuel tanks are fitted. There are two 7.5-gallon tanks in the rocker panels and a 20-gallon tank behind the seats, giving a total of 35 gallons.

Fiberglass bodywork

Apart from the earliest cars, which have aluminum bodywork built by Italian artisans, the bodywork is made of fiberglass. This keeps weight and costs down and makes manufacturing simpler. For competition use you could even specify thinner fiberglass body work with larger wheel openings.

Giugiaro design

The stunning shape was drawn up by a youthful Giorgetto Giugiaro while he was still working with Bertone. It was even more dramatic than the closely related Iso Grifo, also styled by Giugiaro. At just 44 inches high, it made a very strong impression.

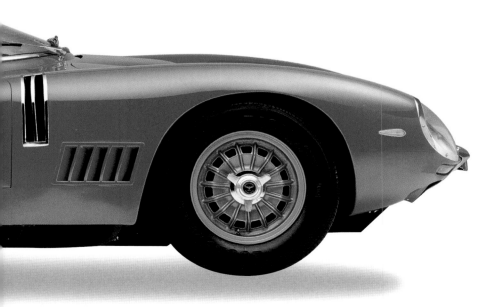

Stripped-out cockpit

True to this car's racing roots, the cabin is not very luxurious. Two narrow bucket seats nestle between the wide sills and transmission tunnel, and the trim is minimal.

Specifications

1966 Bizzarrini GT Strada 5300

ENGINE

Type: V8

Construction: Cast-iron block and heads

Valve gear: Two valves per cylinder operated by a single camshaft with pushrods and rockers

Bore and stroke: 4.00 in. x 3.25 in.

Displacement: 327 c.i.

Compression ratio: 11.0:1

Induction system: Single Holley four-barrel carburetor

Maximum power: 365 bhp at 6,200 rpm

Maximum torque: 344 lb-ft at 4,000 rpm

Top speed: 165 mph

0–60 mph: 6.4 sec

TRANSMISSION

Four-speed manual

BODY/CHASSIS

Separate pressed-steel chassis with two-door coupe body

SPECIAL FEATURES

Ducts behind the front wheels carry hot air away from the cramped engine compartment.

The headlights are concealed behind plastic shrouds.

RUNNING GEAR

Steering: Recirculating ball

Front suspension: Wishbones with coil springs, shock absorbers and anti-roll bar

Rear suspension: De Dion axle with trailing arms, Watt linkage, coil springs and shock absorbers

Brakes: Discs (front and rear)

Wheels: Alloy, 15-in. dia.

Tires: Dunlop, 6.00 x 15 in. (front), 7.00 x 15 in. (rear)

DIMENSIONS

Length: 172.0 in. **Width:** 68.0 in.

Height: 44.7 in. **Wheelbase:** 96.5 in.

Track: 55.5 in. (front), 56.5 in. (rear)

Weight: 2,530 lbs.

BMW M1

Built in small numbers and too late for the racing formula it was designed for, the M1 was turned into BMW's first mid-engined, street-legal supercar with a 277-bhp, twin-cam six.

"...designed as a race car."

"At high speeds, you can feel that the M1 was designed as a racing car. It's as solid as a rock with great reserves of power everywhere. Unfortunately, it is simply too heavy to be a competitive racing car. It takes a lot of effort to drive the M1, with both the clutch and brake needing a firm push...though that's a small penalty. Its steering feel and response is pure BMW, rewarding you with endless confidence and unflappable poise."

The M1's disappointingly unattractive cabin hasn't stood the test of time in the way that the ageless Giugiaro exterior shape has.

Milestones

1972 Paul Bracq, head of BMW styling, creates the Turbo Coupe concept car. The head of BMW Motorsport feels the design could be modified to create a racing car to contest Group 4 endurance events. Giugiaro is asked to style the car.

Giorgetto Giugiaro styled the M1 for BMW.

1978 After many delays, the M1 appears at the Paris Show.

The M635CSi and M1 share same basic 24-valve, six-cylinder engine, but the coupe has more power.

1979 Too late and too heavy to be a competitive racer, BMW and FOCA arrange for the M1 to star in the one-marque 'Procar' series to support Grands Prix.

1981 Production ends after 450 cars have been produced—397 road cars and 53 racers.

UNDER THE SKIN

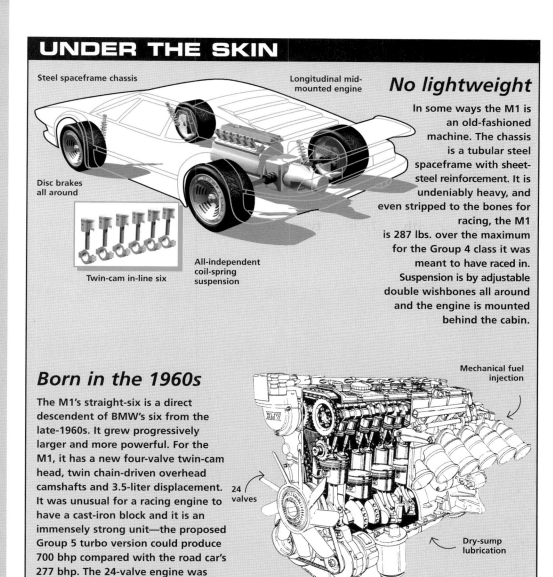

Steel spaceframe chassis

Longitudinal mid-mounted engine

Disc brakes all around

Twin-cam in-line six

All-independent coil-spring suspension

Mechanical fuel injection

24 valves

Dry-sump lubrication

No lightweight

In some ways the M1 is an old-fashioned machine. The chassis is a tubular steel spaceframe with sheet-steel reinforcement. It is undeniably heavy, and even stripped to the bones for racing, the M1 is 287 lbs. over the maximum for the Group 4 class it was meant to have raced in. Suspension is by adjustable double wishbones all around and the engine is mounted behind the cabin.

Born in the 1960s

The M1's straight-six is a direct descendent of BMW's six from the late-1960s. It grew progressively larger and more powerful. For the M1, it has a new four-valve twin-cam head, twin chain-driven overhead camshafts and 3.5-liter displacement. It was unusual for a racing engine to have a cast-iron block and it is an immensely strong unit—the proposed Group 5 turbo version could produce 700 bhp compared with the road car's 277 bhp. The 24-valve engine was later used in the M635CSi (286 bhp) and the M5 (315 bhp).

Effective racer

Racing M1s were tuned to almost 200-bhp more than the road car, and their engines could rev to 9,000 rpm. Although it was an overweight racer, it could still be effective. Hans-Joachim Stuck's M1 led more potent cars at Le Mans one year.

The M1 provided plenty of excitement, running in Procar and Group 4 circuits.

BMW M1

It might not look as spectacular as its exotic Ferrari and Lamborghini rivals, but don't let that fool you. The M1 has one major advantage—it was designed as a real racing car.

Tubular steel chassis
Originally, it made sense to farm out the chassis construction to Lamborghini because they had far more experience than BMW in building tubular steel chassis. Eventually Marchesi of Modena made the chassis.

Fiberglass bodywork
All the M1 body panels are fiberglass and they are both riveted and bonded to the tubular steel frame. The body was produced by Italian company TIR (Transformazione Italiana Resina) to a very high standard.

Twin-cam straight-six
In street-legal form the BMW's six-cylinder, twin-cam engine produces 277 bhp from 3.5 liters.

Pirelli P7 tires
The low-profile Pirelli P7 tire was a huge advance in its day and the car's suspension was set up to suit the tire's characteristics.

Slatted engine cover
Hot air from the engine compartment escapes between these large slats. Rearward vision is very good for a mid-engined supercar, and a glass window behind the driver's head insulates the cockpit from the engine bay.

Air intakes
Slots just behind the nearside, rear window feed air to the engine's induction system. The matching slots on the other side are for engine bay ventilation.

Classic grill

The distinctive BMW grill was kept for the M1 and it is functional because both the radiator and the engine oil cooler are at the front. After the air passes over them, it exits through the vents on top of the hood.

Servo brakes

Street-legal M1s have servo-assisted brakes but these were left off the racers, although the driver could adjust the brake balance between front and rear wheels.

Double-wishbone suspension

Most BMWs have some form of semi-trailing arm suspension at the rear but the M1 is different, with racing-type double wishbones in the front and rear.

Specifications
1980 BMW M1

ENGINE
Type: Straight-six twin cam
Construction: Cast-iron block and alloy head
Valve gear: Four valves per cylinder operated by two chain-driven overhead camshafts
Bore and stroke: 3.68 in. x 3.31 in.
Displacement: 3,453 cc
Compression ratio: 9.0:1
Induction system: Bosch-Kugelfischer mechanical fuel injection
Maximum power: 277 bhp at 6,500 rpm
Maximum torque: 239 lb-ft at 5,000 rpm
Top speed: 162 mph
0–60 mph: 5.7 sec

TRANSMISSION
ZF five-speed manual

BODY/CHASSIS
Fiberglass two-door, two-seat coupe body with tubular steel chassis

SPECIAL FEATURES

Rear screen louvers afforded reasonable rearward vision and helped to keep engine temperatures down.

Dated wheel with Pirelli P7s that are narrow by today's standards.

RUNNING GEAR
Steering: Rack-and-pinion
Front suspension: Double wishbones, coil springs, telescopic shocks and anti-roll bar
Rear suspension: Double wishbones, coil springs, telescopic shocks and anti-roll bar
Brakes: Vented discs front and rear
Wheels: Alloy, 7 in. x 16 in. (front), 8 in. x 16 in. (rear)
Tires: Pirelli P7, 205/55 VR16 (front), 225/50 VR16 (rear)

DIMENSIONS
Length: 171.7 in.   **Width:** 71.7 in.
Height: 44.9 in.   **Wheelbase:** 100.8 in.
Track: 61 in. (front), 60.9 in. (rear)
Weight: 3,122 lbs.

BMW **M3**

In the words of BMW's marketing department, the M3 is one of "the ultimate driving machines." With superb performance and excellent handling, the M3 is certainly one of the world's great GTs.

"...finely-honed super sedan."

"The chin spoiler and rocker panels give the game away. This car says performance. The M3 is one of the finest sport coupes available with a blend of speed, predictable rear-wheel drive handling, and practicality that is simply amazing. In U.S.-spec cars, the engines only make 240 bhp, but with equally strong acceleration and handling characteristics. Luckily, the U.S. M3s are much more affordable."

The interior of the M3 is dark and somber, but it is extremely comfortable with supportive, hip-hugging sports seats.

Milestones

1991 BMW launches
the new E36 3 Series. Initially, the M3 version is not available.

1993 The M3 is introduced in coupe
form only. Its 3.0-liter straight-six engine produces 286 bhp.

The M3 engine saw service again in the M-Roadster.

1994 The M3 is released in the U.S.,
and uses a 240 bhp engine. Performance is mediocre, but the price is low.

The latest 3 Series was first unveiled to the public in 1998.

1996 The European M3 Evolution gets 321
bhp with a slightly larger 3.2-liter engine.

1997 A sequential gearchange is made
available on the M3 SMG.

UNDER THE SKIN

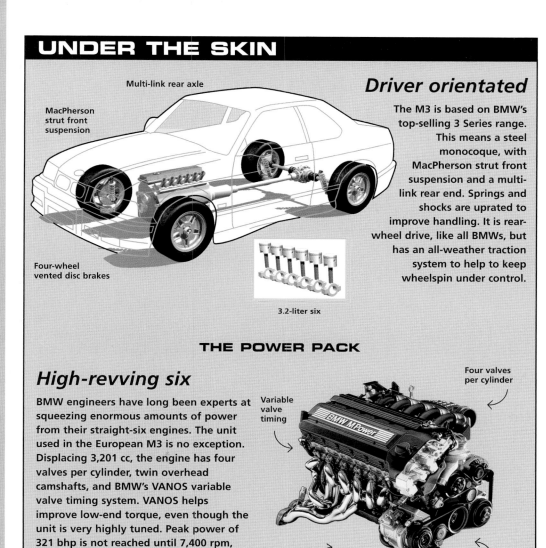

Multi-link rear axle

MacPherson strut front suspension

Four-wheel vented disc brakes

3.2-liter six

Driver orientated

The M3 is based on BMW's top-selling 3 Series range. This means a steel monocoque, with MacPherson strut front suspension and a multi-link rear end. Springs and shocks are uprated to improve handling. It is rear-wheel drive, like all BMWs, but has an all-weather traction system to help to keep wheelspin under control.

THE POWER PACK

High-revving six

BMW engineers have long been experts at squeezing enormous amounts of power from their straight-six engines. The unit used in the European M3 is no exception. Displacing 3,201 cc, the engine has four valves per cylinder, twin overhead camshafts, and BMW's VANOS variable valve timing system. VANOS helps improve low-end torque, even though the unit is very highly tuned. Peak power of 321 bhp is not reached until 7,400 rpm, but maximum torque comes at 3,250 rpm. VANOS isn't used in U.S. spec M3s.

Variable valve timing

Four valves per cylinder

Cast-iron block

Electronic engine management

Drop-top

Although the M3 is available in three body styles—convertible, two-door coupe and four-door sedan—the convertible is without a doubt the most desirable. What it lacks in body stiffness, it more than makes up for with high style.

The convertible offers open-top fun and outrageous performance.

BMW M3

Very few full four-seaters would come near the top of a list of performance cars. One car that would, however, is BMW's M3.

Six-speed transmission

To make the most of the power, the European M3 has a six-speed transmission, whereas the U.S. spec cars use a five speed.

321-bhp engine

The heart of the M3 is its incredible engine. The 24-valve, twin-cam straight-six produces 321 bhp at 7,400 rpm. Peak torque comes at a more down to earth 3,250 rpm thanks to variable valve timing.

Practical trunk

Unlike many cars in the same performance league, the M3 can carry more than just an overnight bag.

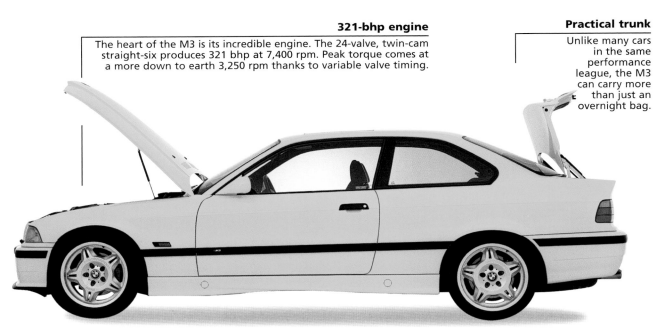

Different body styles

Although it was launched as a two-door coupe, the M3 is now also available as a practical four-door sedan or an eye-catching convertible.

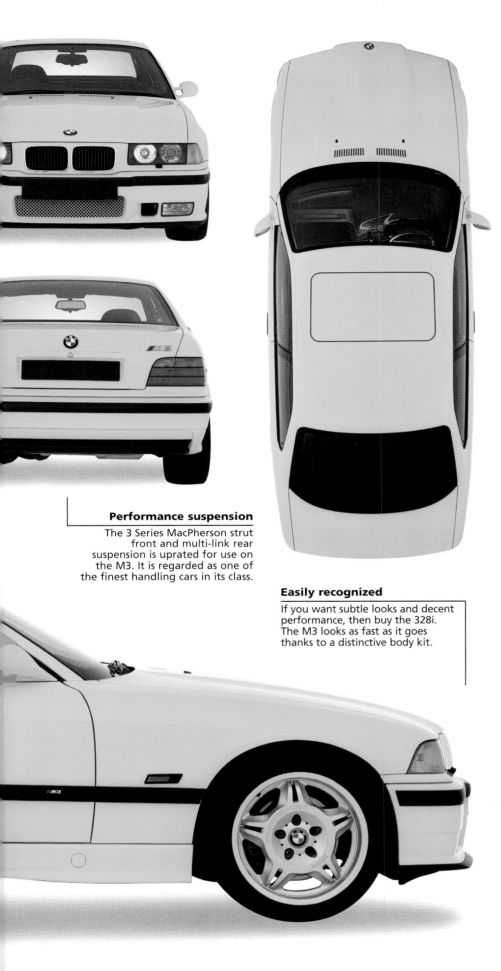

Performance suspension

The 3 Series MacPherson strut front and multi-link rear suspension is uprated for use on the M3. It is regarded as one of the finest handling cars in its class.

Easily recognized

If you want subtle looks and decent performance, then buy the 328i. The M3 looks as fast as it goes thanks to a distinctive body kit.

Specifications

1996 BMW M3 Evolution*

ENGINE

Type: In-line six

Construction: Cast block and alloy head

Valve gear: Four valves per cylinder operated by twin overhead camshafts with VANOS variable valve timing

Bore and stroke: 3.4 in. x 3.58 in.

Displacement: 3,201 cc

Compression ratio: 11.3:1

Induction system: Electronic digital engine management system

Top speed: 140 mph

0–60 mph: 5.6 sec.

TRANSMISSION

Six-speed manual

BODY/CHASSIS

Steel monocoque two-door coupe

SPECIAL FEATURES

The M3 can be easily recognized by its deep chin spoiler.

Wide 17-inch alloy wheels and very low-profile tires help to sharpen the M3's handling.

RUNNING GEAR

Steering: Power-assisted rack-and-pinion

Front suspension: MacPherson struts with arc-shaped lower arms, coils springs, twin-tube shocks and anti-roll bar

Rear suspension: Independent system with coil springs, twin-tube shocks and anti-roll bar

Brakes: Vented discs, 12.4 in. dia. (front), 12.3 in. dia. (rear)

Wheels: Alloy, 17 x 7.5J (front), 17 x 8.5J (rear)

Tires: 225/45ZR-17 (front), 245/40ZR-17 (rear)

DIMENSIONS

Length: 174.5 in.   **Width:** 66.9 in.

Height: 53.7 in.   **Wheelbase:** 106.3 in.

Track: 56 in. (front), 56.6 in. (rear)

Weight: 3,352 lbs.

*Details apply to European-spec M3 Evolution.

BMW Z3 M COUPE

For people who want the really high performance of the M Roadster, but the practicality of a coupe, BMW introduced the M Coupe. It is just as fast but, thanks to its far stiffer structure, handles even better.

"...changes directions instantly."

"What happens when you add a roof? In the case of the M Coupe, it makes the car 2.6 times stiffer, sharpening up the car's responses dramatically. The M Coupe changes direction instantly and turns in sharply, but it's not in the least bit twitchy, always safe and well-behaved, flattering the driver. There's surprisingly strong understeer built in, and it takes real effort to kick the tail out under power (and it's impossible with the traction control switched on). Braking is superb."

Cabin ergonomics are first class, and the figure-hugging seats are practical, too.

Milestones

1993 With the design of the production Z3 convertible pretty well finalized, BMW engineers turn their thoughts to a hot-rod coupe.

1995 The Z3 enters production at first with a 1.9-liter four-cylinder engine.

BMW is currently working on a more expensive sports car, the sleek Z8.

1996 Inevitably, the Z3 gets what it deserves— the in-line six-cylinder engine, with 189 bhp. The M Roadster debuts at the Geneva Show with the M Power 3.2-liter in-line six-cylinder engine under the hood.

The M Roadster has become a common sight on many roads.

1998 A hardtop is grafted onto the M Roadster to form the M Coupe, which has different engine outputs for the U.S. (240 bhp) and Europe (321 bhp).

UNDER THE SKIN

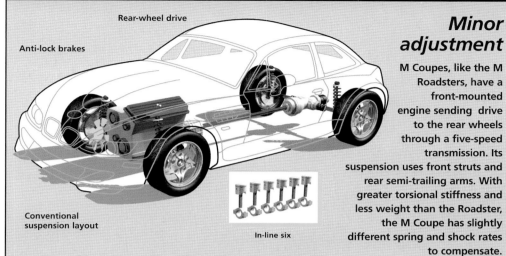

Rear-wheel drive

Anti-lock brakes

Conventional suspension layout

In-line six

Minor adjustment

M Coupes, like the M Roadsters, have a front-mounted engine sending drive to the rear wheels through a five-speed transmission. Its suspension uses front struts and rear semi-trailing arms. With greater torsional stiffness and less weight than the Roadster, the M Coupe has slightly different spring and shock rates to compensate.

THE POWER PACK

Long-stroke design

Powering the M Coupe is the iron-block, alloy-head 3.2-liter engine used in the old M3 rather than the current all-alloy in-line six in the new 3 Series. There are twin chain-driven overhead camshafts, and they operate four valves per cylinder. Helping the long-stroke design produce even more torque is BMW's VANOS system of constantly variable valve timing working on the inlet valves, giving masses of torque below the 3,800 rpm peak. U.S. versions, with 240 bhp, have a lower compression ratio and do without VANOS.

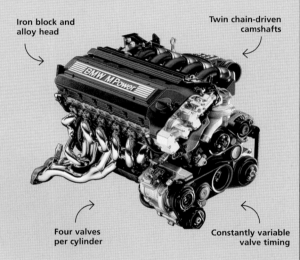

Iron block and alloy head

Twin chain-driven camshafts

Four valves per cylinder

Constantly variable valve timing

Euro power

For real thrills, you need the European-spec M Coupe. It has the 321-bhp engine which *could* take it way beyond its electronically governed 155 mph. It's quicker to 60 mph too—just 4.9 seconds—with the standing ¼-mile completed in 13.6 seconds.

European-spec models are tuned for more outright power than U.S. cars.

BMW Z3 M COUPE

Not many M Coupes will be made, so BMW knew it could take a chance with the controversial styling. It's deliberately a love-it-or-hate-it design intended to make an impact that's impossible to ignore.

Flared arches

The M Coupe shares the same flared wheel arches as the M Roadster. They are greatly extended compared with those on the original Z3. The car is also lower than the Z3.

Six-cylinder engine

European cars have variable intake and exhaust valve timing but U.S. versions have variable intake timing only.

Five-speed transmission

BMW has a six-speed transmission for the European M3 Coupe, but there isn't room for it under the M Coupe's hood, so a five-speed is used. The ratios are kept close so that top gear is a direct ratio and top speed is reached only 200 rpm below the redline.

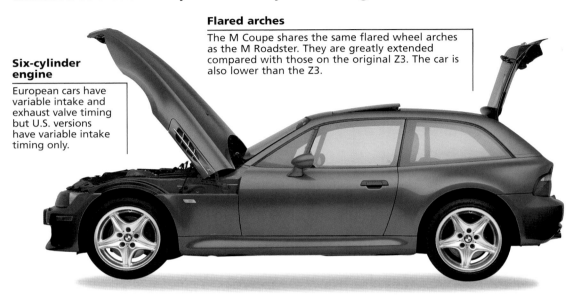

Bigger rear wheels

Although the M Coupe's five-spoke alloys are the same 17-inch diameter front and rear, the rear wheels are wider, reflecting the fact that it is a powerful rear-wheel-drive car.

Stiffer bodyshell

The simple change of adding a roof to the M Roadster dramatically increases the overall rigidity of the car.

Limited-slip differential

With so much power available, a limited-slip differential is essential for maximum traction.

Specifications

1998 BMW Z3 M Coupe

ENGINE

Type: In-line six-cylinder

Construction: Iron block and alloy head

Valve gear: Four valves per cylinder operated by twin chain-driven overhead camshafts

Bore and stroke: 3.40 in. x 3.53 in.

Displacement: 3,152 cc

Compression ratio: 10.5:1

Induction system: Electronic fuel injection

Maximum power: 240 bhp at 6,000 rpm

Maximum torque: 236 lb-ft at 3,800 rpm

Top speed: 139 mph

0–60 mph: 5.1 sec.

TRANSMISSION

Five-speed manual

BODY/CHASSIS

Unitary monocoque construction with steel two-seater coupe body

SPECIAL FEATURES

The hood side vents were developed from the Z3 and the old 507.

The tapered headlamp design is crucial in defining the Coupe's frontal styling.

RUNNING GEAR

Steering: Rack-and-pinion

Front suspension: MacPherson struts with lower control arms and anti-roll bar

Rear suspension: Semi-trailing arms with coil springs, telescopic shock absorbers and anti-roll bar

Brakes: Vented discs, 12.4-in. dia. (front), 12.3-in. dia. (rear)

Wheels: Alloy, 7.5 x 17 in. (front), 9 x 17 in. (rear)

Tires: 225/45 ZR17 (front), 245/40 ZR17 (rear)

DIMENSIONS

Length: 158.5 in.   **Width:** 68.5 in.

Height: 50.4 in.   **Wheelbase:** 96.8 in.

Track: 56.0 in. (front), 58.7 in. (rear)

Weight: 3,131 lbs.

Bugatti EB110

Ettore Bugatti's pre-war supercars inspired one man, Romano Artioli, to reform the company and build a car that Ettore himself might have built if he had lived in our age: the incredible quad-turbo V12 EB110.

"...cutting-edge art."

"This is a staggering tour-de-force supercar in the ultimate sense of the word. But as you pull onto the Autostrada, and the four turbochargers summon the silky V12 to sing in your ears, you notice how civilized this all feels. Yes, this is a mid-engined, all-wheel drive, half-million dollar machine. But in your hands, all this cutting-edge technology combines with art as only a true Italian masterpiece can."

Bugatti made the EB110 one of the easiest supercars to drive with its light controls and outstanding high-speed stability.

Milestones

1956 Bugatti ends production with the unsuccessful Type 101; Ettore Bugatti himself had died in 1947.

1987 Romano Artioli acquires the use of the Bugatti name and builds a new factory in Campogalliano near Modena, Italy rather than Molsheim, France where Bugatti was originally based.

1991 the EB110 is launched on September 15 with a spectacular party in Paris. EB stands for Ettore Bugatti and 110 for the 110th anniversary of his birth.

Standard EB110 GT next to the lightweight EB110S.

1992 The EB110 becomes the world's fastest production car, rivaling the Jaguar XJ220 with a speed of 212 mph. The sports version of the EB110 appears, the EB110S.

1994 The EB110S is renamed the EB110SS (Super Sport) and has a power output of 611 bhp and 477 lb-ft of torque, to give a claimed top speed of 221 mph.

1995 Sales of the EB110 never reach the over-optimistic projected levels and the company finally goes into receivership.

UNDER THE SKIN

Carbon fiber structure

The EB110 has a carbon fiber tub for two reasons: the material is extremely strong and also far lighter than steel or alloy. It covers a four-wheel drive system with the gearbox ahead of the mid-mounted engine and connected to the front differentials via a torque tube. Only 27 percent of the drive goes to the front wheels.

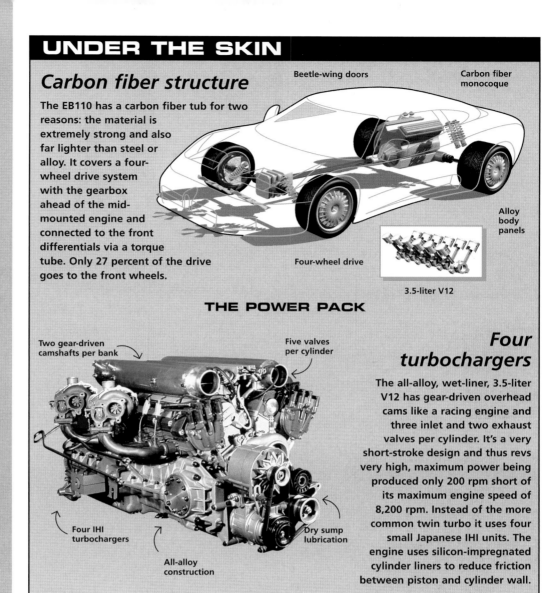

Beetle-wing doors

Carbon fiber monocoque

Alloy body panels

Four-wheel drive

3.5-liter V12

THE POWER PACK

Two gear-driven camshafts per bank

Five valves per cylinder

Four IHI turbochargers

Dry sump lubrication

All-alloy construction

Four turbochargers

The all-alloy, wet-liner, 3.5-liter V12 has gear-driven overhead cams like a racing engine and three inlet and two exhaust valves per cylinder. It's a very short-stroke design and thus revs very high, maximum power being produced only 200 rpm short of its maximum engine speed of 8,200 rpm. Instead of the more common twin turbo it uses four small Japanese IHI units. The engine uses silicon-impregnated cylinder liners to reduce friction between piston and cylinder wall.

Supersport

The S stood for Supersport. It was designed for international GT racing and had a fixed rear wing, no rear side windows and stiffened suspension. The 110SS, as it was later known, was 441 lbs. lighter thanks to carbon fiber body panels, Plexiglas side windows and a stripped interior. An extra 40 bhp raised the already impressive top speed to 221 mph.

The earth-shattering EB110S: 441 lbs. lighter than the standard car.

Bugatti **EB110**

Despite the name, Bugatti was originally a French company. However, when it reformed in the 1990s, it was Italian-owned and the EB110 rivaled other Italian greats, the Ferrari F40 and Lamborghini Diablo.

Four-wheel drive

The Bugatti's 552 bhp is fed to all four wheels, although not in equal amounts: 63 percent of the drive goes to the rear and 37 percent to the front.

Six-speed transmission

To enable the driver to exploit all the power from the rev-happy V12, the EB110 has a six-speed close-ratio transmission mounted in front of the engine.

Four turbochargers

To avoid turbo lag at low engine speeds, the EB110 has no fewer than four small intercooled IHI turbos, two for each bank of cylinders.

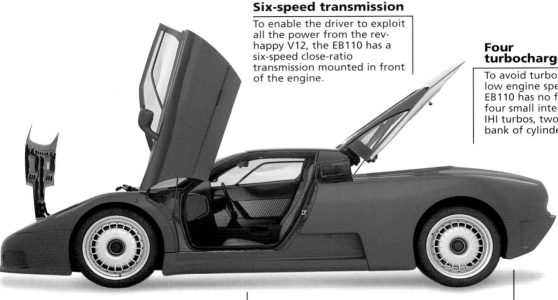

Carbon fiber chassis

Even before the advanced McLaren F1 appeared, the EB110 had a main structural "tub" or chassis made of carbon fiber, making it incredibly strong.

Special Michelin tires

Bugatti's close relationship with Michelin resulted in special ultra low-profile MXX3 tires for the EB110, fitted to alloy wheels inspired by those fitted to the pre-war Bugatti Royale.

Quad-cam V12

The EB110's 3.5-liter V12 revs to 8,200 rpm and produces as much power as the early Cosworth DFV Formula One engines.

Traditional Bugatti grill

Bugatti's horseshoe shaped radiator opening was retained for the EB110, to give it unmistakable links to Bugatti's past.

Anti-pollution devices

Four turbos are complemented by four catalytic convertors and an oil vapor collector to make the EB110 as eco-friendly as possible.

Twin rear shocks

To give the best wheel control, the EB110 uses two shocks on each side of the car's rear double wishbone suspension.

Alloy bodywork

To save weight, the body is made from lightweight aluminum alloy, usually painted traditional Bugatti blue, although some EB110s are silver.

Specifications
1993 Bugatti EB110

ENGINE

Type: V12, quad-cam
Construction: Light alloy block and heads with wet cylinder liners
Valve gear: Five valves per cylinder (three inlet, two exhaust) operated by four overhead camshafts
Bore and stroke: 3.3 in. x 2.2 in.
Displacement: 3,500 cc
Compression ratio: 7.5:1
Induction system: Bugatti multi-port fuel injection with four IHI turbos
Maximum power: 552 bhp at 8,000 rpm
Maximum torque: 450 lb-ft at 3,750 rpm
Top speed: 212 mph
0–60 mph: 3.5 sec

TRANSMISSION

Six-speed manual

BODY/CHASSIS

Alloy two-door, two-seat coupe with carbon fiber monocoque chassis

SPECIAL FEATURES

Like the Lamborghini Diablo, the EB110 has "butterfly" doors. On a car this wide, it would be almost impossible to open conventional doors in a standard size parking space or garage.

RUNNING GEAR

Steering: Rack-and-pinion
Front suspension: Twin wishbones, coil springs, telescopic shocks and anti-roll bar
Rear suspension: Twin wishbones, with twin coil spring/shock units per side
Brakes: Vented discs (front and rear), 12.7 in. with ABS
Wheels: Magnesium alloy 9 in. x 18 in. (front),12 in. x 18 in. (rear)
Tires: Michelin 245/40 (front) and 325/30 (rear)

DIMENSIONS

Length: 173.2 in.
Width: 76.4 in.
Wheelbase: 100.4 in.
Height: 44.3 in.
Track: 61 in. (front), 63.7 in. (rear)
Weight: 3,571 lbs.

Buick GNX

The basic idea of the GNX was to mimic what Buick did with the GSX™ project in 1970. Because 1987 marked the end of the rear-wheel drive Regal™, Buick wanted to build a killer limited edition performance car using its turbo V6 engine.

"...B-B-Bad to the Bone."

"The caption on 1987 Buick GNX promotional poster read: 'The Grand National™ to end all Grand Nationals.' When the simple V6 is fired up it sounds docile. With one foot on the brake and the other on the gas the boost needle rises to 1 psi. Release the brake and drop the accelerator and the 3.8 liter engine quickly makes 15 psi of boost rocketing the car down the ¼ mile in 13.43 seconds at 104 mph. Another Turbo Buick promotion labeled the car as 'B-B-Bad to the Bone'—and it lives up to this reputation."

The standard GN gauges were scrapped in favor of analog instruments from Stewart-Warner.

Milestones

1978 A downsized Buick Regal is launched with a turbo 3.8 liter V6 engine that kicks out 150 bhp.

The turbo V6 was also offered in Regal T-Types.

1982 215 Grand Nationals and 2,022 T-Types are built.

1984 GNs return with an all-black exterior and a 200-bhp turbo V6 engine. Grand Nationals are nothing more than an appearance package on the Buick T-Type.

1986 The Grand National and T-Types get an air-to-air intercooler revised fuel management system and relocated turbocharger. The engine makes 235 bhp.

Buick sold 20,193 GNs in 1987.

1987 Stock turbo Buicks make 345 bhp. Buick and ASC/Mclaren build 547 GNX cars to commemorate the final year of the turbocharged cars.

UNDER THE SKIN

Rear torque arm and Panhard rod

Recalibrated transmission

Auxiliary transmission cooler

Turbocharged V6

Luxury coupe

Beneath the menacing black paint essentially lies a Regal— Buick's mid-size luxury coupe of the late 1980s. For the GNX the suspension has been modified for better handling. Sideloads are absorbed by a Panhard rod, while a torque arm offers better traction off the line. Braking is by power discs at the front and drums at the rear.

THE POWER PACK

Forced-power GNXpress

Under the hood lies the key to the GNX's Corvette-killing performance. It used the standard turbocharged V6 found in the T-Type and GN, but was modified by ASC/McLaren. The intercooler has a greater cooling capacity than a stock GN's. To reduce back pressure a low restriction, dual exhaust system is used. The fuel management system was recalibrated to permit the T-3 Garrett turbocharger with a ceramic impeller to produce a maximum of 15 psi of boost to make 276 bhp at 4,400 rpm and 360 lb-ft of torque at 3,000 rpm.

T-3 Garrett turbocharger with ceramic impeller

Sequential port fuel injection

8:1 compression ratio

modified intercooler

Modern Muscle

During the 1980s late-model muscle cars were beginning to resurface. It was the first time since the 1960s that American cars were running the S/S ¼ mile in under 14 seconds. The Buick GNX was the fastest production car in 1987 and is a landmark car for collectors.

Surprisingly, the 1987 GNX was faster than the new Corvette® that year.

Buick GNX

Buick had three objectives with the GNX; to drop its 0–60 by almost a second over a stock GN, to revise the body and interior in functional areas, and to build a limited number to create exclusivity and collectability. It met them all.

Flared wheel arches

Because of the larger and wider wheels and tires, the front and rear wheel well openings had to be modified and fitted with composite fender flares. They blend in nicely with the rest of the GNX's styling.

Upgraded turbocharged engine

The 3.8 liter SFI turbocharged engines are refitted with a better turbo, improved intercooler, recalibrated fuel management system and a low restriction exhaust system.

Ceramic impeller

The ceramic impeller in the turbocharger greatly reduces turbo lag.

Live axle

The same 8.5-inch rear that is found in the GN and T-Type is retained in the GNX. It also uses the same 3.42:1 axle ratio. All GNX cars came equipped with aluminum rear brake drums to help save weight.

Powermaster brakes

A unique braking system was used on all turbocharged Buicks. Instead of a vacuum-assisted system it uses a hydraulic system that works off the power steering pump.

Modified transmission

A stock GN 200-4R transmission with a 2.74:1 first-gear ratio and an increased stall speed torque converter was used in the GNX. It was recalibrated for increased line pressure, resulting in firmer shifts.

16 x 8-inch alloy wheels

Larger 16 x 8-inch BBS style black mesh wheels were used on all GNXs. It's a very similar wheel used on the Trans Am GTA, but with a different offset.

Stiffer suspension

The GNX has a unique rear suspension. It uses a Panhard rod and torque arm. It also uses the same 19 mm anti-roll bar and Delco shocks found on GNs and T-Types.

Black out

Like all 1984-1987 Grand Nationals, the GNX was only available in black. Tinted glass, black wheel centers and a complete lack of exterior chrome further enhanced its menacing appearance. It did receive special 'GNX' badging on the front fenders, grill and rear trunk lid.

Stewart-Warner gauges

A special Stewart-Warner analog instrument cluster replaces the stock gauges. It includes a 140 mph speedometer, 8,000 rpm tachometer, turbo boost gauge, amp meter, oil pressure and water temperature gauge.

Fender vents

Vents were incorporated into the fenders to reduce engine bay heat.

Specifications

1987 Buick Regal GNX

ENGINE

Type: V6

Construction: Cast-iron block and heads

Valve gear: Two valves per cylinder operated by a camshaft with .389/.411 inch lift and 294/290 degrees of duration

Bore and stroke: 3.80 in. x 3.40 in.

Displacement: 231 c.i.

Compression ratio: 8.0:1

Induction system: SFI with modified intercooler and Garrett T-3 turbocharger

Maximum power: 276 bhp at 4,400 rpm

Maximum torque: 360 lb-ft at 3,000 rpm

Top speed: 124 mph

0–60 mph: 5.5 sec.

TRANSMISSION

Modified GM 200-4R four-speed automatic

BODY/CHASSIS

Steel two-door four-seater

SPECIAL FEATURES

GNXs have special fender vents which release hot air from the engine compartment.

Each GNX is numbered and has a plaque on the dashboard. Also, anyone who ordered one new received a GNX booklet, hat and jacket.

RUNNING GEAR

Steering: Recirculating ball

Front suspension: Double wishbones with shocks and anti-roll bar

Rear suspension: Live axle with Panhard rod, torque arm, trailing links, coil springs, and anti-roll bar

Brakes: Discs, 10.5-in. dia. (front), drums, 9.5-in. dia. (rear)

Wheels: Alloy, 8 x 16 in.

Tires: Goodyear Gatorbacks, 245/50 VR16 (front), 255/50 VR16 (rear)

DIMENSIONS

Length: 200.6 in. **Width:** 71.6 in.

Height: 56.0 in. **Wheelbase:** 108.1 in.

Track: 59.4 in. (front), 59.3 in. (rear)

Weight: 3,545 lbs.

Callaway **CORVETTE SPEEDSTER**

When turbocharging specialist Reeves Callaway built his mighty ZR-1®-beating, twin-turbo Sledgehammer version of the Corvette it was difficult to see what else could match it. The answer was the incredible and amazing-looking Corvette Speedster.

"...astounding acceleration."

"The chopped roof is disconcerting and the wraparound rear window and headrests make it difficult to see out, but practicality is not the Speedster's forté. Acceleration is astounding—it can reach 100 mph in 12.1 seconds. Callaway has reworked the Corvette suspension to increase its handling characteristics. And when you take into account the powerful brakes, enormous grip from the tires and outrageous style, the sky-high price becomes understandable."

The blue-trimmed interior is outrageous—but then so is the performance.

Milestones

1985 Reeves Callaway fits twin

turbos to an Alfa Romeo GTV6, boosting its power output to 230 bhp and taking top speed to 140 mph. Chevrolet is so impressed that it approaches Callaway to develop a twin-turbo version of the Corvette.

Callaway used the standard C4 Corvette as the basis for his turbocharged specials.

1988 Callaway produces the incredible

225-mph, 880-bhp Sledge-hammer version of the Corvette. French Canadian stylist Paul Deutschman is charged with improving the stock Corvette's aerodynamics.

Callaway also has a racing program and has entered Corvettes at Le Mans.

1991 The first Speedster appears at the

Los Angeles Auto Show, and is the first car identified purely as a Callaway. The reception is amazing and Callaway prepares to make the Speedster a special edition; only 50 are built.

UNDER THE SKIN

Fiberglass body panels

All-independent suspension

Four-wheel disc brakes

Twin-turbo V8

Reworked

Callaway has comprehensively reworked the standard C4 Corvette. Composite transverse leaf springs are almost a Corvette trademark, but these have been replaced with coil-over-shock units for all four wheels which give greater chassis tuning possibilities. At the same time the brake system is uprated with a Callaway/Brembo set up with four-piston calipers and vented cross-drilled discs.

THE POWER PACK

Totally revised

Callaway completely stripped and rebuilt the Corvette 350-cubic inch L98 V8, fitting a stronger crankshaft which is made from forged steel rather than cast iron. The compression ratio has been lowered to 7.5:1 using Cosworth or Mahle pistons to allow for turbocharging with twin RotoMaster turbos. The aluminum-alloy heads are milled and have stronger valve springs plus stainless-steel valves, and the standard electronic fuel injection has been recalibrated to help boost the new power output.

Dual intercoolers

Steel crankshaft

Dual RotoMaster turbochargers

7.5:1 compression pistons

Dream Vette®

With its incredible acceleration, superior handling and braking, plus outrageous style and very limited production, the Callaway Corvette Speedster ranks among the most desirable performance car ever built, anywhere.

Only a select few are lucky enough to own a Callaway Speedster.

Callaway CORVETTE SPEEDSTER

Callaway proved that there was no need to go down the ZR-1 route with a complex quad-cam, 32-valve V8. It showed that all you need for huge horsepower is twin intercooled turbochargers producing 420 bhp.

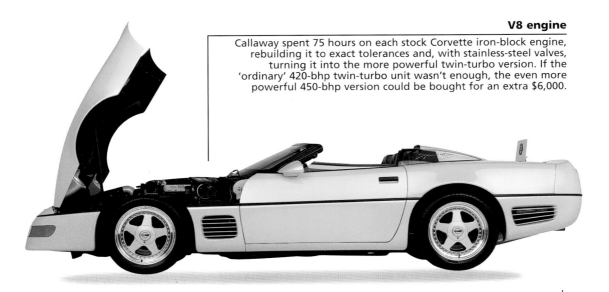

V8 engine

Callaway spent 75 hours on each stock Corvette iron-block engine, rebuilding it to exact tolerances and, with stainless-steel valves, turning it into the more powerful twin-turbo version. If the 'ordinary' 420-bhp twin-turbo unit wasn't enough, the even more powerful 450-bhp version could be bought for an extra $6,000.

Intercooled turbochargers

Most of the increase in power is due to the twin turbochargers. The watercooled RotoMaster units produce power quickly with little lag. The air is fed through twin intercoolers to keep it dense and to help release more power.

Extra vents

The Speedster features a variety of very large vents at both the front and rear to guarantee that the engine receives enough air and that the big brakes are properly cooled. Their exaggerated size is due to style as well as function.

Leather interior

Callaway would fit the very highest quality full-leather trim to the Speedster on request, but it cost an extra $12,000.

Wraparound rear window

The side glass is continued onto the rear deck and complements the prominent twin headrest humps which are a big part of the Speedster theme.

MBT 546

Lowered windshield

Callaway chopped seven inches from the Corvette's A-pillars to lower the windshield. However, it is not a full seven inches lower because of exaggerated rake, but it does aid aerodynamics at high speed.

Exotic colors

Speedsters were available in 12 different colors, but some of the more exotic, including Old Lyme Green, Hot Pink or Nuclear Meltdown Orange, were an expensive option at $7,500.

Specifications

1991 Callaway Corvette Speedster

ENGINE

Type: V8

Construction: Cast-iron block and alloy heads

Valve gear: Two valves per cylinder operated by a single vee-mounted camshaft via pushrods and rockers

Bore and stroke: 4.0 in. x 3.48 in.

Displacement: 350 c.i.

Compression ratio: 7.5:1

Induction system: Electronic fuel injection with Callaway Micro Fueler controller and twin RotoMaster turbochargers

Maximum power: 420 bhp at 4,250 rpm

Maximum torque: 562 lb-ft at 2,500 rpm

Top speed: 185 mph

0–60 mph: 4.5 sec

TRANSMISSION

Six-speed manual

BODY/CHASSIS

Separate steel chassis frame with two-seater fiberglass open speedster body

SPECIAL FEATURES

A lowered windshield prevents air from buffeting inside the cabin.

The Speedster has a special plaque mounted on the console next to the boost gauge.

RUNNING GEAR

Steering: Rack-and-pinion

Front suspension: Double wishbones with coil springs, telescopic shock absorbers and anti-roll bar

Rear suspension: Multi-link with coil springs, telescopic shock absorbers and anti-roll bar

Brakes: Brembo vented discs with four-piston calipers (front and rear)

Wheels: Alloy, 9.5 x 18 in. (front), 11 x 18 in. (rear)

Tires: Bridgestone RE71 285/35 ZR18

DIMENSIONS

Length: 176.5 in.   **Width:** 71.0 in.

Height: 39.7 in.   **Wheelbase:** 92.2 in.

Track: 59.6 in. (front), 60.4 in. (rear)

Weight: 3,200 lbs.

Chevrolet **CAMARO ZL-1**

GM supported the Automotive Manufacturers Association (AMA) ban in the 1960s by only using its 400 cubic-inch and larger engines in full size cars and Corvettes. Through the Central Office Production Order system Vince Piggins, one of Chevrolet's officers, found a loop hole with the ban and created the ultimate Camaro—the ZL-1.

"...the apex of Chevy muscle."

"This is the apex of Chevy's muscle cars. In the driver's seat the car resembles a typical six-cylinder Camaro. When you start it up and listen to the aggressive engine you soon realize you've slid behind the wheel of a true factory-built racer. With the addition of tubular headers, drag slicks and a super tune, one of these nasty Camaros could run the ¼ mile in 11.68 seconds at more than 120 mph. Few cars come close to offering the level of thrill that a ZL-1 can."

Most ZL-1s had stripped cabins, but this one has a deluxe interior with woodgrain trim.

Milestones

1967 In response to the Mustang,

Chevrolet launches the Camaro. The most powerful engine available is the 375 bhp, 396 V8. Because of the AMA ban, GM's intermediates weren't available with engines larger than 400 cubic inches. Meanwhile, a handful of Chevy dealers were installing 427 V8s into these cars, especially Camaros.

In 1967 car dealers were installing 427 V8s into new Camaros.

1968 Don Yenko of

Yenko Sports Cars becomes the largest dealer converting these Camaros. GM's Vince Piggins takes notice. Later that year, Piggins and Yenko get together to offer the conversion package from GM's COPO (Central Office Production Order) department for 1969.

Don Yenko's YSC Camaros got the ball rolling for the ZL-1.

1969 A few hundred COPO Camaros

are built. While most come with cast iron 427s, 69 versions known as ZL-1s are built with aluminum big-block engines. Tuned ZL-1s made 500+ bhp and could cover the ¼ mile in just under 12 seconds.

UNDER THE SKIN

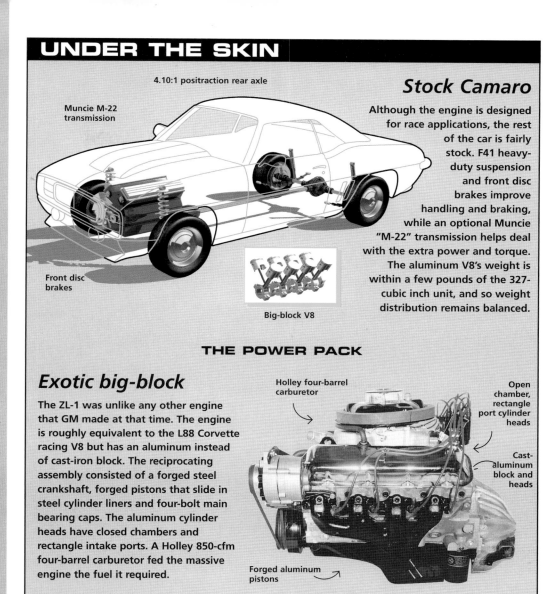

4.10:1 positraction rear axle

Muncie M-22 transmission

Front disc brakes

Big-block V8

Stock Camaro

Although the engine is designed for race applications, the rest of the car is fairly stock. F41 heavy-duty suspension and front disc brakes improve handling and braking, while an optional Muncie "M-22" transmission helps deal with the extra power and torque. The aluminum V8's weight is within a few pounds of the 327-cubic inch unit, and so weight distribution remains balanced.

THE POWER PACK

Exotic big-block

The ZL-1 was unlike any other engine that GM made at that time. The engine is roughly equivalent to the L88 Corvette racing V8 but has an aluminum instead of cast-iron block. The reciprocating assembly consisted of a forged steel crankshaft, forged pistons that slide in steel cylinder liners and four-bolt main bearing caps. The aluminum cylinder heads have closed chambers and rectangle intake ports. A Holley 850-cfm four-barrel carburetor fed the massive engine the fuel it required.

Holley four-barrel carburetor

Open chamber, rectangle port cylinder heads

Cast-aluminum block and heads

Forged aluminum pistons

Pure racer

ZL-1s are ranked with the Hemi Cuda convertible and Ram Air IV™ GTO® as one of the most desirable muscle cars ever produced. With only 69 built with the all-aluminum engine, they attract a premium price and often trade hands for $150,000 or more.

To this day, Chevrolet hasn't built a more powerful production car than the ZL-1.

Chevrolet **CAMARO ZL1**

Most ZL-1s had plain bodies with skinny steel wheels—they didn't even have any badging to designate their model or engine size. This unique ZL-1 has the RS appearance package, vinyl top and 427 badging.

ZL2 cowl hood

All ZL-1s came with cowl induction hoods. It forced cool air into the engine from the high pressure area just below the windshield.

Expensive engine

You had to have a healthy bank account to be able to afford a ZL-1 Camaro. The engine's all-aluminum construction saved 160 lbs. over the cast-iron 427. Because it is virtually hand built, the engine alone cost $4,160—more than most cars of the period.

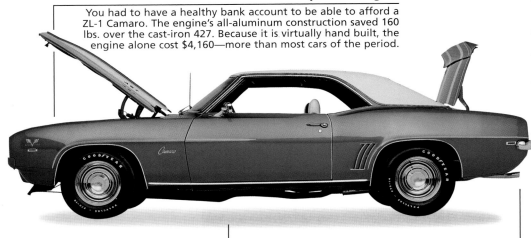

Better balance

Although it is a big-block unit, the ZL-1 engine weighs about 500 lbs. which is roughly the same as a 327, and so these special Camaros actually handle better than the stock SS 396™. However, these cars were designed for use in NHRA Super Stock drag racing events.

Standard exhaust system

ZL-1s left the factory with lots of mismatched parts because the owners were expected to do a lot of race development themselves. The stock exhaust manifolds restrict the flow of exhaust gases and were usually among the first items to be replaced.

The ZL-1 option package

All ZL-1s began life as SS 396s, but the engine and Super Sport™ option were deleted. Instead, the special cars received the ZL-1 option package which included the aluminum engine, F41 suspension, front discs and a cowl induction hood.

Heavy duty suspension components

All ZL-1s were equipped with the heavy duty F41 suspension and front disc brakes. To better handle the 450 lb-ft of torque from the powerful engines, ZL-1s were equipped with 12-bolt rear ends with 4.10 gears.

Performance transmission

Only two transmissions were strong enough to cope with the ZL-1 V8: the Muncie M-22 'Rock Crusher' four-speed or the equally stout TurboHydramatic 400 automatic.

Specifications

1969 Chevrolet Camaro ZL-1

ENGINE
Type: V8

Construction: Aluminum block and cylinder heads

Valve gear: Two valves per cylinder operated by a single camshaft

Bore and stroke: 4.25 in. x 3.76 in.

Displacement: 427 c.i.

Compression ratio: 12.0:1

Induction system: Holley four-barrel carburetor

Maximum power: 430 bhp at 5,200 rpm

Maximum torque: 450 lb-ft at 4,400 rpm

Top speed: 125 mph

0–60 mph: 5.3 sec

TRANSMISSION
Muncie M-22 four-speed manual

BODY/CHASSIS
Unitary steel chassis with two-door hardtop coupe body

SPECIAL FEATURES

Each ZL-1 engine has a special sticker on the valve cover.

Most ZL-1s have exposed headlights, but this car has the RS package.

RUNNING GEAR
Steering: Recirculating ball

Front suspension: Double wishbones with coil springs, telescopic shock absorbers and anti-roll bar

Rear suspension: Live axle with semi-elliptic leaf springs and telescopic shock absorbers

Brakes: Discs (front), drums (rear)

Wheels: Steel, 6 x 15 in.

Tires: Goodyear Wide Tread GT, E70-15

DIMENSIONS
Length: 186.0 in. **Width:** 74.0 in.

Height: 51.0 in. **Wheelbase:** 108.0 in.

Track: 59.6 in. (front), 59.5 in. (rear)

Chevrolet **CORVETTE GS**

With the advent of the new C5 model on the horizon, Chevrolet wanted to send off the fourth generation version in typical Corvette style. So for its final year in production, Chevy® added a 330-bhp LT4 small-block V8 and some interesting graphics that hark back to the original sports racer of the 1960s and called it the Grand Sport.

"...a driving enthusiast's dream."

"Because this is a limited edition Corvette it needed more than radical graphics to give it collectible status. The engine reaches 330 bhp thanks to redesigned cylinder heads and intake manifold. Its stable road manners and flat-out handling leave the driver with a strong feeling of confidence and enthusiasm. The firm suspension, responsive steering and potent brakes mated with the one-year-only engine option are a hard-core driving enthusiast's dream come true."

'Grand Sport' embroidery on each seat back is just one exclusive touch to this special Vette®.

Milestones

1954 The first V8 Corvette
is built. It uses the 195-bhp 'Turbo-Fire' 265-cubic-inch V8.

1967 Most coveted of all
Corvettes is the L88 Sting Ray®. Only 20 are built.

1984 Late-model technology
in the form of a rigid chassis and race-car style suspension is the focus on the fourth-generation model.

The original Grand Sport cars were built for SCCA racing.

1990 'King of the Hill' is the name
given to the ZR-1®. It boasts a special Lotus-designed 32-valve all-alloy engine.

For the Corvette's 40th anniversary in 1993, a special appearance package was offered.

1996 The end of an era coincides
with the one-year-only LT4 small-block V8. Grand Sport production is limited to 1,000 units.

UNDER THE SKIN

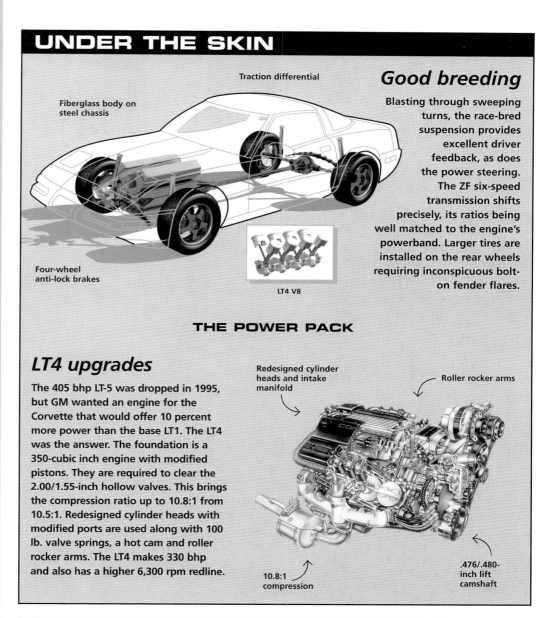

Traction differential

Fiberglass body on steel chassis

Four-wheel anti-lock brakes

LT4 V8

Good breeding

Blasting through sweeping turns, the race-bred suspension provides excellent driver feedback, as does the power steering. The ZF six-speed transmission shifts precisely, its ratios being well matched to the engine's powerband. Larger tires are installed on the rear wheels requiring inconspicuous bolt-on fender flares.

THE POWER PACK

LT4 upgrades

The 405 bhp LT-5 was dropped in 1995, but GM wanted an engine for the Corvette that would offer 10 percent more power than the base LT1. The LT4 was the answer. The foundation is a 350-cubic inch engine with modified pistons. They are required to clear the 2.00/1.55-inch hollow valves. This brings the compression ratio up to 10.8:1 from 10.5:1. Redesigned cylinder heads with modified ports are used along with 100 lb. valve springs, a hot cam and roller rocker arms. The LT4 makes 330 bhp and also has a higher 6,300 rpm redline.

Redesigned cylinder heads and intake manifold

Roller rocker arms

10.8:1 compression

.476/.480-inch lift camshaft

Neat package

Models with the Z51 'Performance Handling Package' have a special attraction. The package increases the Grand Sport's cornering ability by means of thicker anti-roll bars, firmer shocks and stiffer springs. The ride is firm, but the trade-off is worth it.

In addition to its many dynamic qualities, the Grand Sport is very attractive.

Chevrolet **CORVETTE GS**

All Grand Sports were finished in the identical color scheme. This makes the cars very distinctive, while the limited production run guarantees a desirable degree of exclusivity.

Small-block V8

To separate the 330-bhp LT4 small-block from the base LT1, the ignition wires, intake manifold and 'Corvette' lettering on the plastic manifold covers are all painted red.

High-flow heads

The LT4's heads are a completely different casting than the LT1's. The exhaust ports are widened, the intake ports are raised by .100-inch and the radius has been smoothed for better flow. They are assembled with larger 2.00-inch hollow-stem intake valves, and 1.55-inch sodium-filled exhaust valves and use stiffer valve springs.

Distinctive color

All Grand Sports are painted Admiral Blue Metallic with a white stripe down the center of the body and red hash marks on the driver's side front fender.

Six-speed shifting

GM didn't think that an automatic unit would be strong enough to handle the engine's 10 percent power gain. Because of this, all Grand Sports were only available with a strong ZF 6-speed manual transmission.

Performance wheels and tires

High-performance Z-rated Goodyear GS-C tires are fitted to black, powder-coated 17-inch five-spoke wheels. Although they look like ZR-1 wheels, their offset is slightly different.

Special identification

To celebrate the Grand Sport's limited production run of only 1,000 models, Chevrolet gave them a separate serial number sequence.

Aero shape

Although they have a large frontal area, fourth-generation Corvettes slice through the air quite effectively. Special fender flares in the rear have been added to house the wider 315/35 ZR17 tires.

Specifications

1996 Corvette Grand Sport

ENGINE
Type: V8 (LT-4)

Construction: Cast-iron block and aluminum cylinder heads

Valve gear: Two valves per cylinder operated by a centrally-mounted camshaft with pushrods and roller rocker arms

Bore and stroke: 4.00 in. x 3.48 in.

Displacement: 350 c.i.

Compression ratio: 10.8:1

Induction system: Sequential fuel injection

Maximum power: 330 bhp at 5,800 rpm

Maximum torque: 340 lb-ft at 4,500 rpm

Top speed: 168 mph

0–60 mph: 4.7 sec.

TRANSMISSION
Six-speed manual

BODY/CHASSIS
Fiberglass body on steel chassis

SPECIAL FEATURES

The five-spoke wheel design resembles that of the ZR-1, but is in fact unique.

Red 'Grand Sport' seat embroidery is just one of many identifying features.

RUNNING GEAR
Steering: Rack-and-pinion

Front suspension: Independent with aluminum upper and lower control arms, transverse leaf spring, gas shock absorbers and anti-roll bar

Rear suspension: Independent with five-link, transverse leaf spring and anti-roll bar

Brakes: Discs, 12-in. dia. (front and rear)

Wheels: Aluminum, 9.5 x 17 in.

Tires: Goodyear, 275/40 ZR17 (front), P315/35 ZR17 (rear)

DIMENSIONS
Length: 178.5 in.   **Width:** 70.7 in.

Height: 46.3 in.   **Wheelbase:** 96.2 in.

Track: 57.7 in. (front), 59.1 in. (rear)

Weight: 3,298 lbs.

Chevrolet **CORVETTE ZR-1**

With its Lotus-designed quad-cam V8 engine, the ZR-1 has a more advanced powerplant and superior performance than the current C5 Corvette. It is the ultimate Corvette—a genuine world-class supercar.

"...the ultimate Corvette?"

"Above 3,500 rpm, when all 16 injectors are pumping fuel as fast as the engine can use it, the ZR-1's performance is astounding, even for early models. With the later 405 bhp engines there were few cars on the road to challenge the ZR-1's performance. The chassis easily copes with the huge power output. The ride may be harsh and the interior cramped, but this is a supercar with sensitive steering, powerful brakes, and fine rear-wheel drive road manners."

Lateral support in the ZR-1 is excellent, although the cockpit is difficult to enter.

Milestones

1984 A new Corvette

is finally introduced in 1983 as a 1984 model. The fourth-generation Corvette is the best in years, but, although it retains the front-engine rear-drive format, it severely needs more power.

By 1956 the Corvette finally matured, and turned into a serious sports car.

1986 The Corvette roadster

is revived, and goes on sale this year. It is selected as a pace car for the Indianapolis 500.

1990 After much hype,

the ZR-1 finally enters production. It has unique rear end styling to distinguish it from the standard Corvette.

An all-new, fifth-generation Corvette debuted in 1997.

1993 Power is boosted

to 405 bhp and a special 40th anniversary trim package is available on all Corvettes. The ZR-1 returns for two more seasons with new five-spoke alloy wheels.

UNDER THE SKIN

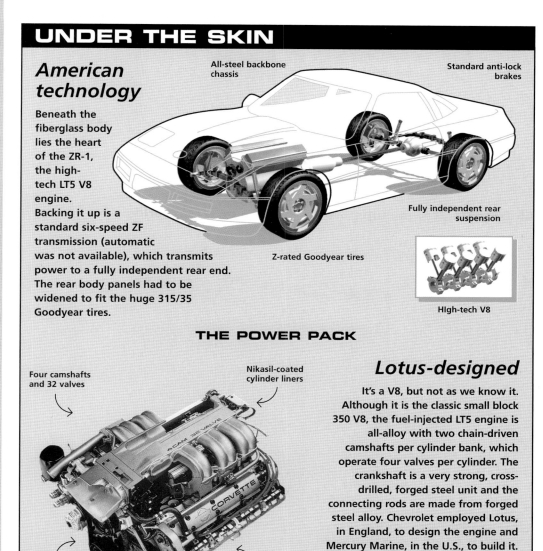

American technology

Beneath the fiberglass body lies the heart of the ZR-1, the high-tech LT5 V8 engine. Backing it up is a standard six-speed ZF transmission (automatic was not available), which transmits power to a fully independent rear end. The rear body panels had to be widened to fit the huge 315/35 Goodyear tires.

All-steel backbone chassis

Standard anti-lock brakes

Fully independent rear suspension

Z-rated Goodyear tires

HIgh-tech V8

THE POWER PACK

Four camshafts and 32 valves

Nikasil-coated cylinder liners

All-alloy construction

Forged steel crankshaft

Lotus-designed

It's a V8, but not as we know it. Although it is the classic small block 350 V8, the fuel-injected LT5 engine is all-alloy with two chain-driven camshafts per cylinder bank, which operate four valves per cylinder. The crankshaft is a very strong, cross-drilled, forged steel unit and the connecting rods are made from forged steel alloy. Chevrolet employed Lotus, in England, to design the engine and Mercury Marine, in the U.S., to build it. The sophisticated design meant that it could be tweaked to produce even more power.

Brute force

In 1993 Chevrolet began to make use of the powerful Lotus-designed LT5 V8, pushing up its output to 405 bhp at 5,800 rpm and the torque to 385 lb-ft. The early ZR-1s may have been fast, but the extra power of the later model really makes them move.

This post-1993 model has an increased power output of 405 bhp.

Chevrolet **CORVETTE ZR-1**

With the ZR-1, Chevrolet proved that an exotic mid-mounted engine and $100,000 price tag are not required to offer true supercar performance.

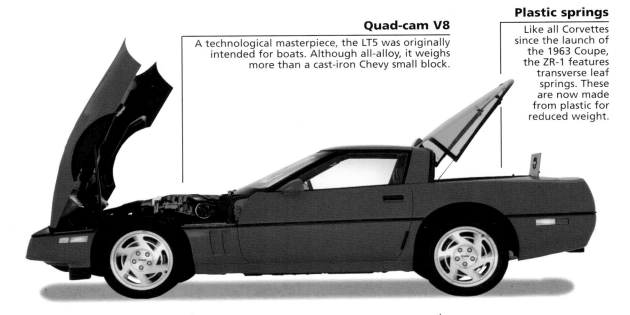

Quad-cam V8
A technological masterpiece, the LT5 was originally intended for boats. Although all-alloy, it weighs more than a cast-iron Chevy small block.

Plastic springs
Like all Corvettes since the launch of the 1963 Coupe, the ZR-1 features transverse leaf springs. These are now made from plastic for reduced weight.

Traction control
Corvettes were often tricky to control on slippery roads. The introduction of ASR (Anti-Slip Regulation) considerably reduced the tendency for the car to slide on wet roads.

Tire-pressure monitor
For 1989 all Corvettes received a tire-pressure monitoring device which warns the driver, by means of a flashing light, if tire pressures are low.

CAGS gear selection
Computer-Aided Gear Selection (CAGS) is a device which skips shifts in low gears at light throttle openings.

Valet key

To prevent certain individuals from experiencing the ZR-1's full performance, a special key can be used to restrict horsepower.

Fiberglass bodywork

The ZR-1, like all Corvettes, retains fiberglass bodywork. The back half of the car had to be widened to fit the ZR-1s large wheels.

Selective ride control

At the touch of a switch the ZR-1 driver can select three different suspension settings: Touring, Sport, or Performance. As speed increases, the shocks are stiffened by a computer that is able to make 10 adjustments per second.

Variable fuel injection

During normal driving, the ZR-1's engine uses only eight primary ports and injectors. With the throttle floored and the engine turning above 3,500 rpm, the eight secondary injectors are brought into action, producing truly awesome performance.

Specifications
1991 Chevrolet Corvette ZR-1

ENGINE

Type: LT5 V8

Construction: Alloy block, heads and cylinder liners

Valve gear: Four valves per cylinder operated by four overhead camshafts

Bore and stroke: 3.90 in. x 3.66 in.

Displacement: 350 c.i.

Compression ratio: 11:1

Induction system: Multi-port fuel injection

Maximum power: 375 bhp at 5,800 rpm

Maximum torque: 371 lb-ft at 4,800 rpm

Top speed: 180 mph

0–60 mph: 5 sec

TRANSMISSION

ZF six-speed manual

BODY/CHASSIS

Separate steel chassis with fiberglass two-door coupe body

SPECIAL FEATURES

A unique feature of the LT5 is the three-stage throttle control.

Prototype ZR-1s retained the original 1984 instrument panel layout.

RUNNING GEAR

Steering: Rack-and-pinion

Front suspension: Double wishbones, transverse plastic leaf springs, and telescopic adjustable shocks

Rear suspension: Upper and lower trailing links, transverse plastic leaf spring, telescopic adjustable shocks, and anti-roll bar

Brakes: Vented discs front and rear, 13 in. dia. (front), 12 in. dia. (rear)

Wheels: Alloy, 17 x 9.5-in. dia. (front), 17 x 11-in. dia. (rear)

Tires: Goodyear Eagle ZR40, 275/40 ZR17 (front), 315/35 ZR17 (rear)

DIMENSIONS

Length: 178.5 in. **Width:** 73.2 in.

Height: 46.7 in.

Wheelbase: 96.2 in.

Track: 60 in. (front), 62 in. (rear)

Weight: 3,519 lbs.

Chevrolet YENKO CHEVELLE

Best known for his hopped-up Camaros®, Don Yenko also offered a small number of hot Chevelles during 1969—made possible due to a GM corporate loophole—powered by 427-cubic inch engines. Properly tuned these cars could run the ¼ mile in around 12 seconds.

"...highly tuned street car."

"If the bold stripes don't tell you that this Chevelle is a highly tuned street car then upon start up, the loud engine note will. Replacing the nasty 375 bhp 396 is an even more belligerent Corvette-spec 427 that cranks out a whopping 450 bhp. During part throttle acceleration, the Yenko Chevelle is notchy and disobedient. But if it's all-out racing excitement you crave, step on the accelerator all the way and listen to the throaty 427 bellow its true intention."

The interior looks stock with the exception of the column-mounted Stewart Warner tach.

Milestones

1967 After building a small number of hot Corvairs, Cannonsburg speed shop owner Don Yenko strikes a deal with Vince Piggins at Chevrolet to build 427 c.i. Camaros. Stock SS 396 models are sent to the Yenko dealership where their engines are swapped out for 427s. A total of 118 are built up to 1968.

The factory Chevelle for 1969 was the SS 396—mainstream muscle.

1969 Using a loophole known as the Central Office Production Order, Yenko convinces Chevrolet to build 427 powered Camaros on the production line. These are then sent to Cannonsburg for installation of decals and trim

Filling the Yenko's shoes in 1970 was the mighty Chevelle SS 454.

1969 Following on from the Camaros are a small number of 427 Chevelles. Yenko orders 99 with SS hoods, 4.10 gears and front disc brakes.

UNDER THE SKIN

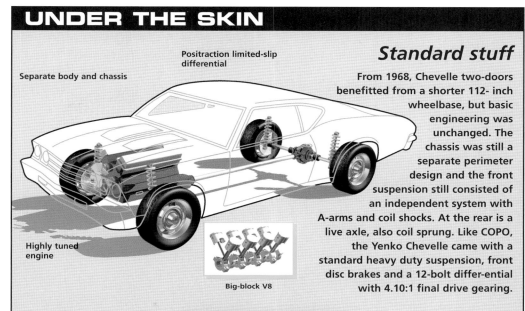

Positraction limited-slip differential

Separate body and chassis

Highly tuned engine

Big-block V8

Standard stuff

From 1968, Chevelle two-doors benefitted from a shorter 112- inch wheelbase, but basic engineering was unchanged. The chassis was still a separate perimeter design and the front suspension still consisted of an independent system with A-arms and coil shocks. At the rear is a live axle, also coil sprung. Like COPO, the Yenko Chevelle came with a standard heavy duty suspension, front disc brakes and a 12-bolt differ-ential with 4.10:1 final drive gearing.

THE POWER PACK

Tyrannical L-72

Due to a corporate edict, the largest engine officially available in the Chevelle in 1969 was a 396. By ordering his cars as COPO specials tuning specialist Don Yenko was able to have 427s factory installed in Chevelles. All these cars have L-72 engines which feature a cast-iron block with four-bolt main bearing caps, rectangular exhaust ports with closed combustion chambers, low restriction exhaust manifolds, an aluminum intake, a solid lifter camshaft and a 800 cfm Holley four-barrel carburetor. GM quoted output at a conservative 425 bhp, however Yenko and the National Hot Rod Association rated them as a more truthful 450 bhp.

Super Car

Only 99 1969 Yenko Chevelles were built. All models had L-72 engines and Positraction 12-bolt rear ends. As some of the quickest GM intermedi-ates of the 1960s, these cars command high prices today and perfectly restored examples sell for $80,000 or more.

Rarest of all Yenko Chevelles are the automatic cars—only 28 were built.

Chevrolet Yenko **CHEVELLE**

Going a step beyond what the factory had to offer, the Yenko Chevelles, adorned with Yenko SC (Super Car) logos, were part of a select band of street warriors and among the finest Detroit muscle cars ever built.

Heavy-duty transmission

The only transmissions deemed strong enough to cope with the raucous 427 were a Muncie M21 and M22 'Rock-crusher' four-speed manual or, as in this car, a strengthened TH400 three-speed automatic.

Big-block engine

All Chevelles built as part of the COPO order received L-72 427-cubic inch V8s with four-barrel carburetors and solid lifters. For an additional charge, Yenko could fit a pair of Mickey Thompson Super Scavenger headers making the Chevelle a genuine 12-second street car.

Heavy-duty rear axle

Intended as straight-line screamers, the 427 COPO Chevelles and Yenkos were fortified with strengthened GM 12-bolt rear ends with 4.10:1 gearing for maximum acceleration. A Posi-traction limited-slip differential was standard.

Gaudy graphics

Yenko liked to dress up his cars, so the Chevelles got side and hood stripes with SC (Super Car) emblems. Like the factory 396SS Chevelles, Yenkos came with a blacked-out Super Sport grill and rear valance along with the intimidating SS hood.

Base interior

As all the 427 Chevelles were part of a COPO order, they received base Malibu interiors, but many had front bench seats and a center console. Some of the Yenko cars also came with three-spoke, wood-rimmed steering wheels and Hurst shifters.

Power front disc brakes

Because it could scream to 60 mph in less than six seconds, the Chevelle needed considerable power to bring it to a halt. Front disc brakes were thus mandatory.

Specifications

1969 Chevrolet Yenko Chevelle

ENGINE

Type: V8

Construction: Cast-iron block and heads

Valve gear: Two valves per cylinder operated by a single camshaft with pushrods and rockers

Bore and stroke: 4.25 in. x 3.76 in.

Displacement: 427 c.i.

Compression ratio: 11.0:1

Induction system: Holley cfm 800 four-barrel carburetor

Maximum power: 450 bhp at 5,000 rpm

Maximum torque: 460 lb-ft at 4,000

Top speed: 110 mph

0–60 mph: 5.7 sec.

TRANSMISSION

TH400 three-speed automatic

BODY/CHASSIS

Separate steel chassis with two-door coupe body

SPECIAL FEATURES

All 427-cubic inch V8s were built at GM's Tonawanda plant in NY.

A vinyl roof was a popular option in the late 1960s.

RUNNING GEAR

Steering: Recirculating ball

Front suspension: Unequal length A-arms, coil springs, telescopic shock absorbers and anti-roll bar

Rear suspension: Live axle, coil springs, lower links and telescopic shock absorbers

Brakes: Discs (front), drums (rear)

Wheels: Steel Rally 7 x 15 in.

Tires: Goodyear Polyglas GT F70-15

DIMENSIONS

Length: 186.4 in.   **Width:** 77.2 in.

Height: 55.6 in.   **Wheelbase:** 112.0 in.

Track: 61.9 (front), 61.0 (rear)

Weight: 3,800 lbs.

De Tomaso MANGUSTA

De Tomaso's first volume production sports car was a mid-engined, supercar designed to challenge Ferrari. It paved the way for the famous Pantera, although in some ways its design was more advanced and more like the racing car from which it was developed.

"...a perfect combination."

"A light front end, flexible chassis and less-than-perfect driving position ensure the Mangusta is a challenge. Against that, there's a perfect combination of power and torque, giving all the performance its shape promises; 100 mph comes up in an impressive 18.7 seconds. The steering is light and the straight line stability good, but don't throw this car into bends too hard; mid-engined cars, particularly this one, don't like it."

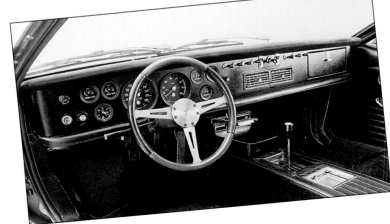

The fully-equipped dashboard gives the Mangusta a strong race car feel.

Milestones

1965 The Turin Motor Show sees an open mid-engined racer, the 70P, appear. It has a central backbone much like De Tomaso's Vallelunga road car, but a 5.0-liter Ford engine rather than a 1.5-liter. It is styled by an ex-GM designer, Pete Brock, and built by coachbuilders Fantuzzi.

Conceived in the early 1960s, the Vallelunga was ahead of its time.

1966 The basic structure of the 70P reappears at the next Turin Show, now covered by the stylish Giugiaro-designed body.

1967 Production of the Mangusta begins with the one-of-a-kind fiberglass show body replaced by sheet metal and aluminum.

The Pantera was built in greater numbers than the Mangusta.

1971 Production ceases after 400 Mangustas (including one convertible) have been made. About 300 were exported to the U.S.

UNDER THE SKIN

Racing heritage

Technically more advanced than the later and more famous Pantera, the Mangusta has a folded and welded sheet steel box-section central backbone. Onto the back of that is mounted the Ford V8 acting, as in a racing car, as a stressed chassis member. Right at the back is the ZF five-speed transmission with long shifter linkage. The classic racing car suspension has double wishbones at the front and rear.

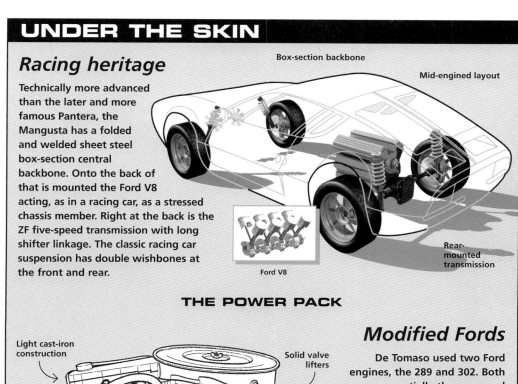

Box-section backbone

Mid-engined layout

Rear-mounted transmission

Ford V8

THE POWER PACK

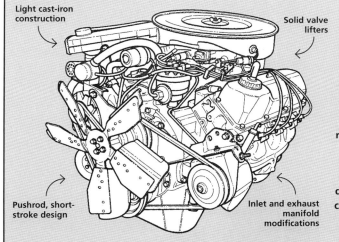

Light cast-iron construction

Solid valve lifters

Pushrod, short-stroke design

Inlet and exhaust manifold modifications

Modified Fords

De Tomaso used two Ford engines, the 289 and 302. Both are essentially the same and share a surprisingly light cast-iron pushrod, short-stroke V8 design. The HiPo 289 with its stronger connecting rods, higher compression ratio and solid rather than hydraulic valve lifters is the unit used in the fast Mustangs, AC Cobras and the Shelby GT350. De Tomaso decided to have the same modifications as Shelby, using improved intake and exhaust manifolds to make the engine breathe better.

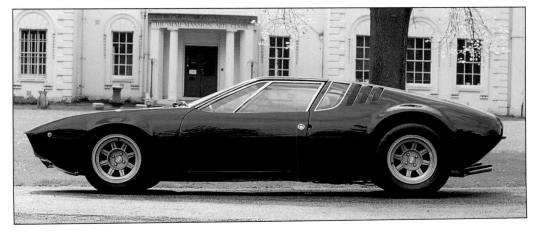

Euro models

Curiously for a car intended for the U.S., the European-spec Mangusta is the one to choose as it has the 289 V8 with 305 bhp compared with 230 bhp from a larger 302. Naturally, the Euro spec cars have quicker acceleration and a higher top speed, too.

European-spec versions are more powerful than those built for the U.S.

De Tomaso MANGUSTA

This is now one of the forgotten supercars, but it would have been a very different story if De Tomaso had given the powerful Mangusta the development its stunning Giugiaro design merited.

Glass engine covers

Giugiaro's solution to engine access was to design two transparent covers which opened up, pivoting from the center. They are an impressive sight when up, but access is awkward nevertheless.

V8 engine

Given De Tomaso's close links with Ford (the later Pantera was a joint Ford/De Tomaso enterprise), it was no surprise that De Tomaso chose to use the 289- and 302-cubic inch Ford V8s. They give plenty of power and are very reliable.

Front radiator

Although De Tomaso mounted the radiator at the front and ran pipes back to the engine to offset the car's weight distribution, the Mangusta was still very rear-heavy.

Rear-biased weight distribution

A combination of the all-iron V8, clutch, final drive and heavy ZF transmission at the back of the car gives the Mangusta a very heavy rear weight bias—as much as 68 percent of the weight at the back.

Giugiaro styling

After he moved on from Bertone, Giorgetto Giugiaro was, for a time, head of styling at Ghia (then owned by De Tomaso). During this time, he designed the body for the Mangusta. It still looks stunning today, more than thirty years after its debut.

Bigger rear tires

With the weight at the back of the car the front and rear tires are different sizes, with 185 HR15s at the front and 225 HR15s at the rear. Time has proven that the car needs even larger, more modern tires for its performance to be safely exploited.

Alloy hood

Strangely, given that the Mangusta's design ensures that it is light at the front, it has an alloy hood which makes the problem worse.

Specifications

1970 De Tomaso Mangusta

ENGINE
Type: V8
Construction: Cast-iron block and heads
Valve gear: Two valves per cylinder operated by single V-mounted camshafts via pushrods and rockers
Bore and stroke: 4.00 in. x 3.00 in.
Displacement: 4,950 cc
Compression ratio: 10.0:1
Induction system: Four-barrel carburetor
Maximum power: 230 bhp at 4,800 rpm
Maximum torque: 310 lb-ft at 2,800 rpm
Top speed: 130 mph
0–60 mph: 6.3 sec

TRANSMISSION
Rear-mounted ZF five-speed manual

BODY/CHASSIS
Sheet steel backbone chassis with engine and transmission as stressed members and alloy and steel two-door coupe body

SPECIAL FEATURES

By way of a nod to Ferrari, the Mangusta has a gated shifter.

The triple line engine vents on the C-pillars are a neat styling touch.

RUNNING GEAR
Steering: Rack-and-pinion
Front suspension: Double wishbones with coil springs, telescopic shock absorbers and anti-roll bar
Rear suspension: Reversed lower wishbone with single transverse link and twin radius arms per side, coil springs, telescopic shock absorbers and anti-roll bar
Brakes: Girling discs, 11.5-in. dia. (front), 11.0-in. dia. (rear)
Wheels: Magnesium alloy, 7 x 15 in. (front), 7.5 x 15 in. (rear)
Tires: 185 HR15 (front), 225 HR15 (rear)

DIMENSIONS
Length: 168.3 in.   **Width:** 72.0 in.
Height: 43.3 in.   **Wheelbase:** 98.4 in.
Track: 54.9 in. (front), 57.1 in. (rear)
Weight: 2,915 lbs.

De Tomaso PANTERA

The combination of an exotic Italian-styled body with the strength, power and reliability of a huge American V8 engine seemed to offer the best of both worlds to some manufacturers, De Tomaso in particular. The Pantera is one of the world's longest-lived supercars.

"Acceleration is shattering."

"That massive engine thunders away just behind your head, shaking the whole car and generating enough heat to make the standard air conditioning absolutely vital. Shifts are made with the ZF 5-speed transaxle, steering is light and handling impressive. The grip on those huge tires is enormous and the Pantera rides flat through the sharpest of turns. Its 5.6-second 0–60 acceleration is shattering and 165 mph top speed is virtually unmatched by any competitor. In fact, the exotic Italian-styled car looks fast even when it's standing still."

The Pantera interior has plush leather seats and instruments that are very easy to see.

Milestones

1969 Ford provides funds to produce the first Pantera. De Tomaso retains European sales rights, while Ford retains the rights in the U.S.

1971 Pantera goes on sale.

The Mangusta was De Tomaso's first V8-engined supercar.

1974 Chassis revisions, better brakes and a 330-bhp 351 'Cleveland' Ford V8 engine are in the European-spec GTS models. Due to emissions regulations, U.S. models produce only 266 bhp. Ford pulls out of the project leaving De Tomaso to build the cars independently.

1982 The GT5 is launched. Tacked-on wheel arch extensions are used to fit wider wheels and tires.

The GT5 gained wheel arch extensions and rear spoiler.

1990 Dramatic revamp is undertaken, although the concept stays the same. The engine is now Ford's popular 5.0 liter that makes 305 bhp with natural aspiration. By adding twin turbochargers, the Pantera makes up to 450 bhp.

UNDER THE SKIN

Mighty monocoque

Unusual for an Italian supercar, the Pantera has a steel monocoque structure. The car was planned to be sold in high volume through Ford dealers, so a separate chassis design would have been too labor-intensive and slow. The big Ford V8 is mounted behind the driver, turning the rear wheels through a rugged ZF five-speed transaxle. Double-wishbone suspension is used on all four wheels.

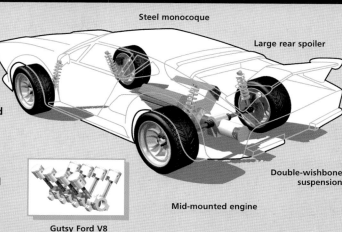

Steel monocoque

Large rear spoiler

Double-wishbone suspension

Mid-mounted engine

Gutsy Ford V8

THE POWER PACK

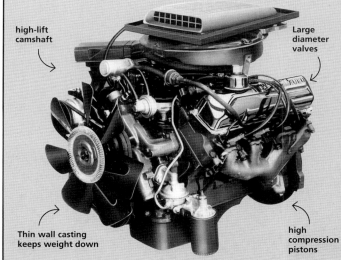

high-lift camshaft

Large diameter valves

Thin wall casting keeps weight down

high compression pistons

Ford power

The best engine to be fitted to the Pantera was the Ford 'Cleveland' V8 (named after the plant where it was built). It is a conventional all-iron V8 with high-lift camshaft and hydraulic lifters, although solid lifters could be specified for higher rpm. Although big, at 5,763 cc, its thin wall casting made it relatively lightweight. The engine could easily be tuned to produce more power with a high compression ratio, big valves, higher lift cams, free-flowing exhaust systems and multiple carburetors rather than one Holley.

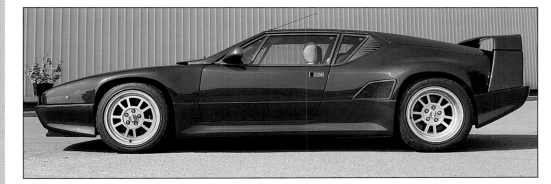

1990s Pantera

The Pantera was totally updated for the 90s with the introduction of the Gandini-styled 450 in 1990. It uses twin turbochargers to boost the power of a smaller 5.0-liter V8 engine to 450 bhp, hence the name. De Tomaso claims a top speed over 180 mph.

Gandini's restyle and twin turbos really brought the Pantera up to date.

De Tomaso PANTERA

The Pantera was built tough to survive on the U.S. market, with a simple and strong Ford V8 engine. It proved to be the right approach and the Pantera stayed in production long after it should have become obsolete.

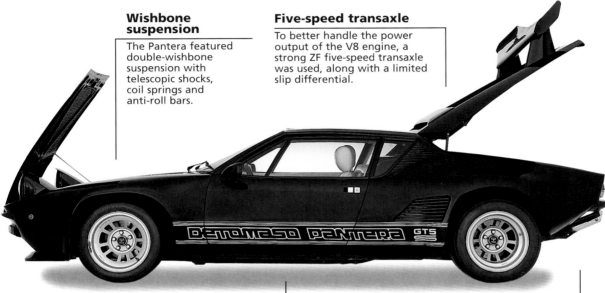

Wishbone suspension

The Pantera featured double-wishbone suspension with telescopic shocks, coil springs and anti-roll bars.

Five-speed transaxle

To better handle the power output of the V8 engine, a strong ZF five-speed transaxle was used, along with a limited slip differential.

Steel monocoque

As it was intended to be built in large numbers for a supercar (Ford hoped for 5,000 a year), it was designed to be built like a mass-production car, with a unitary steel monocoque.

Ford V8 engine

Because the Pantera was to be sold through Ford in the large U.S. market, it used a Ford Cleveland 5,763 cc V8 overhead valve engine design that was used in many early Mustangs.

Front spoiler

Designed to complement that flamboyant extrovert rear wing, the front spoiler plays its part in cutting down the amount of air that can flow under the car.

Carbon fiber rear spoiler

A rear spoiler was optional on the Pantera to provide extra downforce at very high speeds. By the 1980s that spoiler was made of carbon fiber.

Unequal-size wheels

To carry the large rear tires the rear wheels are 13 inches wide, compared with the slimmer 10-inch wide front wheels.

Extra driving lights

Its headlights were never the Pantera's strong suit and the extra driving lights which could be fitted in front of the air dam were a valuable addition.

Specifications
1986 De Tomaso Pantera GT5S

ENGINE

Type: Ford V8
Construction: Cast-iron block and heads
Valve gear: Two valves per cylinder operated by single block-mounted camshaft via pushrods and rockers
Bore and stroke: 4.01 in. x 3.50 in.
Displacement: 5,763 cc
Compression ratio: 10.5:1
Induction system: Single four-barrel Holley 680 cfm carburetor
Maximum power: 350 bhp at 6,000 rpm
Maximum torque: 451 lb-ft at 3,800 rpm
Top speed: 165 mph
0–60 mph: 5.6 sec

TRANSMISSION

ZF five-speed manual transaxle

BODY/CHASSIS

Steel monocoque two-door, two-seat coupe

SPECIAL FEATURES

Wheel vents in the rear arch extensions redirect cool air to the brakes keeping them from getting too hot and fading at high speeds.

Like the Lamborghini Countach, De Tomaso Panteras came with an optional rear spoiler. It was as much for style as function.

RUNNING GEAR

Steering: Rack-and-pinion
Front suspension: Double wishbones with coil springs, telescopic shocks and anti-roll bar
Rear suspension: Double wishbones, coil springs, telescopic shocks and anti-roll bar
Brakes: 11.7 in. discs (front) vented 11.2 in. discs (rear)
Wheels: Alloy, 10 in. x 15 in. (front), 13 in. x 15 in. (rear)
Tires: 285/40 VR15 (front), 345/35 VR15 (rear)

DIMENSIONS

Length: 168.1 in.   **Width:** 77.5 in.
Wheelbase: 99 in.   **Height:** 44.3 in.
Track: 61 in. (front), 62.1 in. (rear)
Weight: 3,202 lbs.

Dodge **CHALLENGER T/A**

With the SCCA's Trans Am wars in full swing, Dodge jumped in to the foray with its aptly-named Challenger T/A. Built for only one year and powered by a 340 cubic inch V8, it was conceived as a road racer but became a factory street rod.

"...mindwarping acceleration."

"Unlike its big-block counterparts, the T/A is a better-balanced package with less weight over the front wheels. It therefore offers more nimble handling. The rev-happy 340 V8 engine, with its triple carburetors and the bulletproof TorqueFlite transmission give mind-warping acceleration. For its time, the power-assisted steering is smooth and the brakes firm, but the sound of the V8 blowing through the side pipes is enough to stir anyone's soul."

Full instrumentation and black upholstery give the interior a real sporty feel.

Milestones

1970 Dodge finally

launches its own ponycar—the Challenger. An R/T performance model is offered with standard big-block power. With the popularity of Trans Am racing Dodge develops a homologation special: the Challenger T/A. Street versions are fitted with a 340-cubic inch V8, a fiberglass lift-off hood, side pipes and large rear tires. Only 2,142 are built this year.

In 1969, the top performing Dodge small block muscle car was the Dart GTS 383.

1971 With factory

support in Trans Am racing on the decline, the T/A does not return, although the big-block R/T makes it second and last appearance. Only 4,630 R/Ts are built and Challenger sales in general are less than half those of 1970.

The 1971 Demon is also powered by a 340-cubic inch V8.

1972 Big-block engines

are no longer available and the performance model is a new Challenger 360 Rallye. The Challenger itself lasts until 1974.

UNDER THE SKIN

3.55:1 or 3.90:1 rear axle ratios

Power front disc brakes

Fiberglass hood

Rallye suspension

Small-block V8

Proven design

In 1970 Chrysler introduced a brand-new E-body design. It shares front-end geometry with the larger B-body Charger and Coronet. The chassis is of unitary construction, with a separate front subframe bolted to it. Suspension is classic Chrysler, with torsion bars up front and a live axle at the rear suspended by leaf springs with increased camber to clear the exhaust outlet and rear tires. Front disc brakes are standard on T/As.

THE POWER PACK

Rev-happy magnum

The T/A proved that the hemi or the 440 Magnum are not necessary to produce real power. The 340-cubic inch unit used in the Dart Swinger is fitted with a special Edelbrock intake manifold, on which sits three two-barrel Holley carburetors. The advertised output was 290 bhp at 5,000 rpm, although this was purely for insurance reasons. With this engine the Challenger T/A and its AAR 'Cuda twin are a serious threat on the street and hydraulic lifters ensured that they were always ready for action.

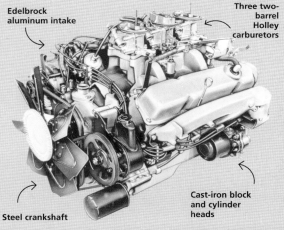

Edelbrock aluminum intake

Three two-barrel Holley carburetors

Steel crankshaft

Cast-iron block and cylinder heads

Loud T/A

In 1970 Dodge finally got serious about SCCA racing and launched its T/A. On the race circuit all cars ran a 305-cubic inch V8 which was nothing more than a destroked 340. To make the street versions more fun, an Edelbrock intake and trio of Holley carbs were added.

The Challenger T/A has handling to match its massive power output.

Dodge CHALLENGER T/A

With its matte black hood and wide stripes, the Challenger T/A might just be one of the most stylish cars Dodge built during the heyday of muscle cars. It was equally at home taking high speed turns or accelerating in a straight line.

V8 engine

When all six barrels of the carburetors are wide open, the 340 has rocket-like acceleration. Though it's a smaller engine than what most Mopar enthusiasts consider to be powerful, the 340 really holds its own against larger-engined cars.

Panther Pink paint

Believe it or not, this color was offered by Dodge. It's called Panther Pink and it's one of the optional High Impact colors.

Limited-slip differential

Despite the larger rear tires, many T/A buyers specified a Positraction limited-slip differential to reduce wheel spin and increase bite.

'Six-pack' carburetors

In order to extract maximum performance out of the 340-cubic inch small-block, Dodge installed three Holley two-barrel carburetors atop the engine. During normal driving only the center carburetor is used, but punching the throttle opens the outboard units and produces astonishing acceleration.

Hardtop body

The Challenger was available in coupe and convertible forms, but all T/A models were hardtop coupes. However, a vinyl roof was available.

Torsion bar suspension

Unlike its rivals, Chrysler used torsion bar front suspension on its cars in the early 1970s. These are more robust than coil springs and result in a smoother ride over rough surfaces.

Big rear wheels

The Challenger T/A was one of the first Detroit production cars to feature different size front and rear tires. At the back are massive G60 x 15 Goodyear Polyglas GTs, which give the T/A excellent straight-line traction.

Four-speed transmission

The standard transmission on the T/A is a Hurst-shifted four-speed with a direct-drive top ratio. The only option was a TorqueFlite three-speed automatic.

Specifications

1970 Dodge Challenger T/A

ENGINE

Type: V8

Construction: Cast-iron block and heads

Valve gear: Two valves per cylinder operated by pushrods and rockers

Bore and stroke: 4.03 in. x 3.31 in.

Displacement: 340 c.i.

Compression ratio: 10.5:1

Induction system: Three Holley two-barrel carburetors

Maximum power: 290 bhp at 5,000 rpm

Maximum torque: 345 lb-ft at 3,200 rpm

Top speed: 125 mph

0–60 mph: 5.8 sec

TRANSMISSION

TorqueFlite three-speed automatic

BODY/CHASSIS

Unitary steel construction with two-door four-seater coupe body

SPECIAL FEATURES

All Challengers are fitted with this racing-style chromed fuel filler cap.

At the rear, Challengers have a single, large back up light behind the Dodge lettering.

RUNNING GEAR

Steering: Recirculating ball

Front suspension: Double wishbones with longitudinal torsion bars, telescopic shock absorbers and anti-roll bar

Rear suspension: Live axle with semi-elliptic leaf springs, telescopic shock absorbers and anti-roll bar

Brakes: Discs (front), drums (rear)

Wheels: Steel discs, 7 x 15 in.

Tires: E60 x 15 (front), G60 x 15 (rear)

DIMENSIONS

Length: 191.3 in.   **Width:** 76.1 in.

Height: 51.7 in.   **Wheelbase:** 110.0 in.

Track: 60.7 in. (front), 61.2 in. (rear)

Weight: 3,650 lbs.

Dodge VIPER GTS-R

The Viper GTS had such a good platform that it cried out to be turned into a racing car. And in GT2 racing, the GTS-R, with its 650-bhp V10, has consistently beaten the best and won its class at the 24 Hours of Le Mans.

"...a raging animal."

"Climb in this raging animal and prepare for the ride of your life. Nail the throttle and dump the clutch and feel yourself catapult to 60 mph in a staggering 3.1 seconds. The thrill doesn't stop there though. This scorching Dodge continues to pull hard through all perfectly matched gears until it reaches its terminal velocity at just over 200 mph. Jam on the massive brakes and you will find that the GTS-R's stopping performance matches its astounding acceleration. "

With five-point harnesses and white-faced gauges this Viper is ready to bite.

Milestones

1995 Chrysler startles viewers in Pebble Beach, California by unveiling its proposed racing version of the hardtop Dodge Viper GTS.

Dodge launched the Viper in 1991, with the RT/10.

1996 Dodge actually takes the GTS-R racing as promised.

1997 Sensibly, Chrysler focuses on the GT2 category in world sportscar racing. It finishes 1-2 in class at the Le Mans 24 Hours. The GTS-R takes the World GT2 championship overall, a first for an American production model. English GTS-R driver Justin Bell takes the driver's championship.

Viper driver Justin Bell (right) celebrates after winning the 1998 24 Hours of Le Mans.

1998 To celebrate its stunning achievements, Dodge offers the GTS-R on sale to the public, on a limited basis.

UNDER THE SKIN

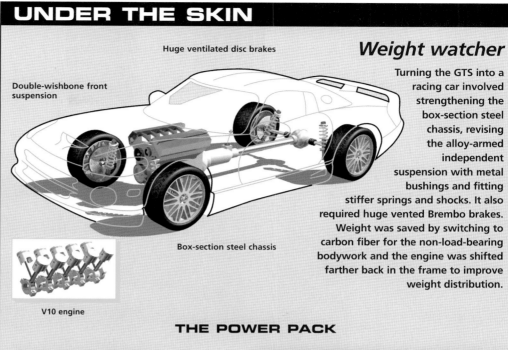

Huge ventilated disc brakes

Double-wishbone front suspension

Box-section steel chassis

V10 engine

Weight watcher

Turning the GTS into a racing car involved strengthening the box-section steel chassis, revising the alloy-armed independent suspension with metal bushings and fitting stiffer springs and shocks. It also required huge vented Brembo brakes. Weight was saved by switching to carbon fiber for the non-load-bearing bodywork and the engine was shifted farther back in the frame to improve weight distribution.

THE POWER PACK

Reworked V10

This engine is nothing like the standard Viper powerplant. For the racing GTS-R, Dodge seriously reworked the all-alloy 8-liter Ferrari eater V10 to give 650 bhp. It is still a single-cam, pushrod engine, but the fully balanced and blueprinted engine benefits from a 12.0:1 compression ratio and stronger forged steel connecting rods. Extensive work is done to both the intake and exhaust systems to extract maximum power. A dry sump oiling system prevents oil from surging when the car takes turns at high speeds. Maximum power is a massive 650 bhp at 6,500 rpm.

Track racer

The GTS-R is a rare model. It has outrageous power at 650 bhp, along with carbon-fiber bodywork, stripped racing interior with digital dashboard meter and a real racing suspension. Of course, a racetrack is needed to get the most out of it.

In GT2, the Vipers have proven almost unbeatable.

Dodge VIPER GTS-R 🇺🇸

Dodge stunned the world when it decided to produce the RT/10 in 1991. It then went
on to impress hard-core endurance racing enthusiasts when it took the FIA
championship in the GT2 class in its fully outfitted GTS-R race car.

V10 engine

The roadgoing versions of the GTS-R, now known as the ACR, do get
more power from their V10s, but nowhere near the 650 bhp of the
racers. However, 460 bhp at 5,200 rpm is more than respectable.

Composite body

Composite paneling is used for the street GTS-R, just as it is in the usual GTS, but for
the serious racing cars the bodywork was made from lightweight carbon fiber.

Front airdam

The GT2 rules allow some bodywork revision in aid of improved aerodynamics. This explains the GTS-R's different, deeper nose and rocker panel extensions. These modifications keep air away from the underside of the car, where it can generate drag and lift.

Adjustable pedals

The ideal driving position is vital in any performance car such as the GTS-R. To help achieve this, electronically controlled foot pedals let the driver get the right relationship between the pedals and steering wheel.

Multilink rear suspension

Rear suspension design is an SLA design with adjustable toe link. Similar to the front suspension the rubber bushings are replaced by spherical bearings and the springs and shocks are all stiffened.

Specifications

1997 Dodge Viper GTS-R

ENGINE

Type: V10

Construction: Alloy block and heads

Valve gear: Two valves per cylinder operated by a single V-mounted camshaft with pushrods and rockers

Bore and stroke: 4.00 in. x 3.88 in.

Displacement: 8.0 Liter

Compression ratio: 12.0:1

Induction system: Electronic fuel injection

Maximum power: 650 bhp at 6,000 rpm

Maximum torque: 650 lb-ft at 5,000 rpm

Top speed: 203 mph

0–60 mph: 3.1 sec

TRANSMISSION

Borg-Warner six-speed manual

BODY/CHASSIS

Separate steel box-section chassis with either carbon-fiber or glass-fiber two-door coupe body

SPECIAL FEATURES

With a sure-shifting six speed, it is easy to row through the gears in a Viper GTS-R.

The twin tailpipes help the GTS-R to produce a fantastic exhaust note.

RUNNING GEAR

Steering: Rack-and-pinion

Front suspension: SLA with coil springs, telescopic shock absorbers, spherical bearings and anti-roll bar

Rear suspension: SLA with extra toe-adjustment link, coil springs, telescopic shocks and anti-roll bar

Brakes: Ventilated discs, 13.0-in. dia.

Wheels: Alloy, 18 x 11(F), BB5 3-piece 18 x 13(rear)

Tires: Michelin Pilot SX Radial Slicks 27/65-18(front), 30/80-18(rear)

DIMENSIONS

Length: 176.7 in.　　**Width:** 75.7 in.

Height: 45.1 in.　　**Wheelbase:** 96.2 in.

Track: 59.8 in. (front), 60.9 in. (rear)

Weight: 2,750 lbs.

Ferrari **360 MODENA**

The latest in a great line of midengined Ferraris, the 360 Modena puts its competition to shame. Its incredible Pininfarina-styled bodywork not only looks good but works for a living. It produces an incredible amount of downforce without the need for add-on spoilers.

"...out of this world."

"If you have driven an older midengined Ferrari, you will be surprised when you step into the 360. The interior is much more spacious and user-friendly, but you still know this is a real road racer. On the road the V8 comes on strong at 4,000 rpm, but doesn't run out of steam until 8,500 revs. Combined with the in-street F1 gearshifts, the acceleration feels out of this world. Handling is excellent, but turn off the traction control at your own risk."

Ferrari has taken great pains to make the 360 more comfortable than previous cars.

Milestones

1967 Ferrari launches its
first mid-engined production car. The Dino 206GT uses a 2.0-liter V6. A bigger 2.4-liter engine is fitted to the revised Dino 246GT in 1969.

Ferrari's first midengined production car was the Dino, launched in 1967.

1973 The V6 Dino is replaced
by the new 308 range, using Ferrari's first-ever V8 engine mounted midship. The first model to be launched is the 308GT4, styled by Bertone.

The 360 Modena replaces the older Ferrari F355.

1999 After several other
generations of mid-engined V8 Ferraris, the company launches its latest offering, the 360 Modena. Its 3.6-liter V8 produces an almighty 394 bhp, and its Pininfarina wind-tunnel-crafted body produces unheard of amounts of downforce.

UNDER THE SKIN

Alloy wonder

The 360 is the first Ferrari to use all-aluminum construction. Its spaceframe/monocoque means it is 134 pounds lighter than its predecessor, the F355, despite an increase in overall size. Aluminum double wishbone suspension is used in conjunction with coil springs, anti-roll bars, and adaptive shock absorbers, which react to conditions to give the best possible damping in any given situation. Huge vented disc brakes ensure the 360 stops.

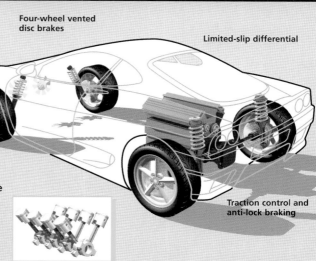

Four-wheel vented disc brakes

Limited-slip differential

Traction control and anti-lock braking

High-tech V8

THE POWER PACK

High-revving V8

The V8 engine powering the 360 is a completely redesigned unit. Displacing 3.6 liters, it has five valves per cylinder (three intake and two exhaust) like the old F355 unit. The valves are actuated by two overhead camshafts per cylinder bank with hydraulic tappets. The block, oil pan and cylinder heads are all cast in light alloy to keep the weight down. Connecting rods are made of titanium, and the pistons are made of forged aluminum. This engine has one of the world's highest specific power outputs at 111 bhp per liter. It produces its maximum power of 394 bhp at a dizzy 8,500 rpm.

Downforce

Despite its lack of big wings or spoilers, the 360 Modena produces more downforce at 70 mph than the F355 could at its top speed. It took thousands of hours in the wind tunnel for Pininfarina to produce this beautiful, yet very functional, design.

Wind tunnel testing shows the 360 to have a drag coefficient of 0.34.

Ferrari **360 MODENA**

With the arrival of the latest Porsche 911, Ferrari was forced to raise its game. With the stunning new 360 Modena, the company has done just that. Fantastic looks and technology to match put it at the top of the supercar league.

3.6-liter V8 engine
The 40-valve V8 engine displaces only 3.6 liters yet produces an enormous 394 bhp—that's 111 bhp per liter.

Aluminum suspension
Aluminum is used for the double-wishbone suspension that is fitted in all four corners. Coil springs and adaptive shock absorbers are also featured.

Aluminum construction
The 360 is the first Ferrari to use all-aluminum construction. It is therefore lighter than the F355 despite an increase in size. It is also stiffer.

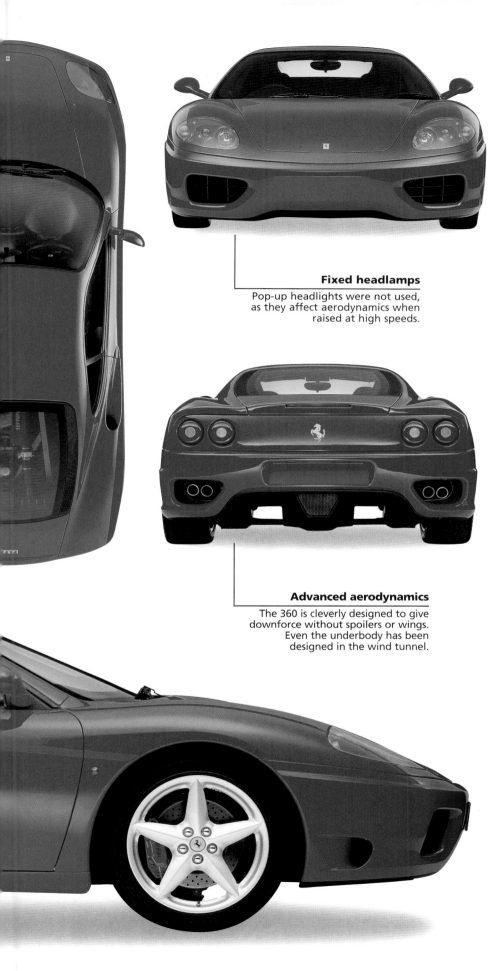

Fixed headlamps

Pop-up headlights were not used, as they affect aerodynamics when raised at high speeds.

Advanced aerodynamics

The 360 is cleverly designed to give downforce without spoilers or wings. Even the underbody has been designed in the wind tunnel.

Specifications

1999 Ferrari 360 Modena

ENGINE

Type: V8

Construction: Alloy block and heads

Valve gear: Five valves per cylinder operated by two overhead camshafts per cylinder bank

Bore and stroke: 3.40 in. x 3.16 in.

Displacement: 3,586 cc

Compression ratio: 11.0:1

Induction system: Bosch multipoint fuel injection

Maximum power: 394 bhp at 8,500 rpm

Maximum torque: 275 lb-ft at 4,750 rpm

Top speed: 185 mph

0–60 mph: 4.5 sec

TRANSMISSION

Six-speed semi-automatic

BODY/CHASSIS

Aluminum spaceframe/monocoque

SPECIAL FEATURES

Despite all-new styling, the traditional round rear lights are retained.

Once again, Pininfarina has penned stunning lines for a Ferrari.

RUNNING GEAR

Steering: Rack-and-pinion

Front suspension: Double wishbones with coil springs, adaptive shock absorbers and anti-roll bar

Rear suspension: Double wishbones with coil springs, adaptive shock absorbers and anti-roll bar

Brakes: Vented discs (front and rear)

Wheels: Alloy, 18-in. dia.

Tires: 215/45 ZR18 (front), 275/40 ZR18 (rear)

DIMENSIONS

Length: 176.3 in.   **Width:** 75.7 in.

Height: 47.8 in.   **Wheelbase:** 102.4 in.

Track: 65.7 in. (front), 63.7 in. (rear)

Weight: 3,065 lbs.

Ferrari **550 MARANELLO**

It is fitting that Ferrari should choose the name of its home town for its first new front-engined two-seater supercar since 1968. It is the fastest Ferrari currently available, yet is also one of the most practical ever built.

"...blistering performance."

"You are unlikely to come away dissatisfied after driving the 550. As well as blistering performance and a magnificently responsive V12 engine, the Maranello has a sensational chassis that is fluid and minutely adjustable at the throttle. Add in great Brembo brakes, and smooth-shifting six-speed transmission and you have an awesome sports car. It also has lightning fast steering that enables you to negotiate sharp corners with complete confidence."

There are few places that a driver would rather be than behind the wheel of this car.

Milestones

1992 Ferrari launches

the 456 GT, the first of a new breed of front-engined V12 supercars. The new car replaces the ageing, mid-engined 512 TR, itself little more than just a Testarossa with a facelift.

Ferrari's previous flagship model was the Testarossa, which was later known as the 512 TR.

1996 Ferrari invites Michael Schumacher

to its famous Fiorano test track to launch the 550 Maranello and impress the motoring media with his driving skill at the wheel.

The Ferrari 456 GT was the first series production Ferrari with the new V12 engine.

1997 Carrozzeria Scaglietti is a buyers'

plan that allows the owners to personalize their 550 Maranellos by choosing from a large list of trim, luxury, and performance enhancements.

UNDER THE SKIN

State-of-the-art

Underneath the Pininfarina-styled body, the 550's ancestry closely follows the Ferrari 456 GT. It shares the same basic chassis layout, V12 engine, and suspension, which means double wishbones all around, coil springs, anti-roll bars and adjustable shocks. To improve weight distribution, the transaxle is mounted at the rear in front of the differential.

All-independent suspension

Rear-mounted transmission

Four-wheel disc brakes

5.5-liter V12

THE POWER PACK

Nikasil-coated cylinder liners

All-alloy construction

Four valves per cylinder

Four overhead camshafts

Operatic V12 power

Ferrari took the V12 engine from the 456 GT and engineered an extra 49 bhp of power. The unit features all-aluminum construction, four overhead camshafts, four valves per cylinder, and variable-geometry inlet and exhaust systems. Equally impressive, this phenomenally powerful engine meets all worldwide emissions requirements. The only disappointment is the sound, which has been muted by noise pollution regulations.

Options list

There is only one 550 model, but the standard specification is impressively complete. An options list is available which allows you to personalize your car. Items include a handling package, carbon-fiber trim, modular wheel rims and tailored luggage.

The 550 is the fastest Ferrari currently available.

Ferrari **550 MARANELLO**

Replacing the mid-engined 512M, the new Ferrari 550's appeal is much more broad. The only disappointment is the styling, which critics say fails to meet Pininfarina's highest standard.

Unique wheels and tires

The five-spoke wheels were designed by Pininfarina specifically for the 550. The tires were also specially developed for this model.

V12 power

The 5.5-liter all-alloy V12 engine has a remarkable torque curve, delivering more than 369 lb-ft of torque between 3,600 and 7,000 rpm.

Pininfarina styling

The famous Italian design house Pininfarina was asked to produce a shape which would be a spiritual successor to the great Daytona of the 1970s.

Spacious practicality

Practicality played as large a part in the Maranello's development process as optimum performance. Hence, the car is easy to get into and it has a 6.5 cubic foot capacity trunk.

ASR traction control

Traction control stops the rear wheels from spinning under acceleration. But it is possible to turn it off.

Luxurious interior

The occupants have unrivaled levels of comfort. Standard equipment in the Maranello includes eight-way electrically-adjustable seats, Jaeger LCD analogue instrumentation, air-conditioning, leather upholstery, and a Sony multi-CD player/radio.

Strong aluminum bodywork

The light aluminum body is welded to a steel frame using a special material called Feran. The frame boasts tremendous torsional rigidity of 207 lb-ft/degrees.

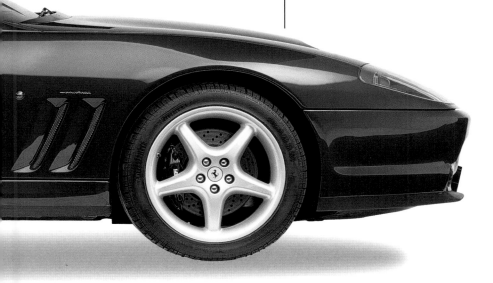

Specifications

1998 Ferrari 550 Maranello

ENGINE

Type: V12

Construction: Alloy cylinder block and heads

Valve gear: Four valves per cylinder operated by four overhead camshafts

Bore and stroke: 3.46 in. x 2.95 in.

Displacement: 5,474 cc

Compression ratio: 10.8:1

Induction system: Bosch 5.2 Motronic fuel injection

Maximum power: 485 bhp at 7,000 rpm

Maximum torque: 398 lb-ft at 5,000 rpm

Top speed: 199 mph

0–60 mph: 4.4 sec

TRANSMISSION

Six-speed manual

BODY/CHASSIS

Steel frame with two-door aluminum coupe body

SPECIAL FEATURES

Cooling vents behind the front wheel arches hark back to the 275 GTB.

 **It may be a brand-new car, but some things never change on a Ferrari. The 550 Maranello has a traditional alloy shifter gate.**

RUNNING GEAR

Steering: Power-assisted rack-and-pinion

Front suspension: Double wishbones with coil springs, telescopic shocks and anti-roll bar

Rear suspension: Double wishbones with coil springs, telescopic shocks and anti-roll bar

Brakes: Vented discs (front and rear)

Wheels: Alloy, 18-in. dia.

Tires: Specially-designed 255/40 ZR18 (front), 295/35 ZR18 (rear)

DIMENSIONS

Length: 179.1 in.   **Width:** 76.2 in.

Height: 50.3 in.   **Wheelbase:** 98.4 in.

Track: 64.3 in. (front), 62.4 in. (rear)

Weight: 3,726 lbs.

Ferrari DAYTONA

Until the arrival of the 550 Maranello, the Daytona was the last front-engined Ferrari supercar. Despite the old-fashioned layout, the Daytona is still one of the fastest supercars of all time.

"...meant to be driven hard."

"Ferrari made no compromises with the Daytona. It was meant to be driven fast and driven hard. At speed, the heavy unassisted steering—which makes parking a huge chore—lightens up. Drive the Daytona the way it was intended—hard—and it repays you. It seems to shrink around you and, despite its weight, it's agile and well behaved. You'll believe it was the fastest car of its time as it accelerates savagely long after other supercars have faded. The Daytona can easily go from 0–100 mph in just under 13 seconds."

The interior is classic Ferrari with a gated shifter and a steering wheel with a central Prancing Horse.

Milestones

1968 Ferrari unveils the 365 GTB/4 at the Paris Motor Show. The press calls it 'Daytona' in honor of Ferrari's success at the 1967 24-hour race. The name is unofficial, however, and never appears on the bodywork.

Daytona's predecessor was the 275 GTB, which also had a V12 engine.

1969 Production begins of both the coupe and convertible models. Ferrari also produces competition models. They have more power, with 400 bhp at 8,300 rpm and can reach more than 180 mph at tracks like Le Mans.

1971 Retractable headlights replace the original perspex-covered type.

1972 A competition Daytona wins its class at the 24 Hours of Le Mans, an achievement repeated in 1973 and 1974.

Daytonas took class victories at the 24 Hours of Le Mans in 1973 and 1974.

UNDER THE SKIN

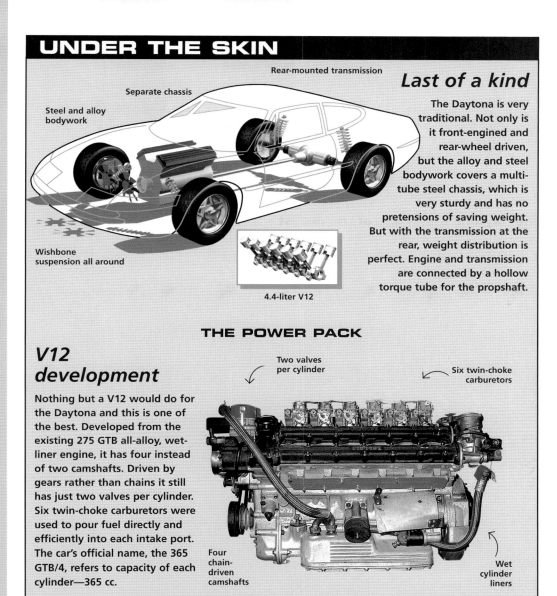

Rear-mounted transmission

Separate chassis

Steel and alloy bodywork

Wishbone suspension all around

4.4-liter V12

Last of a kind

The Daytona is very traditional. Not only is it front-engined and rear-wheel driven, but the alloy and steel bodywork covers a multi-tube steel chassis, which is very sturdy and has no pretensions of saving weight. But with the transmission at the rear, weight distribution is perfect. Engine and transmission are connected by a hollow torque tube for the propshaft.

THE POWER PACK

V12 development

Nothing but a V12 would do for the Daytona and this is one of the best. Developed from the existing 275 GTB all-alloy, wet-liner engine, it has four instead of two camshafts. Driven by gears rather than chains it still has just two valves per cylinder. Six twin-choke carburetors were used to pour fuel directly and efficiently into each intake port. The car's official name, the 365 GTB/4, refers to capacity of each cylinder—365 cc.

Two valves per cylinder

Six twin-choke carburetors

Four chain-driven camshafts

Wet cylinder liners

Easy conversion

The rarest of the Daytonas is the Spyder. A little over 100 were built, although there are many fakes converted from the coupes. For factory and faker alike, the conversion was easy because the car has a strong separate chassis, so it does not rely on the roof for its strength.

Desirable and rare, the factory Spyder has often been copied.

Ferrari **DAYTONA**

The end of an era...but what a way to go! The combination of Pininfarina's perfectly proportioned body and a 4.4 liter Ferrari V12 makes it an instant classic, not to mention one of the world's fastest cars.

Engine air vents

After cool air has passed through the tiny front opening and through the V12's big radiator, it leaves the car via the two unobtrusive sunken vents in the hood.

Quad-cam V12

The 365 GTB/4 model name helps explain the engine. The 365 stands for the size of each cylinder (which multiplied by the number of cylinders gives its 4.4 liter displacement). The 4 stands for the number of camshafts.

Rear-mounted transmission

The five-speed transmission shares the same alloy housing as the final drive. Because this is a two-seater with a short cabin, the length of gear linkage from the driver to the transmission is not excessive.

Square-tube chassis

In the late-1960s, Ferrari was a very traditional manufacturer, so the Daytona's chassis is made up of many small-diameter square section tubes welded together. It is strong but heavy.

Front-to-rear torque tube

The engine and rear-mounted transmission are rigidly connected by a torque tube that houses the driveshaft.

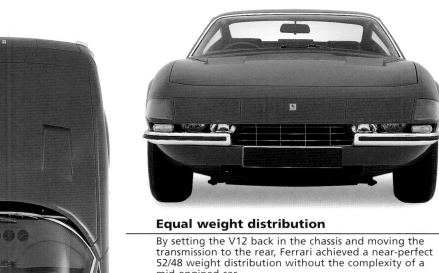

Equal weight distribution

By setting the V12 back in the chassis and moving the transmission to the rear, Ferrari achieved a near-perfect 52/48 weight distribution without the complexity of a mid-engined car.

Wishbone suspension

Double wishbone suspension is fitted all around. To help the packaging, the rear spring/shock units are mounted above the top wishbone.

Alloy and steel body

The doors, hood and trunk lid are made of weight-saving alloy. The rest of the bodywork is steel.

Specifications
1970 Ferrari 365 GTB/4 Daytona

ENGINE
Type: V12
Construction: Alloy block and heads with wet liners
Valve gear: Two valves per cylinder operated by four gear-driven overhead camshafts
Bore and stroke: 3.19 in. x 2.8 in.
Displacement: 4,390 cc
Compression ratio: 9.3:1
Induction system: Six Weber 40DCN 20 downdraft carburetors
Maximum power: 352 bhp at 7,500 rpm
Maximum torque: 330 lb-ft at 5,500 rpm
Top speed: 174 mph
0–60 mph: 5.6 sec

TRANSMISSION
Rear-mounted, five-speed manual

BODY/CHASSIS
Steel square tube separate chassis with alloy and steel two-door coupe or convertible body

SPECIAL FEATURES

Wrap-around front direction indicators were often mimicked after the Daytona's launch.

Four round tail lights and four exhausts tell you you've just been overtaken by a Daytona.

RUNNING GEAR
Steering: Recirculating ball
Front suspension: Double wishbones with coil springs, telescopic shocks and anti-roll bar
Rear suspension: Double wishbones with coil springs, telescopic shocks and anti-roll bar
Brakes: Vented discs, 11.3 in. dia. (front), 11.6 in. dia. (rear)
Wheels: Alloy, 7.5 in. x 15 in.
Tires: 215/7015

DIMENSIONS
Length: 174.2 in.   **Width:** 69.3 in.
Wheelbase: 94.5 in.   **Height:** 49 in.
Track: 56.7 in. (front), 56.1 in. (rear)
Weight: 3,530 lbs.

Ferrari **F40**

The F40 did exactly what Ferrari demanded of it—restore its reputation as a builder of the world's most desirable sports cars. The cars had been getting heavier and less hard-edged. The F40 changed all of that.

"…mind-numbing acceleration!"

"Squeeze yourself into the F40's cockpit—there's no doubt that you are in the ultimate road racer. The heavy clutch bites sweetly and the steering is light, even at a crawl. Designed for triple-digit cornering speeds, the stiff suspension gives a jarring ride over urban roads. But flex your foot on the throttle and there's a blur of mind-numbing acceleration. The power is truly explosive, arriving with a ferocity that no other road car can match. Serious recalibration of your senses is needed to adjust to this Ferrari's outrageous performance."

Despite the stripped-down interior, the F40 still has the classic Ferrari alloy gate for the shifter.

Milestones

1947 The first Ferrari

is built by Enzo Ferrari. His philosophy is to build cars which he races as an advertisement for the production models, which benefit from experience gained on the track. This begins Ferrari's road-racing tradition.

A 250 SWB Berlinetta racing in 1961.

The years between...

Enzo once said that he made cars for young men that only old men could afford. Sadly, the Ferraris that are the most desirable are those competition cars like the GTO, the 250 SWB, and the 288 GTO—cars that ride hard, are noisy and have as few passenger car qualities as possible.

1987 Ferrari's 40th anniversary

is celebrated by the appearance of the F40, the latest in the line. Sliding plastic windows are standard to save weight and the trunk has room for a spare wheel or luggage, but not both.

1992 Production ends

after an estimated 1,315 F40s are produced by the Maranello factory.

... strength with amazing lightness

The chassis consists of a tubular steel space-frame to which the engine and other mechanical components are attached. This is stiffened with bonded composite panels made of woven carbon fiber and Kevlar, or Nomex, and glued into place, achieving strength with amazing lightness. Each door weighs less than 3.5 lbs.

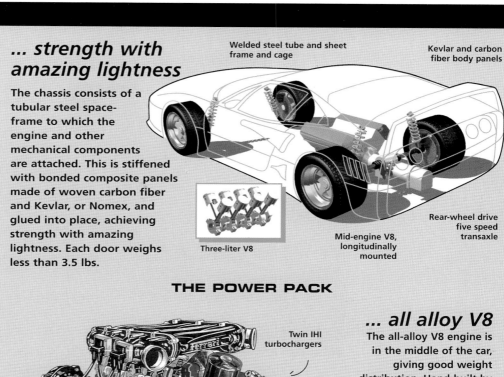

Welded steel tube and sheet frame and cage

Kevlar and carbon fiber body panels

Three-liter V8

Mid-engine V8, longitudinally mounted

Rear-wheel drive five speed transaxle

THE POWER PACK

Twin IHI turbochargers

Four valves per cylinder

Two overhead camshafts per bank

Silumin alloy block and heads

... all alloy V8

The all-alloy V8 engine is in the middle of the car, giving good weight distribution. Hand-built by Ferrari craftsmen, the F40 engine has four camshafts and four valves per cylinder. The exhaust valves are sodium-filled to aid heat dispersion. There are three oil pumps—two for the engine and one for the transaxle. Each engine was bench tested before it was installed in the car.

Racing version

Ferrari developed a racing version of the F40, the F40 LM (for 'Le Mans'). This upgraded and more powerful car debuted in the IMSA series at Laguna Seca in October 1990, finishing a respectable third with Jean Alesi behind the wheel.

Ferrari F40 LM: Power was upped to 630 bhp from the road car's 478 bhp.

Ferrari **F40**

The F40 was designed to be the fastest car that could be driven on European roads. It was the most exciting street-legal Ferrari in 20 years—so exciting that none could be brought to the U.S. for use on the road.

Ground effect

The F40 has a flat bottom, carefully shaped nose and strategically placed air intakes that lead to zero lift in front and downforce at the rear.

Modular wheels

Modular wheels are all light alloy, bolted together with nuts on the inside. Pirelli P-Zero ZR-rated tires were designed for the F40.

Adjustable suspension

Rear suspension has easily adjustable camber (tilting the top of the wheel inward or outward) to tailor handling to suit the driving conditions.

Dual turbos

Dual turbos use exhaust gas to drive them. The compressed air feeds through an intercooler before it enters the engine—the denser the air, the higher the power.

Rear wing

Rear downforce is created by the inverted aerofoil section rear wing.

Three-liter twin-turbo V8

Double overhead cams for each bank of cylinders are driven by a toothed belt. The cylinder heads have two intake and two exhaust valves per cylinder.

Shock absorbers

Front and rear shock absorbers lower height at about 50 mph, improving aerodynamics and handling.

Triple exhaust pipes

Three exhaust pipes exit in the center: one for each bank of cylinders, one for the turbo wastegates.

Cockpit

Brakes and steering have no power boost so that the driver can feel the controls better. There is a choice of three seat sizes.

Dual fuel tanks

Dual fuel tanks have quick-fill caps, 30-gallon capacity. Fuel is fed into the engine by Marelli-Weber fuel injection.

Specifications

1992 Ferrari F40

ENGINE

Type: V8, 90°

Construction: Light alloy, heads, block, Nikasil cylinder liners

Bore and stroke: 3.32 in. x 2.74 in.

Displacement: 2,936 cc

Compression ratio: 7.8:1

Induction system: Two IHI turbos, intercoolers, Marelli-Weber fuel injection, two injectors per cylinder

Ignition: distributorless Marelli-Weber

Maximum power: 478 bhp at 7,000 rpm

Maximum torque: 423 lb-ft at 4,000 rpm

Top speed: 201 mph

0–60 mph: 4.2 sec

TRANSMISSION

Transaxle: Five speeds forward + reverse (non-synchro optional); pump lubricated; limited slip differential

BODY/CHASSIS

Carbon fiber and Kevlar body panels with welded steel tube cage and suspension mounts

SPECIAL FEATURES

The engine cover is louvered to allow the heat generated by the big V8 and twin turbochargers to be dispersed.

If 478 bhp wasn't enough, a factory kit could add an additional 200 bhp.

RUNNING GEAR

Front suspension: Unequal length wishbones with coil-over shock absorbers, anti-roll bar

Rear suspension: Unequal length wishbones, coil-over shock absorbers, anti-roll bar

Brakes: Vented discs, multi-piston calipers front and rear, separate handbrake caliper

Wheels: Modular light alloy 17 in.

DIMENSIONS

Length: 171.5 in.

Width: 77.5 in.

Height: 44.5 in.

Wheelbase: 96.5 in.

Track: 62.7 in. (front), 63.2 in. (rear)

Weight: 2,425 lbs.

Ferrari **F50**

Ferrari decided to celebrate 50 years of racing and road cars by building the nearest thing possible to a Formula 1 racing car for the road. The result was the incredible F50.

"...the supercar of supercars."

"Formula 1 cars are almost unmanageable for ordinary drivers, but the F50, the supercar of supercars, is very user-friendly. The clutch is hard but progressive, and so you don't immediately stall. The gear shift is very quick and precise. The handling is not in the least twitchy. The F50 is biased to the slightest of understeer, grips the road with force and has a decent ride, but most of all you'll remember the incredible acceleration accompanied by a Grand Prix soundtrack."

The F50's interior is stylish and functional but also extremely basic to keep its weight down.

Milestones

1987 The Ferrari F40 appears as a
celebration of the 40th anniversary of the first Ferrari road car—the 166 Inter with its tiny 1.5-liter V12 engine.

The 288 GTO preceded the F40 and was a homologation special.

1990 Plans are laid for the F50 and Ferrari
starts looking at the then-current Formula 1 engine, used to power the cars of Alan Prost and Nigel Mansell, to assess whether it can be adapted as a road car engine.

The F40 was built to celebrate 40 years of Ferraris.

1997 The F50 is built to celebrate 50
years of producing racing and road cars. The racing link explains why Ferrari has built a car with the Formula 1-derived V12 engine and carbon fiber construction. Ferrari intends to make a limited number to make the F50 truly exclusive.

UNDER THE SKIN

Racing derived

It is as advanced as a Formula 1 car for the road should be, with the mid engine mounted rigidly to a carbon fiber monocoque and working through a six-speed transmission with its own heat exchanger. Suspension is by racing-type double wishbones. Pushrods operate the remote mounted shock absorbers and adaptive damping detects the difference between bumps and roll through corners.

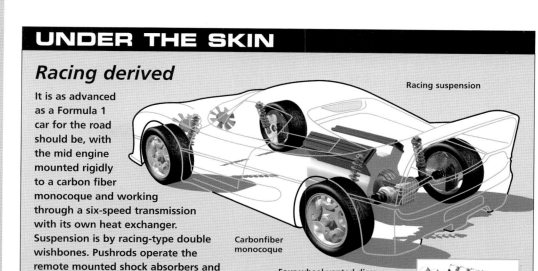

Racing suspension

Carbonfiber monocoque

Four-wheel vented discs

65-degree V12

THE POWER PACK

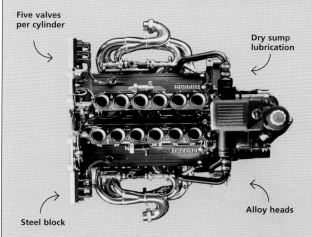

Five valves per cylinder

Dry sump lubrication

Steel block

Alloy heads

Detuned V12

Sometimes referred to as a detuned 1990-era Ferrari F1 engine, there is more to the F50's 65-degree V12 than that. The stroke is lengthened to increase the displacement from the F1's 3.5 liters to 4.7 liters, and this unit revs to only 8,700 rpm rather than 14,000 rpm. Otherwise, it has a cast-iron block with dry-sump lubrication and titanium connecting rods and, of course, four chain-driven camshafts operating 60 valves in total—three intake and two exhaust, per cylinder.

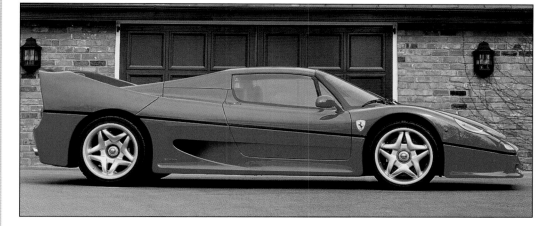

Sleek and fast

The F50 was designed to be driven roofless, even though there is a hardtop. To produce the world's fastest roadster, Ferrari had to make sure that the aerodynamics around the cockpit were right so that wind did not buffet the driver even at high speed.

The F50 looks good with or without its hard top.

Ferrari **F50**

An enlarged Formula 1 engine, carbon fiber construction and racing car pushrod suspension produced the most astounding and fastest street-legal Ferrari ever built.

Formula 1 size brakes

The F50's brakes were as good as those from Formula 1 cars before they switched from metal discs to carbon fiber. They are huge vented discs, nearly 14 inches in diameter at the front.

V12 engine

Power was everything with the F1 engine that formed the basis of the F50's unit. Despite making it 1.2 liters larger, the 4.7-liter V12 still produces only 347 lb-ft of torque compared with its power output of 513 bhp.

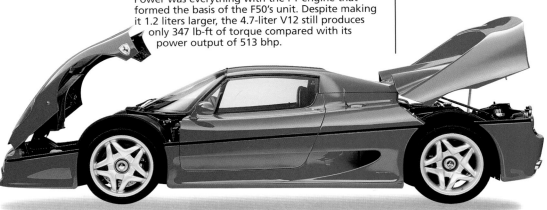

Manual windows

The F50 does not have power windows, because the electric motors would add unwanted weight and not be in keeping with a stripped-down road racer.

Adaptive suspension

Electronically-controlled Bilstein shock absorbers are fitted. Sensors determine the difference between bumps in the road and roll as the car corners, so the shocks stiffen in corners, almost acting as an anti-roll bar.

Huge downforce

The F50 needs all the downforce it can produce and there is at least 350 lbs. available. This is due to the huge rear wing and the shape of the underbody, which generates a venturi effect that sucks the car onto the road.

Front cooling vents

Air for the front-mounted radiator is drawn in through the main opening in the nose, and then through the radiator and out of the two huge vents in what would be the hood in an ordinary car.

Rigid-mounted steering

To give the most responsive steering possible, there is no power assistance and the steering rack is mounted rigidly to the body.

Carbonfiber construction

There was never any doubt that the F50 should be made from carbon fiber like an F1 car. Far lighter than steel and also far stronger, it gives the F50 immense torsional rigidity.

Specifications

1997 Ferrari F50

ENGINE

Type: V12

Construction: Steel block and alloy heads

Valve gear: Five valves per cylinder (three inlet, two exhaust) operated by four chain-driven overhead camshafts

Bore and stroke: 3.37 in. x 2.72 in.

Displacement: 4,698 cc

Compression ratio: 11.3:1

Induction system: Bosch Motronic electronic injection

Maximum power: 513 bhp at 8,000 rpm

Maximum torque: 347 lb-ft at 6,500 rpm

Top speed: 202 mph

0–60 mph: 3.7 sec

TRANSMISSION

Six-speed manual

BODY/CHASSIS

Carbon fiber unitary construction roadster body with separate carbon fiber hardtop

SPECIAL FEATURES

The inboard springs and shock absorbers are actuated with pushrods.

The engine sits under a louvered composite cover.

RUNNING GEAR

Steering: Rack-and-pinion

Front suspension: Double wishbones with inboard pushrod-operated coil springs and shock absorbers with electronic control

Rear suspension: Double wishbones with inboard pushrod-operated coil springs and shock absorbers with electronic control

Brakes: Vented discs, 14-in. dia. (front and rear)

Wheels: Magnesium, 8.5 x 18 in. (front), 13 x 18 in. (rear)

Tires: Goodyear GS-Fiorano, 245/35 ZR18 (front), 335/30 ZR18 (rear)

DIMENSIONS

Length: 176.4 in.   **Width:** 78.2 in.

Height: 44.1 in.   **Wheelbase:** 101.6 in.

Track: 63.8 in. (front), 63.1 in. (rear)

Weight: 3,080 lbs.

Ford GT40

The GT40 showed that when a company the size of Ford decides to go into racing, their vast resources will ensure success. After some initial teething trouble, the mighty V8 Ford humiliated the Ferraris with a sweep at Le Mans in 1966.

"...V8 thumps you in the back."

"Even in the road car, with its milder engine and rubber-bushed suspension it's easy to get a realistic impression of what it was like to drive the GT40s through the June heat at Le Mans. The open road and wide, sweeping corners soon beckon; somewhere you can floor the throttle and feel the gutsy V8 thump you in the back as it tears to 100 mph in just 12 seconds. If it's this good on the road, it must have been fantastic on the Mulsanne Straight."

The cabin is small and claustrophobic. Tall drivers cannot even fit in and miss out on one of the greatest driving experiences available.

Milestones

1963 After failing to buy Ferrari, Ford joins forces with Lola to turn the Lola GT into the prototype Ford GT.

1964 Now known as the GT40, the Ford makes its racing debut at the Nurburgring 1000 km. It is forced to retire, as it does in every race this year.

GT40 was so named because its overall height was 40 inches.

1965 Production starts for homologation and a GT40 wins its first race: the 2000-km Daytona Continental.

1966 The big-block cars finish 1-2-3 at Le Mans and win the International Sports Car Championship for GTs.

GT40 won Le Mans in 1968 and '69 after Ford had withdrawn from sports car racing in '67.

1967 Once again the car wins both the International Sports Car Championship and the 24 Hours of Le Mans. Although Ford withdraws from racing at the end of '67, the GT40 races on in the hands of the Gulf team, winning Le Mans again in '68 and '69.

UNDER THE SKIN

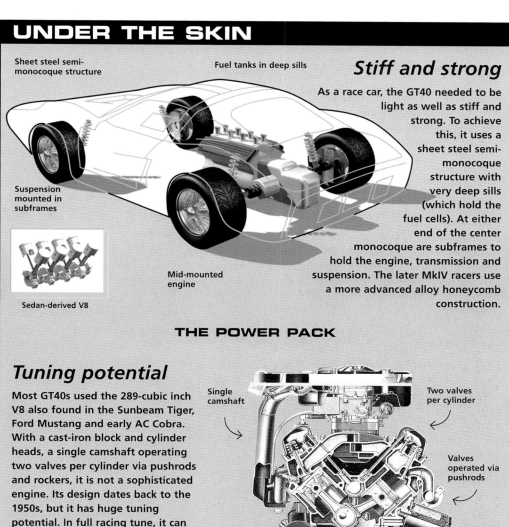

Sheet steel semi-monocoque structure

Fuel tanks in deep sills

Suspension mounted in subframes

Sedan-derived V8

Mid-mounted engine

Stiff and strong

As a race car, the GT40 needed to be light as well as stiff and strong. To achieve this, it uses a sheet steel semi-monocoque structure with very deep sills (which hold the fuel cells). At either end of the center monocoque are subframes to hold the engine, transmission and suspension. The later MkIV racers use a more advanced alloy honeycomb construction.

THE POWER PACK

Tuning potential

Most GT40s used the 289-cubic inch V8 also found in the Sunbeam Tiger, Ford Mustang and early AC Cobra. With a cast-iron block and cylinder heads, a single camshaft operating two valves per cylinder via pushrods and rockers, it is not a sophisticated engine. Its design dates back to the 1950s, but it has huge tuning potential. In full racing tune, it can produce around 400 bhp which was more than enough to blow past the more sophisticated, but often less reliable, Ferraris.

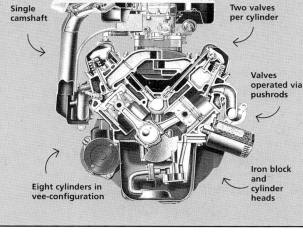

Single camshaft

Two valves per cylinder

Valves operated via pushrods

Iron block and cylinder heads

Eight cylinders in vee-configuration

Big blocks

Ford's first Le Mans-winning GT40 used the big-block 427-cubic inch engine; a unit that proved in the tough world of NASCAR racing it had the strength required for 24-hour racing. Only a few big-block cars were built.

Big-block cars had extra power and strength to compete in endurance racing.

Ford GT40 🇺🇸

Fast and immensely strong, the GT40 showed what a production car company could do when it wanted to go racing, particularly with Carroll Shelby, father of the AC Cobra, running the racing program.

Final specification

Although this car first raced in 1965, it was later brought up to the final racing specs, those of the Le Mans-winning cars of 1968 and '69.

Mid-engined design

By the 1960s, it was obvious that a successful racing car had to be mid-engined and Ford followed suit. The engine is behind the driver, mounted lengthwise, and by 1968, the displacement of the small-block engine had risen to 302 cubic inches. With Gurney-Weslake-developed cylinder heads, as on this car, power output was up to 435 bhp.

Front-mounted radiator

Ford decided to keep the radiator in its conventional position rather than mounting it alongside or behind the engine as on some modern mid-engined designs.

Four-speed transmission

The first racers are equipped with a four-speed Colotti transmission with right-hand change. Road cars have a ZF five-speed box with conventional central shifter.

Opening side windows

GT40s get incredibly hot inside and although the main side windows do not open, there are small hinged windows to allow air to pass through the cockpit.

Fiberglass body

The GT40's body played no structural role, so it was made from fiberglass and consisted basically of two large hinged sections, which gave the best access during pit stops.

Radiator outlet

By 1968, the air passing through the radiator was exhausted through this one large vent. It has a small upturned lip on the leading edge to accelerate air flow through the radiator.

Competition record

This car was one of the first driven at Le Mans, in 1965 by Bob Bondurant, but it failed to finish after cylinder head gasket failure. Three years later, it came fourth in the 1000 km at Spa Francorchamps.

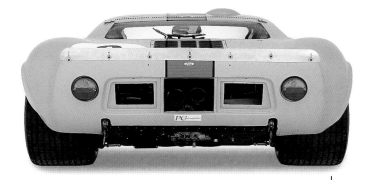

Magnesium suspension components

The GT40 is a heavyweight racing car, but some effort was still made to save weight—the magnesium suspension uprights, for example.

Halibrand wheels

The wide Halibrand wheels are made from magnesium, so they are very light. The design also provides good cooling for the disc brakes. They are a knock-off design for quick changes at pit stops.

Specifications
1967 Ford GT40 MkIII (road spec)

ENGINE

Type: V8
Construction: Cast-iron block and heads
Valve gear: Two valves per cylinder operated by single camshaft via pushrods and rockers
Bore and stroke: 4 in. x 2.87 in.
Displacement: 289 c.i.
Compression ratio: 10.5:1
Induction system: Single four-barrel Holley carburetor
Maximum power: 306 bhp at 6,000 rpm
Maximum torque: 328 lb-ft at 4,200 rpm
Top speed: 165 mph
0–60 mph: 5.5 sec

TRANSMISSION

Five-speed ZF manual transaxle

BODY/CHASSIS

Sheet steel central semi-monocoque with front and rear subframes and fiberglass two-door, two-seat GT body

SPECIAL FEATURES

The GT40 was made as low as possible to help its aerodynamics. On this car, to help fit a driver with helmet into the cockpit, this bump was added onto the roof.

To help achieve a low overall height, the exhaust pipes run over the top of the transmission.

RUNNING GEAR

Steering: Rack-and-pinion
Front suspension: Double wishbones with coil springs, telescopic shocks and anti-roll bar
Rear suspension: Trailing arms and wishbones with coil springs, telescopic shocks and anti-roll bar
Brakes: Discs, 11.5 in. dia. (front), 11.2 in. dia. (rear)
Wheels: Halibrand magnesium 6.5 in. x 15 in. (front), 8.5 in. x 15 in. (rear)
Tires: 5.5 in. x 15 in. (front), 7 in. x 15 in. (rear)

DIMENSIONS

Length: 169 in.   **Width:** 70 in.
Height: 40 in.   **Wheelbase:** 95.3 in.
Track: 55 in. (front), 53.5 in. (rear)
Weight: 2,200 lbs.

Ford MUSTANG BOSS 429

The Boss 429 Mustang was built to satisfy Ford's need to qualify at least 500 production vehicles with its new engine for NASCAR racing. Rather than putting the engine in the mid-size Torinos it ran in stock car racing, Ford put the engine in the sleek and exciting Mustang fastback instead.

"...a rippling mass of power."

"Those who expected the Mustang Boss 429 to be a Corvette® killer were disappointed by its true intent. With a semi-hemi engine that offered high-revving performance, the Boss 429 was a rippling mass of power, but was somewhat disappointing behind the wheel. It's at 6000 rpm and above where the 429 NASCAR engine makes its power, so its not much of a street dominator. It's hard to imagine why Ford made such a car. But the Boss 429 was actually a successful homologation exercise."

All Boss 429s were treated with plush interiors and an 8,000 rpm tachometer.

Milestones

1969 The Mustang

is redesigned with a sleeker body. Performance models include 857 Boss 429s, built to sanction Ford's new NASCAR 429 V8 engine. Once the Boss 429s were homologated for NASCAR, race-prepared Torinos known as Talladegas used the massive V8s. Ford took the title away from Dodge's Hemi Daytonas with more than 30 wins in the 1969 season thanks to the brawny 429 engines.

The early Shelby GT350 was the forerunner of the Boss Mustang.

1970 Mild restyling

for the second, and last, year of the Boss 429 includes a new nose, a revised tail light panel, plus a black hood scoop. Minor engine modifications include solid lifters. Again, Ford uses the same combination for NASCAR. Unfortunately, Plymouth's aerodynamic Hemi Superbird proves to be more successful.

The fearsome 428 Cobrajets were more fun on the street than the Boss 429s.

UNDER THE SKIN

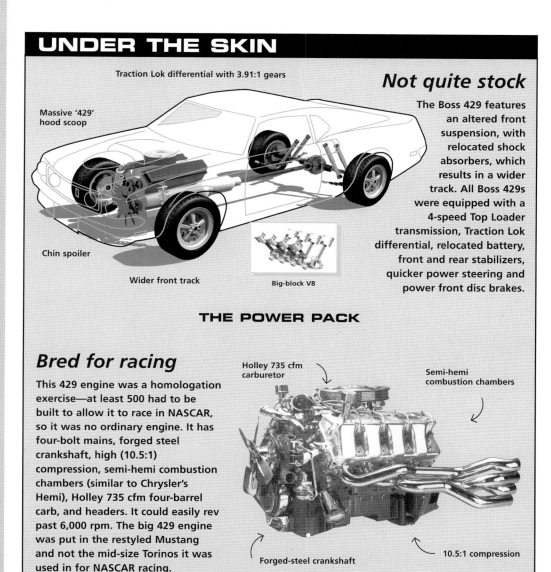

Traction Lok differential with 3.91:1 gears

Massive '429' hood scoop

Chin spoiler

Wider front track

Big-block V8

Not quite stock

The Boss 429 features an altered front suspension, with relocated shock absorbers, which results in a wider track. All Boss 429s were equipped with a 4-speed Top Loader transmission, Traction Lok differential, relocated battery, front and rear stabilizers, quicker power steering and power front disc brakes.

THE POWER PACK

Bred for racing

This 429 engine was a homologation exercise—at least 500 had to be built to allow it to race in NASCAR, so it was no ordinary engine. It has four-bolt mains, forged steel crankshaft, high (10.5:1) compression, semi-hemi combustion chambers (similar to Chrysler's Hemi), Holley 735 cfm four-barrel carb, and headers. It could easily rev past 6,000 rpm. The big 429 engine was put in the restyled Mustang and not the mid-size Torinos it was used in for NASCAR racing.

Holley 735 cfm carburetor

Semi-hemi combustion chambers

Forged-steel crankshaft

10.5:1 compression

Race-bred?

In 1969, muscle car fans thought Ford had built a car to run with the big-block Corvettes. They were saddened to learn that the car was made to homologate the engine for use in NASCAR racing. Despite being a rev-happy engine, the Boss 429 could run the ¼ mile in 14 seconds. It was the most expensive non-Shelby Mustang.

Solid lifters, which allow for higher rpm, were used in 1970 Boss 429s.

Ford **MUSTANG BOSS 429**

Built for just two model years, the Boss 429 is one of the rarest and most valuable of all Mustangs. The homologated high-performance Boss 429 engine, however, earned Ford 30 wins in the 1969 NASCAR season.

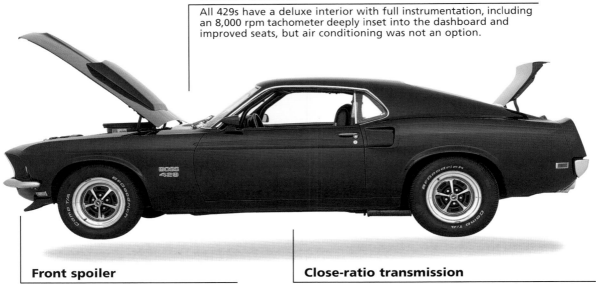

Deluxe interior
All 429s have a deluxe interior with full instrumentation, including an 8,000 rpm tachometer deeply inset into the dashboard and improved seats, but air conditioning was not an option.

Front spoiler
A functional front airdam was optional. At highway speeds, it offers little aerodynamic advantage, however.

Close-ratio transmission
A close-ratio, four-speed manual is the only transmission available on the Boss 429. Automatics weren't strong enough and couldn't handle the 429's torque.

Trunk-mounted battery
The huge and heavy V8 leaves little room for anything else in the tightly-packed engine bay, including the battery. Ford engineers were forced to relocate it to the trunk.

Modified front suspension

As well as having the stiffest springs fitted to any Mustang up to that time, the Boss 429 has a thick, $^{15}/_{16}$-inch diameter, front anti-roll bar and revalved shocks.

429-cubic inch engine

The 429s cylinder heads were so wide that not only did the battery have to be mounted in the trunk, but the shock towers had to be spread apart just to get the engine to fit.

Specifications

1969 Ford Mustang Boss 429

ENGINE

Type: V8

Construction: Cast-iron block and aluminum cylinder heads

Valve gear: Two valves per cylinder operated by a block-mounted camshaft

Bore and stroke: 4.36 in. x 3.59 in.

Displacement: 429 c.i.

Compression ratio: 10.5:1

Induction system: Four-barrel carburetor

Maximum power: 375 bhp at 5,200 rpm

Maximum torque: 450 lb-ft at 3,400 rpm

Top speed: 118 mph

0–60 mph: 6.8 sec.

TRANSMISSION

Top Loader close-ratio manual transmission

BODY/CHASSIS

Steel-frame chassis with steel two-door fastback body

SPECIAL FEATURES

These distinctive side scoops are unique to the 1969 model Boss 429.

The engine left no room for a battery or an air conditioning compressor.

RUNNING GEAR

Steering: Recirculating ball

Front suspension: Upper and lower wishbones, coil springs, telescopic shocks and anti-roll bar

Rear suspension: Live axle with semi-elliptical leaf springs, staggered telescopic shocks and anti-roll bar

Brakes: Discs front, drums rear

Wheels: Magnum 500, 7 in. x 15 in.

Tires: Goodyear Polyglas GT F60 x 15 in.

DIMENSIONS

Length: 187 in.   **Width:** 72 in.

Height: 49 in.   **Wheelbase:** 108 in.

Track: 59.3 in. (front), 58.8 in. (rear)

Weight: 3,870 lbs.

Ford ROUSH MUSTANG

Although the standard Mustang GT now boasts 260 bhp, there are still those who crave more. For them, Roush Performance offers its own monster Mustang, customized as required and offering up to 315 bhp.

"...the torque is right there."

"An extra 35 bhp coupled with side exhausts gives the cammer V8 a wake-up call. Unlike the Cobra, the torque is right there when you hit the gas. The Roush will really move from the lights, helped by a smooth-shifting transmission. Thanks to huge discs, the car will stop as well as it goes, and although the ride is stiff, relegating the car to weekend use, revised suspension tuning means you can really shuffle this 'Stang through corners."

Although Mustangs have been restyled on the outside, the interior is little changed.

Milestones

1988 Jack Roush builds
a special 351-powered, 400-bhp, twin-turbo Mustang as a 25th anniversary edition, but high costs result in Ford rejecting the idea.

Steve Saleen is one of the most notable builders of specialty Mustangs.

1995 Roush Performance
is formed as an offshoot of Roush Racing. Using its competition experience, the company sets to work on building a street-legal, high-performance, Mustang-based car.

Ford's standard high performance Mustang is the stout 320 bhp SVT Cobra with an independent rear suspension.

1998 The Roush Mustang
goes on sale. The car wins a 'Best of Show' award at the SEMA (Speciality Equipment Manufacturers' Association) Show.

1999 New for 1999
are optional bigger tires.

UNDER THE SKIN

Short 3.55:1 rear gearing

Stiff unibody

Lowered suspension

Single overhead cam V8

A step further

Roush Performance takes a stock Mustang GT and comprehensively upgrades it to deal with the extra power. The main improvements include revalved shocks, stiffer anti-roll bars and springs (also lowered) and special Roush lower control arms at the back. This results in considerably better handling, and the brakes—with cross-drilled rotors and Brembo calipers—ensure safe, quick stopping.

THE POWER PACK

Tweaked cammer

Ford's current 4.6-liter modular V8 has huge potential. A virtually equal bore and stroke gives high-revving ability, as does a single overhead camshaft per bank of cylinders. For 1999 Ford has bumped up the Mustang GT engine from 225 to 260 bhp, mainly due to higher lift and longer duration camshafts, larger valves, more efficient combustion chambers and straighter intake runners. The V8 now produces its peak power and torque higher up in the rev range, but the punch is more noticeable. Roush does offer an ignition kit and an Eaton belt-driven supercharger as part of the 1999 Stage II package.

Two's best

Roush offers several different versions of its Mustang. In 1998, a 400-bhp Cobra-based Stage II version was offered, but the 1999 GT Stage II is a much better-balanced package making more sense as a real world high performance automobile.

Bigger wheels and tires are the major technical changes for 1999.

Ford ROUSH MUSTANG

By virtue of its side-mounted exhaust and huge wheels and tires, the Roush Stage II is guaranteed to attract attention. With up to 315 bhp under the hood it has ample performance to back up the brag, too.

Alloy V8

Responding to criticisms of not having enough power, Ford gave the SOHC V8 a welcomed 35 extra bhp for 1999. In Stage II form, Roush cars have stock engines save for a side exhaust system.

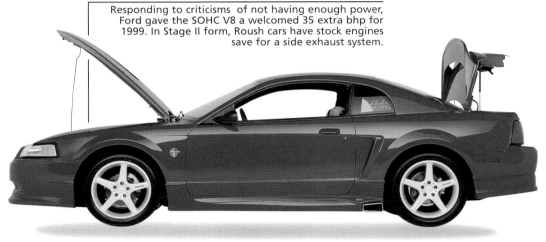

Larger brakes

Even though the standard 1999 GT has 10.8-inch vented discs at the front and 10.5-inch discs at the rear, the Roush cars have huge 13-inch Brembos at the front. To ensure maximum cooling and effeciency, they are vented and cross drilled.

Body extensions

Adding side extensions and new front and rear valances make the already mean-appearing Mustang look positively wild. These bolt-on items are available in the Roush catalog.

Traction control

One improvement the 1999 Mustang GT boasts is a traction control system as an option. When one slipping driven wheel is detected, the spark and fuel supply is cut to one or more cylinders and finally the brakes are applied.

Saving weight

Keeping weight down was of prime importance when redesigning the Mustang for 1999, thus the hood and decklid are now composite instead of steel on the 1994-98 models. A single scoop replaces the twin small vents on the hood of the 1998 Mustang.

Specifications

1999 Roush Mustang Stage II

ENGINE

Type: V8

Construction: Cast-iron block and heads

Valve gear: Two valves per cylinder operated by a single overhead camshaft per bank

Bore and stroke: 3.55 in. x 3.54 in.

Displacement: 281 c.i.

Compression ratio: 9.0:1

Induction system: Sequential multipoint electronic fuel injection

Maximum power: 260 bhp at 5,250 rpm

Maximum torque: 302 lb-ft at 4,000 rpm

Top speed: 150 mph

0–60 mph: 5.8 sec.

TRANSMISSION

Five-speed manual

BODY/CHASSIS

Unitary steel chassis with two-door coupe with a composite and steel body

SPECIAL FEATURES

Roush Mustangs come with a tool kit, mounted to the underside of the decklid.

For 1999, the Roush Mustang gets a bigger deck lid spoiler in place of the stock item.

RUNNING GEAR

Steering: Rack-and-pinion

Front suspension: MacPherson struts with lower control arms and anti-roll bar

Rear suspension: Live axle with four links, coil springs, telescopic gas shock absorbers and anti-roll bar

Brakes: Vented and cross-drilled discs, 13.0-in. dia. (front), 10.5-in. dia. (rear)

Wheels: 9 x 18 in.

Tires: 265/35 ZR18 (front), 295/35 ZR18 (rear)

DIMENSIONS

Length: 182.5 in.   **Width:** 71.8 in.

Height: 52.5 in.   **Wheelbase:** 101.3 in.

Track: 60.8 in. (front), 58.7 in. (rear)

Weight: 3,471 lbs.

Ford SHELBY GT 350

When dynamic Texan Carroll Shelby worked his magic on the best-selling Ford Mustang, he created a classic. The rare top-of-the-line 350-bhp Shelby Mustang GT350 was a great champion—and you could rent the street-legal 306-bhp version from Hertz for $35 a day!

"...tons of upper end power."

"'Rough...nasty...noisy...hard steering...I love it!' were the comments most testers made back in 1965, and it hasn't changed since. The special Detroit Locker limited slip differential makes loud ratcheting noises on slow corners, then locks with a bang when you hit the accelerator. The engine is smaller than most other American muscle cars of the time, but the GT350 is a winner at the track or on the street. Suspension is stiffer than the stock Mustang and really helps the car negotiate sharp turns. The high-performance 289 offers lots of torque and tons of upper end power."

With full instrumentation and a stripped-out interior, it is obvious that the GT350 means business.

Milestones

1964 Mustang introduced in April

and showrooms are mobbed. The first V8 comes slightly later, followed by a bigger V8, then a 271-bhp version (code name 'K'), which is the basis for the GT350.

The Mustang was launched in 1964 as a 'pony' car.

1965 Shelby

American takes time out from building Cobras to produce 100 GT350s and qualifying them to run as SCCA sports cars. They win four out of five of the B-Production regional wins in 1965, and take the overall championship that year and in 1966 and 1967.

1966 Hertz Rent-a-Car

buys about 1,000 GT350Hs (for Hertz), painted with gold stripes—most have automatic transmissions. There are stories about people renting them, racing them, then returning the Rent-a-Racers with brakes smoking and tires worn out.

Hertz gained publicity from renting Shelby Mustangs.

UNDER THE SKIN

New suspension

Engine is mounted in the front, driving through a special Borg Warner T-10 four-speed transmission to a heavy-duty rear axle, taken from a Ford Galaxie station wagon. The Mustang monocoque is steel with Shelby adding a rear seat replacement panel and fiberglass hood (with air scoop). Shelby added a wooden steering wheel—a sports car must-have at the time.

Koni adjustable shocks

Spare tire on fiberglass rear seat panel

Optional alloy wheels

Braces from cowl to suspension towers

Front-mounted V8

THE POWER PACK

Two valves per cylinder

Holley 4-barrel carburetor

10.5:1 Compression ratio

high- lift camshaft

Aluminum oil pan

Ford 'Hi-Po' 289

Basically a Mustang GT unit, the high-performance 289-cubic inch Ford small block started at 271 bhp before Shelby began working on it, a substantial improvement on the 101 bhp of the first six-cylinder Mustangs. The engine of the GT350 street car with a Holley four-barrel carburetor developed 306 bhp, and the mighty GT350R had another 44 bhp. The main modifications were a higher compression ratio, high-lift cam, larger valves, and improved breathing with the performance carburetor.

The GT350R

Only 37 examples of the 'R' (for race) version were built. With a stout 350-bhp engine and stripped interior, it won championships in the Sports Car Club of America's (SCCA) hot B-Production class against Corvettes, Ferraris, Cobras, Lotuses and E-type Jaguars.

GT350R has a fiberglass apron which increased airflow to the radiator.

Ford SHELBY GT 350

Ford's Mustang was selling well, but it lacked the high-performance image of the Corvette. So Ford asked Carroll Shelby to develop the GT350, which beat the Corvette on the race track and outperformed it on the road.

High performance 289 V8

Shelby modified Ford's 'Hi-Po' version of the small-block V8 with 10.5:1 compression ratio, improved valve timing and better breathing. This gave 306 bhp at 6,000 rpm.

Rear-exiting exhaust system

The original GT350s had side-exiting exhausts which were noisy and not permitted in some states. 1966 models were given a conventional rear-exiting exhaust system.

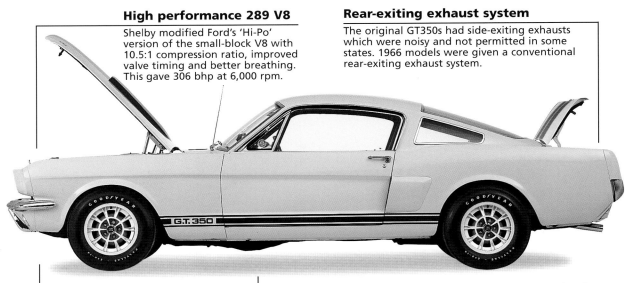

Optional Cragar alloy wheels

Conventional steel wheels were standard wear on the GT350, but many owners opted for the lighter Cragar alloys approved by Shelby.

Functional side scoops

The 1966 GT350 had side scoops which fed air to the rear brakes, distinguishing it from the standard fastback Mustang.

Rear drum brakes

The GT350's extra performance dictated the use of Kelsey-Hayes front discs, but drums were retained at the rear.

Acrylic rear quarter windows

On the 1966 models the standard Mustang fastback louvers were replaced by acrylic windows to make the car lighter.

Improved front suspension

The standard Mustang front suspension was improved for the GT350 with stiffer springs, revalved Koni shocks and relocated control arms.

Custom fuel cap

The 1966-model GT350s were given their very own fuel cap in the middle of the rear of the car, carrying the Cobra logo.

Limited slip differential

Early Shelbys were fitted with the Detroit Locker limited slip differential to improve cornering traction and eliminate wheelspin.

Specifications
1966 Shelby Mustang GT350

ENGINE
Type: V8
Construction: Cast-iron block and heads, aluminum intake manifold, tubular steel exhaust manifolds
Valve gear: Two valves per cylinder operated by single block-mounted camshaft via pushrods and rockers
Bore and stroke: 4.02 in. x 2.87 in.
Displacement: 289 c.i.
Compression ratio: 10.5:1
Induction system: Holley four-barrel carburetor
Maximum power: 306 bhp at 6,000 rpm
Maximum torque: 329 lb-ft at 4,200 rpm
Top speed: 135 mph
0–60 mph: 5.7 sec.

TRANSMISSION
Borg Warner T-10 four-speed with close-ratio gears and aluminum case

BODY/CHASSIS
Standard steel Mustang fastback body with Shelby grill; fiberglass hood, removed rear seat, Mustang monocoque with subframes

SPECIAL FEATURES

Goodyear tires were the performance rubber to have on your 1960s muscle car.

Shelby Mustang ID plate is mounted on left fenderwell.

RUNNING GEAR
Front suspension: Wishbones, coil springs, Koni shocks and anti-roll bar
Rear suspension: Live axle with semi-elliptic leaf springs, Koni shocks and traction control arms
Brakes: Kelsey-Hayes disc brakes 11.3 in. dia. (front), drums (rear)
Wheels: Steel 6 in. x 14 in. or magnesium alloy 7 in. x 14 in.
Tires: Goodyear crossply Blue Dot 775-14

DIMENSIONS
Length: 181.6 in.   **Width:** 68.2 in.
Height: 55 in.   **Wheelbase:** 108 in.
Track: 56.5 in. (front), 57 in. (rear)
Weight: 2,792 lbs.

Ford FAIRLANE THUNDERBOLT

In 1963 Ford campaigned race-prepped Galaxies in Super Stock drag racing. Because they were too heavy, the Max Wedge Mopars and Super Duty Pontiacs beat Ford's finest every time. In 1964 Ford modified its smaller Fairlane, added a full race suspension, and a high-strung 427 V8. It slaughtered the competition.

"...specialized racing machine."

"Let it be known that this is not a car for the faint hearted. The stripped-out interior, light weight and 13:1 compression engine were designed to win NHRA's highly competitive Super Stock drag racing class. The fiberglass body panels, tuned racing suspension and trunk-mounted battery give the T-bolt a traction advantage over the competition. Six out of seven NHRA divisional championships were won by these specialized racing machines."

In the interest of light weight, the sun visors, sound-deadening and mirrors were removed.

Milestones

1963 With its Total Performance

campaign underway Ford launches a new 427 engine. It enables the big Galaxies to run 12.07 ETs. Unfortunately, the cars fail to win an NHRA championship. Rhode Island Ford dealer Bob Tasca stuffs a 427 in a Fairlane and goes to the NHRA Nationals, but fails to win a race.

50 1963 lightweight Galaxies were the first 427 race cars.

1964 In order to combat

the Mopar threat, Ford puts the 427 engine into 100 lightweight Fairlanes. They give Ford the manufacturer's trophy and racer Gas Ronda wins the NHRA driver's championship.

In the 1990s, Ford rereleased its potent 427 for specialized racing.

1966 A 427-powered Fairlane

intended for the street is offered, although it proves more successful at the drag strip than on the road.

UNDER THE SKIN

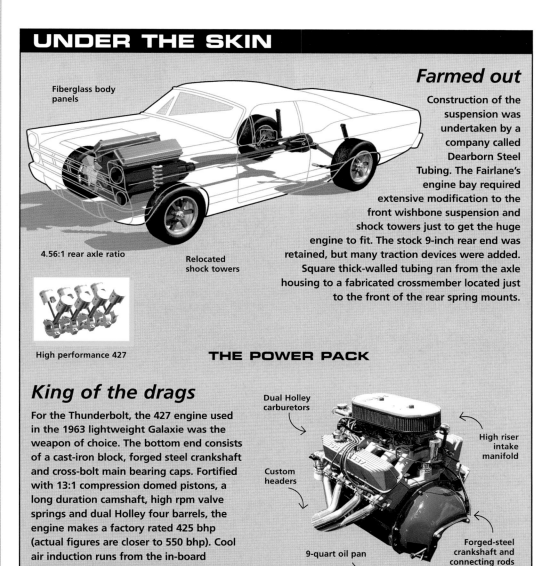

Fiberglass body panels

4.56:1 rear axle ratio

Relocated shock towers

High performance 427

Farmed out

Construction of the suspension was undertaken by a company called Dearborn Steel Tubing. The Fairlane's engine bay required extensive modification to the front wishbone suspension and shock towers just to get the huge engine to fit. The stock 9-inch rear end was retained, but many traction devices were added. Square thick-walled tubing ran from the axle housing to a fabricated crossmember located just to the front of the rear spring mounts.

THE POWER PACK

King of the drags

For the Thunderbolt, the 427 engine used in the 1963 lightweight Galaxie was the weapon of choice. The bottom end consists of a cast-iron block, forged steel crankshaft and cross-bolt main bearing caps. Fortified with 13:1 compression domed pistons, a long duration camshaft, high rpm valve springs and dual Holley four barrels, the engine makes a factory rated 425 bhp (actual figures are closer to 550 bhp). Cool air induction runs from the in-board headlight housings to the dual carbs, while special tubular headers release the exhaust.

Dual Holley carburetors

High riser intake manifold

Custom headers

9-quart oil pan

Forged-steel crankshaft and connecting rods

High prices

Because of their rarity, Thunderbolts are highly sought after today and prices reflect this. If you're interested in a weekend racer then one of these cars is ideal, since they are among the fastest in their class. They are unsuitable for street driving, however.

Only approximately 100 Thunderbolts were built in 1964.

Ford **FAIRLANE THUNDERBOLT**

Although the Thunderbolt was street legal and anyone could walk into a Ford dealer and buy their own factory drag car, it wasn't meant to be driven on the street. It was the most brutal ¼-mile race car that Ford has ever produced.

Teardrop hood

The aluminum air box sits too high on the engine to fit under a conventional flat hood. So a teardrop shaped hood bulge is molded into the fiberglass hood for adequate clearance. Two larger cut-outs in the rear section of the teardrop allow hot air in the engine compartment to escape.

427 engine

With its high compression ratio, long-duration cam and other heavy duty components. The 427 V8 was able to churn out much more than the factory rated 425 bhp.

Maximum traction

For maximum traction, the left rear is suspended by a two-leaf spring, while the right side has a three-leaf spring.

Custom headers

Tubular headers replace the cast iron exhaust manifolds. They were used not only for their tremendous performance gain, but also because the engine bay was too tight for the stock units.

Stripped-out interior

All non-essentials were removed from the interior including the sun visors, heater, radio, armrests and sound deadening. In addition, the stock front seats were replaced with lightweight buckets, the window cranks for the rear windows were removed and an unpadded rubber mat covers the floor pan.

Severe duty rear suspension

Square-tubed radius arms are welded from the crossmember directly to the rear axle housing. This design prevents the chassis from rolling above the axle unless something bends or breaks.

Body modifications

All Thunderbolts were built with fiberglass front fenders, hoods and trunk lids. While the front windshield is standard safety glass, all other windows have been replaced with lightweight Plexiglas.

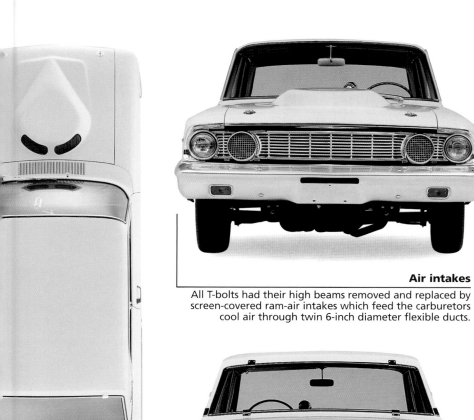

Air intakes

All T-bolts had their high beams removed and replaced by screen-covered ram-air intakes which feed the carburetors cool air through twin 6-inch diameter flexible ducts.

Modified front suspension

Many modifications had to be made to the Thunderbolt's front suspension to get the 427 to fit. The shock towers were trimmed and a flat steel plate welded in place to retain body strength. The upper A-arms were shortened and their pivot points moved out 1 inch.

Specifications

1964 Ford Fairlane Thunderbolt

ENGINE

Type: V8

Construction: Cast-iron block and heads

Valve gear: Two valves per cylinder operated by pushrods and rockers

Bore and stroke: 4.23 in. x 3.78 in.

Displacement: 427 c.i.

Compression ratio: 13:1

Induction system: Two Holley four-barrel carburetors

Maximum power: 425 bhp at 6,000 rpm

Maximum torque: 480 lb-ft at 3,700 rpm

Top speed: 130 mph

0–60 mph: 4.7 sec.

TRANSMISSION

Borg-Warner T10 four-speed

BODY/CHASSIS

Steel unitary chassis with two-door sedan body

SPECIAL FEATURES

Twin air scoops replace the stock inner headlights to give the engine cool air.

A 125-lb. battery is located in the trunk for better traction off the line.

RUNNING GEAR

Steering: Recirculating ball

Front suspension: Modified shock towers, unequal length wishbones with coil springs and telescopic shocks

Rear suspension: Custom fabricated suspension, live axle with multi-leaf springs and telescopic shocks

Brakes: Drums (front and rear)

Wheels: Steel discs, 15-in. dia.

Tires: Goodyear bias ply (front), Mickey Thompson slicks (rear)

DIMENSIONS

Length: 190.3 in.   **Width:** 73.6 in.

Height: 56.9 in.   **Wheelbase:** 115.5 in

Track: 58.6 in. (front), 55.3 in. (rear)

Weight: 3,225 lbs.

Honda **NSX-R**

The Type-R is the hottest version of the NSX, the stock version of which is sold with Acura badging in the U.S. This performance option is not available on U.S. cars and therefore the Type-R is badged as a Honda and not an Acura.

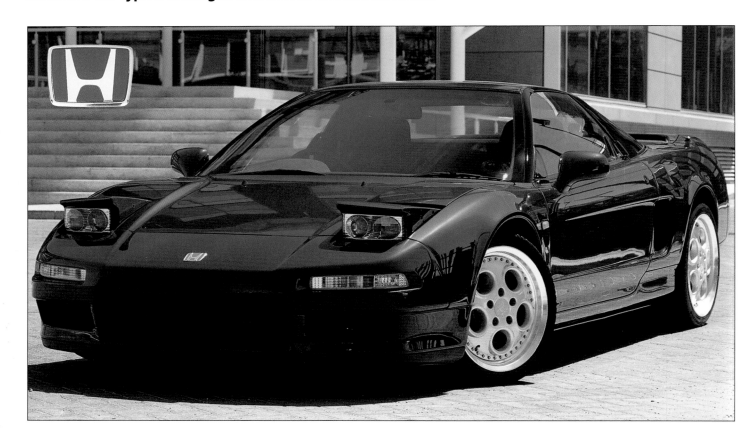

"...tremendous traction."

"Some of the more civilized auto enthusiasts feel the NSX Type-R is a serious and hard-core race car because of its incredibly hard suspension settings. Those settings come into their own on smooth roads, where the car hurtles through corners dead flat with the driver held firm in the Recaro seats. Doubling the effect, the limited-slip differential gives tremendous traction. The Honda is still the easiest car in the world to drive at very high speeds with superb handling and plenty of feedback."

Although the Type-R is a lightweight racer, the cabin contains many modern conveniences.

Milestones

1984 Honda starts its ambitious
NSX project. Research includes looking at the world's best supercars to find out how to improve them.

The light Integra Type-R uses techniques honed on the NSX.

1989 The NSX makes its debut
at the Chicago Auto Show in February, over a year before it's due for production.

The NSX is sold with Acura badging only in the U.S.

1990 Production starts at
a totally new factory dedicated to the NSX at the Tochigi Technical Center.

1992 Honda reveals the
lightweight NSX Type-R. This follows a Mugen version with lowered, stiffened suspension and some carbon-fiber bodywork, as well as a 3.2-liter engine.

1997 The 170-mph NSX S.zero
is released using principles of the Type-R.

UNDER THE SKIN

Showcase

The mid-engined NSX is an absolute showcase of advanced technology with more use of aluminum than any other car. The monocoque body/chassis unit is alloy, with three different thicknesses used—1.2 mm for the outer panels, just 1.0 mm for the roof and 3.0 mm for the inner structural members. Even the suspension arms are alloy to save weight, as are the subframes on which they are mounted. More than 250 lbs. has been saved.

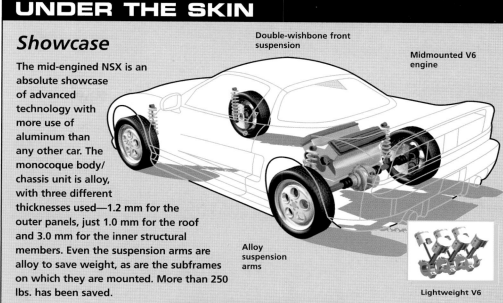

Double-wishbone front suspension

Midmounted V6 engine

Alloy suspension arms

Lightweight V6

THE POWER PACK

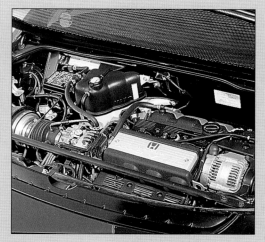

Racing expertise

Honda's experience in building some of the world's best racing engines shone through in the original NSX's 274-bhp, 3.0-liter V6. The block and heads are naturally made from alloy and the engine is a compact short-stroke design with four belt-driven overhead camshafts working four valves per cylinder. It benefits from titanium connecting rods that allow the engine to have an 8,000 rpm redline. Not only is there variable valve timing coming into operation around 5,800 rpm, but there is also a variable volume intake system. It operates at the same rpm to give the engine much greater airflow. This raises power to 280 bhp.

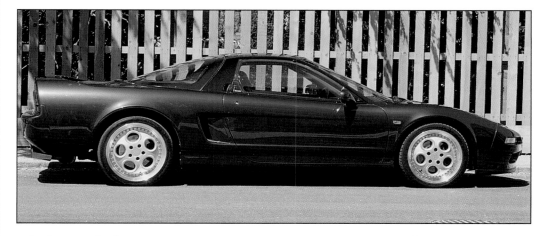

Lightweight

Although the regular NSX set the benchmark for supercar handling, the Type-R is more agile with even higher levels of grip and more responsive steering. The trade-off, however, is a very punishing ride on all but the smoothest surface.

The NSX Type-R is a sleek, purposeful performance machine.

Honda **NSX-R**

Don't be fooled by its looks. The NSX-R retains the beautiful Ferrari-inspired lines of the standard NSX road car, but underneath there is a blueprinted engine and suspension almost as stiff as a racing car's.

V6 engine

For the Type-R, the 3.0-liter DOHC V6 was fully balanced and blueprinted to withstand competition use. Advertised power and torque remained virtually unchanged at 280 bhp and 209 lb-ft.

Alloy wheels

Not only are the NSX's wheels made from alloy, but they are forged rather than cast to give extra strength. They are also lighter than typical cast-aluminum wheels. The spare tire was deleted to save weight.

VTEC-variable valve timing and lift

By 5,800 rpm, the intake and exhaust valves open farther and longer, thus increasing the engine's power. A hydraulically actuated mechanism locks the cam followers to follow the high lift cam profile.

Weight-saving program

To save 268 lbs., Honda took drastic measures. It scrapped the air conditioning, underseal, stereo, the standard seats and other pieces of electrical equipment.

Wishbone rear suspension
Very wide-based wishbones are used at the rear, and what looks like a steering track rod on each side is in fact an adjustable arm to change the toe angle of the wheels. This gives a measure of passive rear-wheel steer, toeing-in under cornering load.

Alloy body
There was little scope to lighten the body, except for the plastic-covered steel bumpers. For the best compromise between strength and weight, they were changed to alloy.

Specifications

1993 Honda NSX Type-R

ENGINE
Type: V6

Construction: Alloy block and heads

Valve gear: Four valves per cylinder operated by two belt-driven overhead camshafts per bank of cylinders with VTEC-variable valve lift

Bore and stroke: 3.54 in. x 3.07 in.

Displacement: 2,997 cc

Compression ratio: 10.2:1

Induction system: Electronic fuel injection

Maximum power: 280 bhp at 7,300 rpm

Maximum torque: 209 lb-ft at 5,400 rpm

Top speed: 169 mph

0–60 mph: 5.1 sec

TRANSMISSION
Five-speed manual

BODY/CHASSIS
Aluminum-alloy monocoque with alloy two-door coupe body

SPECIAL FEATURES

The rear window lifts up to give better access to the NSX's midmounted engine.

The alloy wheels are unique to the NSX Type-R and are ultra-lightweight.

RUNNING GEAR
Steering: Rack-and-pinion

Front suspension: Double wishbones with coil springs, telescopic shock absorbers and anti-roll bar

Rear suspension: Double wishbones with coil springs, telescopic shock absorbers and anti-roll bar

Brakes: Vented discs, 11.1-in. dia.

Wheels: Alloy 6.5 x 15 in. (front), 8.0 x 16 in. (rear)

Tires: 205/50 ZR15 (front), 225/50 ZR16 (rear)

DIMENSIONS
Length: 173.4 in.   **Width:** 71.3 in.

Height: 46.1 in.   **Wheelbase:** 99.6 in.

Track: 59.4 in. (front), 60.2 in. (rear)

Weight: 2,712 lbs.

Iso **GRIFO**

This car was conceived by Renzo Rivolta as a rival to Ferraris and Lamborghinis. But beneath the Grifo's elegant Italian lines beats the heart of an all-American Chevrolet Corvette V8.

"...seriously underrated."

"The Grifo is probably the best marriage of Italian engineering and style with the power and durability of a Detroit powerplant. The Corvette V8 may lack the pure-bred feel of an Italian V12, but it produces the necessary horsepower. To match its raw power, the Grifo carves corners perfectly, with enough power to limit its tendency to understeer while going through turns. This is a seriously underrated car."

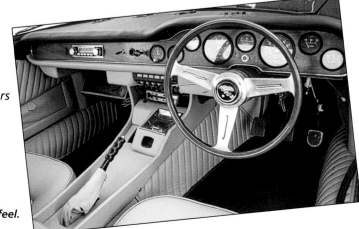

Inside, the Grifo was sumptuously furnished with leather trim. Optional air-conditioning and wood trim contributes to its luxury feel.

Milestones

1963 A stunningly

beautiful A3 Lusso (road car) and a competition racer (A3/C) debut at the Turin Motor Show.

1965 The Grifo,

with its exotic Italian styling and American V8 power, enters production. A racing variant makes its debut at Sebring in 1964, but fails to make its mark.

The Iso A3/C competition racer ran in 1964 and 1965.

1968 Iso introduces

a second Grifo. Called the 7-Liter, this has a longer front end and raised hood housing a 427-cubic inch big-block V8. It is capable of speeds of up to 170 mph.

The four-seater Iso Lele competed with Lamborghini's Espada.

1970 A facelift

introduces a much lower nose housing semi-retractable headlights. The standard engine is a 327 (5.4 liter) V8.

1974 Rising insurance

rates and the oil crisis spell the demise for the Grifo and production ends.

UNDER THE SKIN

Clever chassis

The Grifo was effectively constructed by hand. Stamped steel pressings were welded to the floorpan for maximum stiffness. The independent front suspension used coil springs and unequal length wishbones. The rear consists of a de Dion axle with twin radius arms and a Watt linkage. It also uses Dunlop four-wheel disc brakes.

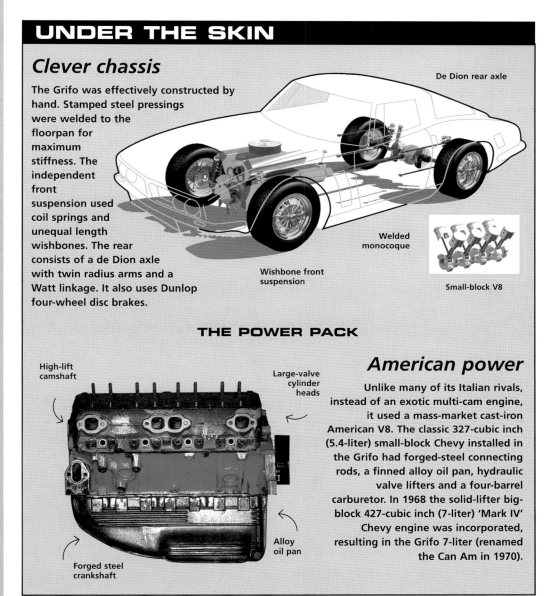

De Dion rear axle

Welded monocoque

Wishbone front suspension

Small-block V8

THE POWER PACK

High-lift camshaft

Large-valve cylinder heads

Forged steel crankshaft

Alloy oil pan

American power

Unlike many of its Italian rivals, instead of an exotic multi-cam engine, it used a mass-market cast-iron American V8. The classic 327-cubic inch (5.4-liter) small-block Chevy installed in the Grifo had forged-steel connecting rods, a finned alloy oil pan, hydraulic valve lifters and a four-barrel carburetor. In 1968 the solid-lifter big-block 427-cubic inch (7-liter) 'Mark IV' Chevy engine was incorporated, resulting in the Grifo 7-liter (renamed the Can Am in 1970).

Small changes

During the course of its life cycle, Grifo styling was evolutionary. The new 1968 7-Liter model introduced a bulged hood and longer front end. Half-covered headlights were fitted for 1970, updating the car's looks for the new decade.

The post-1969 Grifos boast slightly cleaner front-end styling.

Iso GRIFO

Iso may not have the heritage of some of its rivals, but for a brief moment in the 1960s, the Italian company produced one of the fastest production supercars in the world.

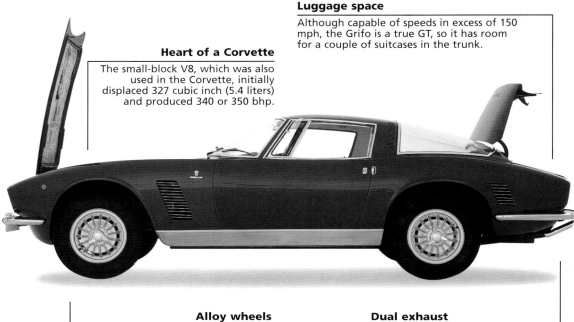

Heart of a Corvette
The small-block V8, which was also used in the Corvette, initially displaced 327 cubic inch (5.4 liters) and produced 340 or 350 bhp.

Luggage space
Although capable of speeds in excess of 150 mph, the Grifo is a true GT, so it has room for a couple of suitcases in the trunk.

Alloy wheels
Most Grifos are fitted with these handsome cast-alloy wheels, complete with knock-off spinners.

Dual exhaust
To exploit the V8s power, dual exhaust is mandatory and gives a fantastic exhaust note.

Excellent visibility
A large rear window offers great visibility and came with a standard built-in defroster.

Wishbone suspension

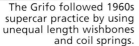

The Grifo followed 1960s supercar practice by using unequal length wishbones and coil springs.

Elegant shape

The Grifo was designed by a young Giorgetto Giugiaro, who has been responsible for many of the world's most elegant cars.

Specifications

1967 Iso Grifo

ENGINE

Type: V8

Construction: Cast-iron block and heads

Valve gear: Two valves per cylinder operated by pushrods and rocker arms

Bore and stroke: 4.0 in. x 3.25 in.

Displacement: 5,359 cc

Compression ratio: 10.5:1

Induction system: Single four-barrel Holley carburetor

Maximum power: 350 bhp at 5,800 rpm

Maximum torque: 360 lb-ft at 3,600 rpm

Top speed: 163 mph

0–60 mph: 6.4 sec.

TRANSMISSION

ZF five-speed manual

BODY/CHASSIS

Monocoque two-door coupe

SPECIAL FEATURES

Side scoops on the front fenders are functional and vent hot air from the engine bay.

Bertone was responsible for building the beautiful coupe body.

RUNNING GEAR

Steering: Burman recirculating ball

Front suspension: Upper and lower wishbones with coil springs and telescopic shocks

Rear suspension: De Dion axle with coil springs, telescopic shocks, anti-roll bar, Watt linkage, and radius arms

Brakes: Servo-assisted disc brakes all around

Wheels: Cast-alloy knock-off

Tires: Pirelli Cinturato 205HS/15

DIMENSIONS

Length: 174.7 in.   **Width:** 69.5 in.

Height: 47 in.   **Wheelbase:** 106.3 in.

Track: 55.5 in. (front and rear)

Weight: 3,036 lbs.

Jaguar **D-TYPE**

Jaguar designed the D-type with one aim in mind—to create a car that could win the most important race in the world, the 24 Hours of Le Mans. It achieved three straight victories in the mid-1950s.

"...tractable in traffic."

"By any standards, the D-type is an astonishing car with straight-line power to frighten many current supercars. A lack of cockpit space is emphasized by the big central rib, and the steering wheel feels big and skinny. The gearshift is positive, but heavy. None of the other controls are unduly heavy. Surprisingly for a race car, the D-type is tractable in traffic. But find an open road and it rockets to 60 mph in just over 5 seconds and tops 162 mph."

A bulky transmission tunnel results in a snug fit inside the cockpit.

Milestones

1953 Jaguar's XK120C Mk 2 is first seen in October, when it achieves nearly 180 mph on a closed Belgian highway.

The C-type started Jaguar's run of success at Le Mans.

1954 Now known as the D-type, three cars are entered in the 24 Hours of Le Mans. Two drop out, but the third car takes second place.

1955 Fitted with longer noses, two D-types take first and third at Le Mans.

Jaguar's next specialist racer was the lightweight E-type.

1956 An Ecurie Ecosse D-type wins at Le Mans, with a poor showing from the works cars.

1957 Jaguar no longer campaigns the D-type, but an Ecurie Ecosse car wins Le Mans again. New regulations result in the D-type's demise.

UNDER THE SKIN

Proven and new

The D-type's chassis owes as much to aircraft-industry thinking as to conventional race-car engineering. Whereas most racing sports cars in the mid-1950s still relied on a ladder-type frame, or at best a tubular spaceframe, the D-type uses a strong central monocoque with a separate subframe to support the engine and front suspension. Like its predecessor, the D-type has a live rear axle and four-wheel disc brakes.

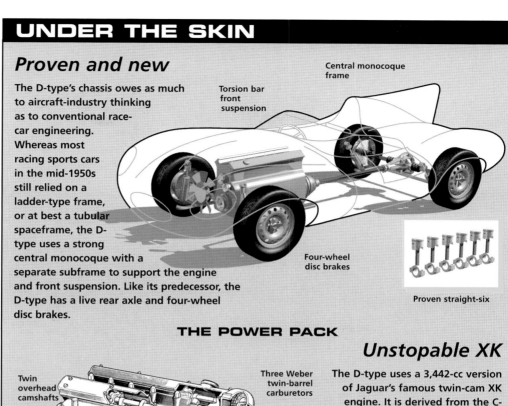

Torsion bar front suspension

Central monocoque frame

Four-wheel disc brakes

Proven straight-six

THE POWER PACK

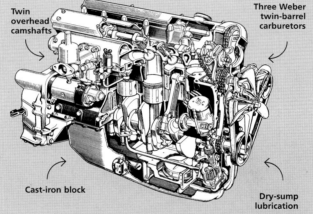

Twin overhead camshafts

Three Weber twin-barrel carburetors

Cast-iron block

Dry-sump lubrication

Unstopable XK

The D-type uses a 3,442-cc version of Jaguar's famous twin-cam XK engine. It is derived from the C-type's iron-block, alloy-head unit, but has a dry sump, bigger inlet valves, a new exhaust manifold and hotter camshafts. In its original form, with three twin-barrel Weber carburetors, it produces 250 bhp—more than 30 bhp more than the C-type unit. This unit was later increased to 3,781 cc and with fuel injection and an improved cylinder head, it produces up to 304 bhp.

Road racer

If the D-type is a little too stark for your tastes, the roadgoing version—the XKSS—is the one to choose. This later model is fitted with a proper windshield and a folding soft top. It has a road-car style interior without the central divider.

The last 16 cars were XKSS versions and were fully street legal.

Jaguar **D-TYPE**

Jaguar's D-type broke new ground with its semi-monocoque construction and aerodynamic design. It was perfectly at home on the fast circuit of Le Mans, where it won for three consecutive years (1955–1957).

Dry-sump lubrication

Although the D-type's XK engine is essentially identical to that used in Jaguar's roadgoing sports cars, it has a dry sump rather than a conventional wet one. The oil is kept in a separate tank and circulated by a pump, which prevents oil surge during high-speed cornering.

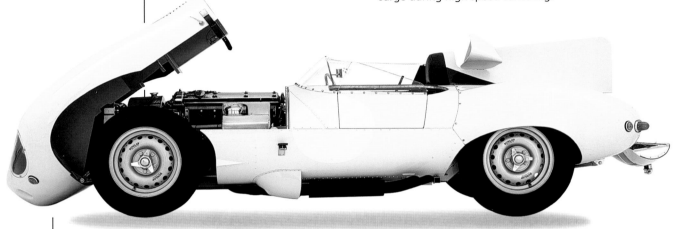

Disc brakes front and rear

Jaguar pioneered the use of disc brakes in motor racing with the C-type. The Dunlop system was also used in the D-type, being employed both front and rear.

Two-seater bodywork

Racing regulations decreed that the D-type had to be a two-seater. In reality, it raced with just a driver; a fixed cover was put over the second seat to aid aerodynamics.

Rear stabilizing fin

Part of the aerodynamic package designed by ex-Bristol Aircraft aerodynamicist Malcolm Sayer is the fin that runs back from behind the driver's headrest. This provides important directional stability when racing on very fast circuits like Le Mans.

Monocoque center section

To give it the very stiff but light structure needed for a racing car, the D-type pioneered the use of an alloy monocoque to replace the spaceframe chassis used on the C-type. It is not a full monocoque, however, as the engine and front suspension are held in a separate subframe.

Specifications

1957 Jaguar D-type*

ENGINE

Type: In-line six

Construction: Cast-iron block and alloy head

Valve gear: Two valves per cylinder operated by two overhead camshafts

Bore and stroke: 3.27 in. x 4.17 in.

Displacement: 3,442 cc

Compression ratio: 9.0:1

Induction system: Three Weber sidedraft carburetors

Maximum power: 250 bhp at 6,000 rpm

Maximum torque: 242 lb-ft at 4,000 rpm

Top speed: 162 mph

0–60 mph: 5.4 sec.

TRANSMISSION

Four-speed manual

BODY/CHASSIS

Center monocoque with separate front subframe

SPECIAL FEATURES

The spare wheel is stored in a small trunk which hinges down for access.

A leather strap on each side keeps the clamshell hood secured.

RUNNING GEAR

Steering: Rack-and-pinion

Front suspension: Double wishbones with longitudinal torsion bars and telescopic shock absorbers

Rear suspension: Live axle with single transverse torsion bar, trailing links, single A-bracket and telescopic shock absorbers

Brakes: Dunlop discs (front and rear)

Wheels: Dunlop light alloy Center-lock, 5.5 x 16 in.

Tires: Dunlop racing, 6.50 x 16 in.

DIMENSIONS

Length: 154.0 in.   **Width:** 65.4 in.

Height: 44.0 in.   **Wheelbase:** 90.0 in.

Track: 50.0 in. (front), 48.0 in. (rear)

Weight: 2,460 lbs.

* Model illustrated is a Lynx replica

Jaguar **E-TYPE LIGHTWEIGHT**

The E-Type was never meant to be a race car but encouraging results in competition persuaded Jaguar to build a limited number of very special Lightweight cars. With their alloy bodywork and highly-tuned engines, they were very different from the standard car, and very competitive.

"...an extraordinarily fast car."

"That the Lightweight E-Type is an extraordinarily fast car is never in doubt. Off the line, it gulps up the track, pelting through the 60-mph barrier in five seconds and careening on up to a top speed close to 160 mph. The tires are skinny by today's standard and you certainly know all about power oversteer by the end of the first lap. The handling is superb, with almost no body roll and tremendous stability. The disc brakes are sharp, progressive, and full of feel."

The Lightweight's dashboard is fully stocked with every necessary gauge.

Milestones

1961 In the year of the E-Type's launch, the standard car achieves several competition wins in the hands of Graham Hill, Roy Salvadori and others.

The Lightweight E-Type was never as successful as the D-Type.

1962 The factory produces some cars with lighter-gauge steel and aluminum hoods, and competes at the 24 Hours of Le Mans.

The Lightweight was based on the open top monocoque.

1963 Competition (Lightweight) E-Types take to the track and immediately start winning; one takes ninth place at Le Mans but most success is scored in club racing.

1964 Lightweights again compete at the 24 Hours of Le Mans without much success.

UNDER THE SKIN

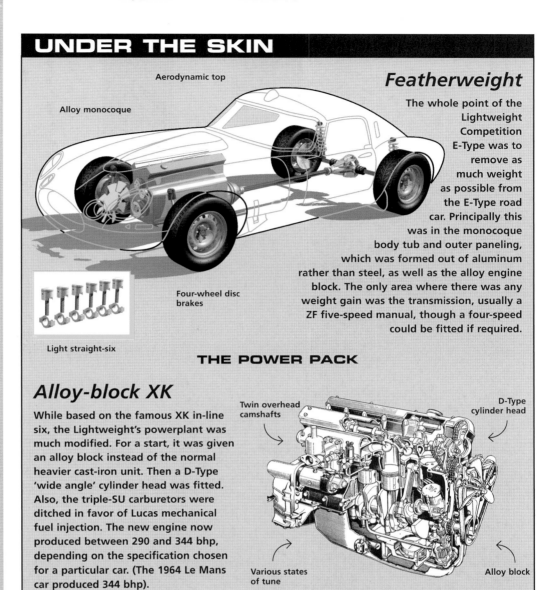

Aerodynamic top

Alloy monocoque

Four-wheel disc brakes

Light straight-six

Featherweight

The whole point of the Lightweight Competition E-Type was to remove as much weight as possible from the E-Type road car. Principally this was in the monocoque body tub and outer paneling, which was formed out of aluminum rather than steel, as well as the alloy engine block. The only area where there was any weight gain was the transmission, usually a ZF five-speed manual, though a four-speed could be fitted if required.

THE POWER PACK

Alloy-block XK

While based on the famous XK in-line six, the Lightweight's powerplant was much modified. For a start, it was given an alloy block instead of the normal heavier cast-iron unit. Then a D-Type 'wide angle' cylinder head was fitted. Also, the triple-SU carburetors were ditched in favor of Lucas mechanical fuel injection. The new engine now produced between 290 and 344 bhp, depending on the specification chosen for a particular car. (The 1964 Le Mans car produced 344 bhp).

Twin overhead camshafts

D-Type cylinder head

Various states of tune

Alloy block

Lightweight

Among E-Type aficionados, the one car they would all dearly love to own is a Lightweight Competition car. Apart from extreme rarity—only 12 were ever made—they have terrific pedigree and most have their own unique racing history attached to them.

With only 12 built, the Lightweight E-Type is highly desirable.

Jaguar E-TYPE LIGHTWEIGHT 🇬🇧

Following the racing success of the great Jaguar C-Type and D-Type was never going to be easy, and the E-Type had to be radically transformed by lightening it significantly to be competitive.

Alternative nose treatments

Most Lightweights had a hood like that of the roadgoing E-Type, except that it was made of aluminum. Several race cars, such as this model, were fitted with longer noses designed by Malcolm Sayer. This car competed in the 1964 Le Mans.

Bigger brakes

Even the standard roadgoing E-Type had all-around disc brakes, so all the Lightweight needed were slightly larger brake discs and uprated calipers.

Choice of rear axle formats

Some Lightweights used the conventional Power-Lok differential, but others used ZF or Thornton units. There was a choice of rear axle ratios depending on how you planned to use the E-Type.

Fixed hardtop

The Lightweights were all based on the lighter open-topped body but to add extra rigidity they were all fitted with an aluminum non-removable hardtop. Usually the shape echoed that of the road car's hardtop, but an alternative 'low-drag' fastback was also designed by aerodynamicist Malcolm Sayer for fast events such as Le Mans. The shape of the roof on this Lindner Nocker Lightweight was unique.

All-aluminum body

While the roadgoing E-Type had a steel monocoque and body panels, the Lightweight used aluminum exclusively throughout. This reduced the car's overall weight by nearly 500 lbs.

No bumpers

In an effort to save weight, no bumpers were fitted front or rear. Other weight-saving omissions included badges, brightwork, sliding windows and a stripped-out interior.

Uprated suspension

Much of the suspension was shared with the highly effective roadgoing E-Type. However, certain components were uprated. Up front, stiffer torsion bars and anti-roll bar, uprated shock absorbers and special upper and lower fulcrum housings were used. At the rear there was a stiffer cage bottom plate, lightened hub carriers, modified wishbones, shock absorbers with integral bump-stops and stiffer mountings.

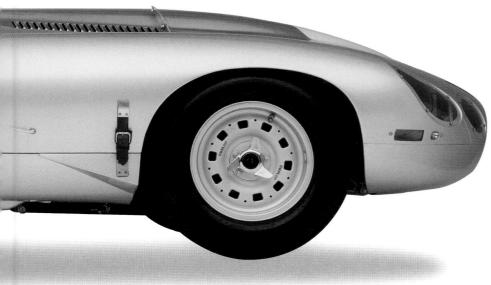

Specifications

1963 Jaguar E-Type Lightweight

ENGINE

Type: In-line 6-cylinder

Construction: Aluminum cylinder block and head

Valve gear: Two valves per cylinder operated by twin chain-driven overhead camshafts

Bore and stroke: 3.43 in. x 4.17 in.

Displacement: 3,781 cc

Compression ratio: 9.5:1

Induction system: Lucas mechanical fuel injection

Maximum power: 344 bhp at 6,500 rpm

Maximum torque: 314 lb ft at 4,750 rpm

Top speed: 157 mph

0–60 mph: 5.0 sec.

TRANSMISSION

Four or five-speed manual

BODY/CHASSIS

Unitary monocoque construction with aluminum fixed hardtop coupe body

SPECIAL FEATURES

A racing-type fuel filler allows quick mid-race fuel stops.

The blue light over the windshield is for signaling to the pits.

RUNNING GEAR

Steering: Rack-and-pinion

Front suspension: Wishbones with torsion bars, anti-roll bar and telescopic shock absorbers

Rear suspension: Lower wishbone, upper driveshaft link, radius arms, coil springs, anti-roll bar and telescopic shock absorbers

Brakes: Discs (front and rear)

Wheels: Alloy 15-in dia.

Tires: 5.50 x 15 (front), 6.00 x 15 (rear)

DIMENSIONS

Length: 175.3 in.   **Width:** 65.2 in.

Height: 48.0 in.   **Wheelbase:** 96.0 in.

Track: 50.0 in. (front), 50.0 in. (rear)

Weight: 2,220 lbs.

Jaguar **XJ13**

Number 13 turned out to be unlucky for this spectacular Jaguar racing car. Conceived so that Jaguar could relive its Le Mans glories of the 1950s, it never raced but its legacy lived on in the V12-powered Jaguar road cars.

"...unforgettable experience."

"Although the XJ13 is nearly 75 inches wide, half of that width is taken up by the sills and the cockpit is incredibly cramped—the two occupants actually have to overlap shoulders. Fire it up and the sound is unforgettable: ear-splittingly loud, almost violent. The twin-plate clutch is very jerky and the gearshift is awkward, but once out on the circuit all this is forgotten as the XJ13 unleashes its true potential."

The XJ13's driving position might be snug, but it wasn't designed for cruising.

Milestones

1964 Jaguar completes the prototype of its V12 engine project.

1965 Construction of the XJ13 bodyshell begins.

Jaguar's D-type proved highly successful in the late 1950s.

1966 The XJ13 sports racer is completed and in July breaks the British speed record for a closed circuit run at 161.6 mph. However, Jaguar merges with BMC and the XJ13 project is permanently put on hold.

The most recent Jaguar supercar is the limited production XJ220.

1971 During a promotional event Norman Dewis rolls the XJ13 after a wheel collapses and almost destroys it.

1972 New Jaguar chief executive 'Lofty' England discovers the XJ13 under dust sheets and has it restored.

UNDER THE SKIN

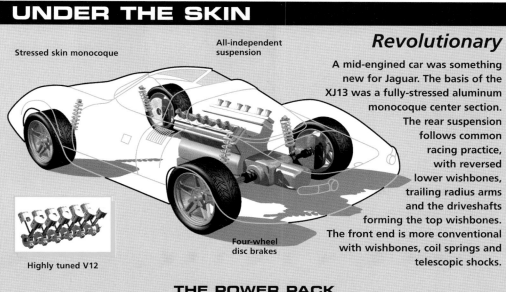

Stressed skin monocoque

All-independent suspension

Highly tuned V12

Four-wheel disc brakes

Revolutionary

A mid-engined car was something new for Jaguar. The basis of the XJ13 was a fully-stressed aluminum monocoque center section. The rear suspension follows common racing practice, with reversed lower wishbones, trailing radius arms and the driveshafts forming the top wishbones. The front end is more conventional with wishbones, coil springs and telescopic shocks.

THE POWER PACK

Monster V12 engine

Many years before Jaguar announced the famous V12 engine which powers the E-Type and XJ sedans, the company developed a very special and quite different V12 for the XJ13. The alloy block had dry liners and boasted a displacement of 5.0 liters, dry sump lubrication and two-stage chain drive to its four camshafts. It is a heavy engine, weighing 639 lbs. Initially, the engine produced 430 bhp at 7,500 rpm, but fine tuning increased power to 502 bhp at 7,600 rpm during one static engine test.

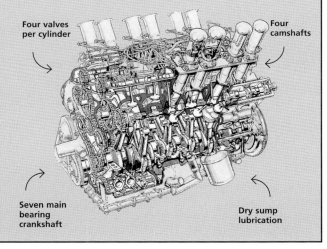

Four valves per cylinder

Four camshafts

Seven main bearing crankshaft

Dry sump lubrication

One and only

The one XJ13 that was built is today jealously guarded by Jaguar. It occasionally appears at classic car shows when Jaguar brings the old beast out of retirement from its museum. However, only a very lucky few are allowed to take the wheel.

Only one original XJ13 was produced, but there are a number of replicas.

Jaguar **XJ13** 🇬🇧

Even as Jaguar drew the curtains on its racing program in the 1950s, insiders were planning a spectacular comeback. The XJ13 was the result, but politics and changing regulations caused its demise.

Ultra wide tires

For maximum grip, the XJ13 was fitted with 10-inch front tires and 13.6 rear tires. It was very unusual for a car of the 1960s to have tires this wide.

Stressed engine

Following the lead of the Lotus 25 Formula 1 car, the XJ13's engine is a stressed part of the monocoque structure.

Unique V12 engine

The XJ13 engine is a complex, double overhead camshaft racing unit, while the eventual roadgoing V12 used in the E-Type S3 is a much more practical single overhead camshaft design and is far more reliable.

Six ZF transmissions

Jaguar had six ZF 5DS25/2 transaxles made for the XJ13 because it was easier to change the transmission than just the differential. Each of the six units had a different final drive ratio.

Alloy wheels

The magnesium alloy wheels were cast especially for the XJ13, and featured knock-on spinners. When the car was restored in the mid-1970s, an entirely new set of wheels were fitted as the existing ones were showing signs of fatigue.

Timeless elegance

The XJ13's graceful lines were styled by Malcolm Sayer, the very gifted designer of the great C-Type and D-Type racers of the 1950s. He also penned the immortal E-Type. The overall shape is very aerodynamically efficient, with a low body and minimal frontal area. It is claimed that its drag coefficient is superior to that of the Ford GT40.

Aluminum monocoque

The key to the XJ13's light weight is its superb monocoque made entirely of aluminum. It is fully stressed and clothed in light alloy bodywork by Abbey Panels of Coventry, England. The engine is mounted directly to the monocoque, and doesn't use rubber bushings.

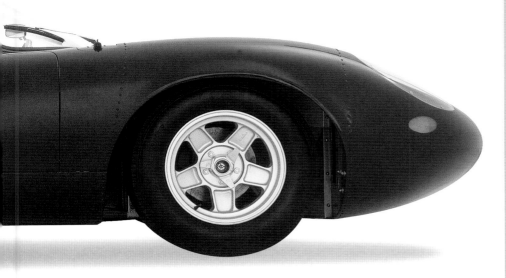

Specifications
1966 Jaguar XJ13

ENGINE
Type: V12

Construction: Aluminum cylinder block and heads

Valve gear: Two valves per cylinder operated by two chain-driven overhead camshafts per bank

Bore and stroke: 3.42 in. x 2.75 in.

Displacement: 4,991 cc

Compression ratio: 10.4:1

Induction system: Lucas fuel injection

Maximum power: 502 bhp at 7,600 rpm

Maximum torque: 365 lb-ft at 5,500 rpm

Top speed: 161 mph

0–60 mph: 4 sec.

TRANSMISSION
Five-speed manual

BODY/CHASSIS
Aluminum monocoque with two-door open-roof coupe body

SPECIAL FEATURES

The intake tubes dominate the view of the engine from the rear.

For maximum grip the one-off Jag uses 15-inch alloys with 10-inch wide tires in the front and 13.6-inch tires on the rear.

RUNNING GEAR
Steering: Rack-and-pinion

Front suspension: Double wishbones with coil springs, shocks and anti-roll bar

Rear suspension: Trailing links with fixed length driveshafts, bottom A-frame with coil springs, shocks and anti-roll bar

Brakes: Vented discs (front and rear)

Wheels: Magnesium alloy, 15-in. dia.

Tires: Dunlop Racing, 4.75/10.00 x 15 (front), 5.30/13.60 x 15 (rear)

DIMENSIONS
Length: 176.4 in.   **Width:** 73 in.

Height: 37.9 in.   **Wheelbase:** 95.9 in.

Track: 55.9 in. (front), 55.9 in. (rear)

Weight: 2,477 lbs.

Jaguar **XJ220**

Hand-made by craftsmen and race-proven at Le Mans, the XJ220 was to be the ultimate sporting Jaguar for the 21st Century. Yet the prototype of this superb machine was built without funding by Jaguar's engineers on their own time.

"...a predator ready to pounce."

"Sit in most supercars and you will find that creature comforts definitely take second place to performance. But the XJ220 is unique, cocooning you in traditional Jaguar luxury. The interior reeks of sumptuous leather. Air conditioning? Of course! Settle back—there's room for the tallest driver. But make no mistake, this cat crouches low like a predator ready to pounce. 100 mph is reached in just 7.3 seconds when you floor the accelerator. The mid-rear engine placement assures beautiful balance and the chassis offers massive structural integrity."

The wrap-around dash houses a complete set of instruments. Despite the car's performance, this is no stripped-down racing car, but a luxury Jaguar.

Milestones

1988 The XJ220

prototype is unveiled to cheers at the British International Auto Show. Designed in secret, it has a 12-cylinder 5,999-cc motor, all-wheel drive and a planned top speed of 200 mph plus. Dozens of potential buyers come forward saying, "We'll have one—at any price."

The XJ220 made full use of Jaguar's endurance racing technology.

1989 Jaguar

announces "the XJ220 you can buy" with a 24-valve V6 turbocharged engine, rear-wheel drive—and a planned top speed of more than 220 mph; 350 orders are accepted from 1,000 applications.

1992 In testing at

Nardo, Italy an XJ220 achieves 217.3 mph, making it the world's fastest production road car—a tag now assumed by the smaller McLaren F1. Given a long enough straightaway, it should be possible for the XJ220 to reach the magic 220 mph.

1994 The last of the

281 production run of XJ220s come off the line. A price of $706,000 made it impossible to sell every car in a world hit by recession, but those who did take delivery, like rock star Elton John, own the fastest Jaguar ever.

UNDER THE SKIN

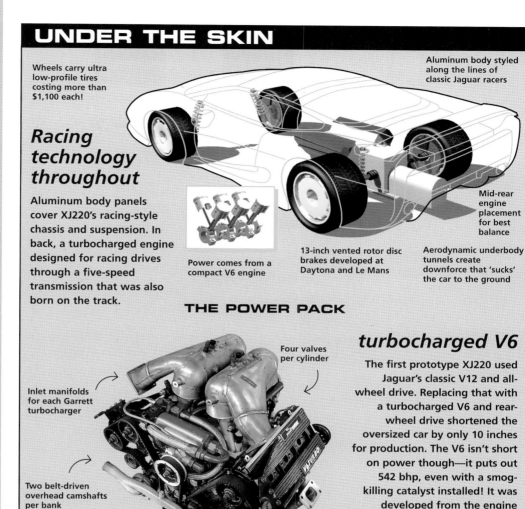

Aluminum body styled along the lines of classic Jaguar racers

Wheels carry ultra low-profile tires costing more than $1,100 each!

Racing technology throughout

Aluminum body panels cover XJ220's racing-style chassis and suspension. In back, a turbocharged engine designed for racing drives through a five-speed transmission that was also born on the track.

Power comes from a compact V6 engine

Mid-rear engine placement for best balance

13-inch vented rotor disc brakes developed at Daytona and Le Mans

Aerodynamic underbody tunnels create downforce that 'sucks' the car to the ground

THE POWER PACK

Four valves per cylinder

Inlet manifolds for each Garrett turbocharger

Two belt-driven overhead camshafts per bank

Dry sump with remote oil tank

turbocharged V6

The first prototype XJ220 used Jaguar's classic V12 and all-wheel drive. Replacing that with a turbocharged V6 and rear-wheel drive shortened the oversized car by only 10 inches for production. The V6 isn't short on power though—it puts out 542 bhp, even with a smog-killing catalyst installed! It was developed from the engine Jaguar raced at Le Mans, with four belt-driven overhead cams, 24 valves and 3.5 liters.

Elegant strength

Although constructed mostly from aluminum, the XJ220 is no lightweight. Its smooth, sensuous lines hide an extremely advanced honeycomb construction. The immensely strong panels and chassis give the car massive structural integrity—after its government crash test, the XJ220's glazing remained intact, and all doors and rear panels opened normally!

Open lids of radiator, engine and tiny luggage compartment.

Jaguar **XJ220**

Elegant and smooth, the XJ220 took its styling cues from the XJ13, a still-born Jaguar racer of the 1960s. But under the skin it's right up to date, with state-of-the-art racing technology.

Baggage space

This is a car for traveling light. The rear end is full of engine, and the front is full of radiators to cool it. The trunk is just big enough for a briefcase or two.

Transparent engine cover

The hood on the XJ220 is a lift-up glass panel that puts the powerful turbo motor permanently on show.

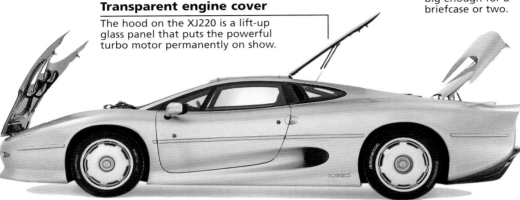

Aluminum-honeycomb chassis

Designed to be simple and easy to produce (because the first XJ220 was built in Jaguar engineers' spare time), the chassis is bonded together with adhesive, not welded.

Aluminum body

Lightweight aluminum is used for the body. Each car was hand-assembled before being painted one of five standard colors—all metallics. Cars were available in silver, grey, blue, green and maroon.

V6 turbo engine

Light and compact, the engine was designed for Jaguar's IMSA race cars in the late-1980s. Adapted for road use, it produces 542 bhp, more than the big V12 originally planned for the car.

Luxury interior

Leather seats, lush carpets and a top-level sound system ensure that XJ220 owners know they're in a Jaguar.

King-size wheels and tires

Specially-designed tires and wheels are so big there's no room for a spare. If a tire goes flat, it's filled with a special aerosol mixture and can be driven up to 60 miles at 30 mph.

Aerodynamic styling

Designed to look as elegant as a Jaguar should, the XJ220 is also aerodynamically efficient. At high speeds, the car develops over nearly 600 lbs. of downforce to hold it on the road.

Street legal

The XJ220 is legal for road use in most parts of the world, but not in the U.S. Jaguar never exported any cars to the States, although 10 were sent there for a TV race series in 1993.

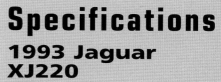

Specifications
1993 Jaguar XJ220

ENGINE

Type: V6 turbocharged, 60°
Construction: Aluminum alloy block and heads
Bore and stroke: 3.7 in. x 3.3 in.
Displacement: 3,494 cc
Compression ratio: 8.3:1
Induction system: Electronic injection with twin Garrett turbochargers with air-to-air intercoolers and wastegate control
Maximum power: 542 bhp at 7,200 rpm
Maximum torque: 475 lb-ft at 4,500 rpm
Top speed: 208 mph
0–60 mph: 3.8 sec.

TRANSMISSION

Transaxle: FF Developments all-synchromesh, five-speed manual transaxle with triple-cone synchronizer on first and second gears; Viscous control limited-slip differential

BODY/CHASSIS

Aluminum alloy honeycomb monocoque with alloy two-door, two-seat body

SPECIAL FEATURES

Stylish air outlets for radiator compartment at front.

Vents behind doors feed air to engine's twin intercoolers.

RUNNING GEAR

Front suspension: Independent, double unequal-length wishbones, push-rod and rocker-operated spring/shock units, anti-roll bar
Rear suspension: Independent, unequal-length double wishbones, rocker-operated twin spring/shock units, anti-roll bar
Brakes: Vented 13 in. (front), 11.8 in. (rear), four-piston calipers
Wheels: Die-cast aluminum alloy. 9 in. x 17 in. (front),
10 in. x 18 in. (rear)
Tires: 255/45 ZR17 (front), 345/35 ZR18 (rear)

DIMENSIONS

Length: 194 in.   **Width:** 87.4 in.
Height: 45.3 in.
Wheelbase: 103.9 in.
Track: 67.3 in. (front), 62.5 in. (rear)
Weight: 3,241 lbs.

Jaguar XKR

Not since the legendary E-Type has Jaguar produced an incredibly high-performance convertible with extraordinary handling to match. The 370-bhp supercharged XKR has plenty of old-world charm, albeit for a new age.

"...supercharged excitement."

"Combining outstanding handling prowess with a soft, supple ride is not easy, but Jaguar has done a remarkable job—there is perfect handling balance and enormous feel through the reworked power steering. Supercharged excitement comes from the blown V8 making the XKR very quick indeed. Its mid-range torque helps to move you along in near total silence, even at speeds above 100 mph. It is a refined cruiser of the highest order."

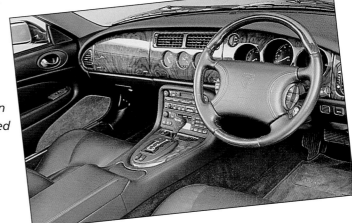

Plenty of wood and leather upholstery give the interior incredible panache.

Milestones

1996 Jaguar chooses the prestigious
Geneva Show to unveil the new XK8 in coupe and convertible versions. Both are powered by the new lightweight alloy AJ-V8 4.0-liter engine with 290 bhp. Sales begin in October.

The XKR takes its styling cues from the legendary E-Type.

1997 Overshadowing the XK8
is a new Jaguar sedan, the XJR. Bolting an Eaton supercharger to the 4.0-liter V8 gives loads of performance—0–60 mph in 5.6 seconds and a limited 155-mph top speed.

Regular XK8s continue in production alongside the XKR.

1998 A tricked-out XK8 is
launched at this year's Geneva Show. Known as the XKR, it packs a supercharged engine that results in an earth-shattering 370 bhp. Other upgrades include a new suspension and bigger wheels and tires. A Mercedes-Benz transmission is used to handle the engine's extra torque.

UNDER THE SKIN

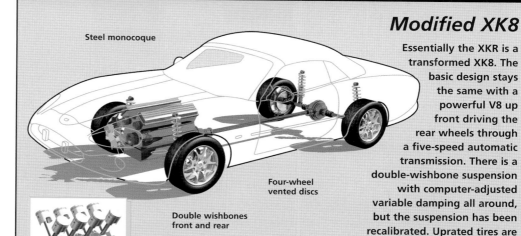

Steel monocoque

Four-wheel vented discs

Double wishbones front and rear

All-alloy V8

Modified XK8

Essentially the XKR is a transformed XK8. The basic design stays the same with a powerful V8 up front driving the rear wheels through a five-speed automatic transmission. There is a double-wishbone suspension with computer-adjusted variable damping all around, but the suspension has been recalibrated. Uprated tires are also specified.

THE POWER PACK

Modern masterpiece

Thanks to Ford, Jaguar's parent company, the XKR's V8 engine is a masterpiece. It is all alloy and the lightest in its class, yet is extremely stiff thanks to its split-block construction and structural oil pan. Four valves in large combustion chambers are opened by dual chain-driven overhead camshafts for each bank of cylinders. The normally aspirated engine gets its spread of power from variable camshaft timing, which is electronically controlled. On the XKR, the emphasis is on the Eaton M112 mechanically driven supercharger, which gives this luxury hot rod 28 percent more power than its normally aspirated sibling.

Fixed roof

Two bodystyles are offered and the choice is really down to your individual preference. The convertible is more expensive, but the coupe can better harness the power, due to its more rigid structure. It also comes with a firmer suspension for even better handling.

For touring aficionados, the convertible represents a better choice.

Jaguar **XKR**

Like the E-Type, the XKR convertible has perfect looks to go with the performance. It lacks the immediate visual impact of the 1960s icon, but is still one of the most dramatic-looking cars around.

Huge brakes

This amount of power and weight takes some controlling, and Jaguar's solution is huge, 12-inch-diameter vented discs front and rear. The XKR has uprated higher-friction pads to cope with the higher temperatures.

Quad-cam V8

The four-cam 32-valve engine is a lightweight all-alloy unit with the pistons running on Nikasil-coated bores. This dispenses with the need for liners and enables it to take increased power with few modifications. Each cylinder has its own individual coil.

Traction control

Despite the huge tires, traction control is standard on the XKR. When one rear wheel begins to spin, braking is applied.

Power top

It takes just the press of a button and the Jaguar's lined insulated top folds away in 20 seconds. It also features a zip-out heated glass rear window.

Leather interior

Standard interior equipment for the XKR includes leather-faced, multi-adjustable, power front seats; maple trim; climate control; a six-CD changer and cruise control. A memory function for the driver's seat is optional.

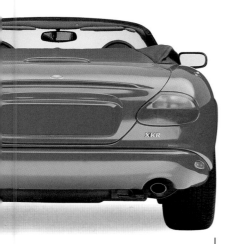

Larger rear wheels

Partly to accommodate the huge brakes and partly for style, the XKR has very tall, 18-inch wheels.

Hood vents

For supercharged engines that run at higher temperatures, extra engine-bay cooling really helps. For this reason, the XKR has twin hood vents.

Specifications

1999 Jaguar XKR

ENGINE

Type: V8

Construction: Alloy block and heads

Valve gear: Four valves per cylinder operated by twin chain-driven overhead camshafts per bank of cylinders

Bore and stroke: 3.38 in. x 3.38 in.

Displacement: 3,996 cc

Compression ratio: 9.0:1

Induction system: Electronic fuel injection with Eaton mechanically driven supercharger

Maximum power: 370 bhp at 6,150 rpm

Maximum torque: 387 lb-ft at 3,600 rpm

Top speed: 155 mph

0–60 mph: 5.1 sec.

TRANSMISSION

Five-speed automatic

BODY/CHASSIS

Unitary monocoque construction with steel coupe or convertible body

SPECIAL FEATURES

Jaguar's customary J-gate is retained, but Mercedes-Benz supplies the transmission.

The chrome mesh grill distinguishes the XKR from the basic XK8.

RUNNING GEAR

Steering: Rack-and-pinion

Front suspension: Double wishbones with coil springs, Bilstein shock absorbers and anti-roll bar

Rear suspension: Double wishbones with coil springs, Bilstein shock absorbers and anti-roll bar

Brakes: Vented discs (front and rear)

Wheels: Alloy, 8 x 18 in. (front), 9 x 18 in. (rear)

Tires: Pirelli P Zero, 245/45 ZR18 (front), 255/45 ZR18 (rear)

DIMENSIONS

Length: 187.4 in.   **Width:** 79.3 in.

Height: 51.4 in.   **Wheelbase:** 101.9 in.

Track: 59.2 in. (front), 58.9 in. (rear)

Weight: 3,850 lbs.

Jensen **INTERCEPTOR**

Unveiled in 1966, the Interceptor had everything: Italian styling, American V8 power and well-balanced handling. The original Interceptor remained in production, virtually unaltered, for 10 years and gained a cult following which lives on today.

"...a sense of refinement."

"More of a grand tourer than a sports car, the Interceptor has deep, comfortable seats. The powerful American V8 and automatic transmission are perfectly suited to a laid-back approach to driving and give the car a sense of refinement. Despite its mannerisms, the car is still quick and can reach 60 mph in just over six seconds. Despite its weight, the Jensen has predictable handling, but the brakes are hard pressed to stop the it from speeds above 124 mph."

Full instrumentation is standard and the interior trim is of the highest quality.

Milestones

1966 Jensen
presents two vehicles styled by Vingale at the London Motor Show. One is fitted with a specially-developed four-wheel drive system.

Jensen's 1954 541 had triple carburetors and four-wheel disc brakes

1969 An improved
Mk II Interceptor is launched. It has a bigger fuel tank, radial tires, and restyled bumpers.

1971 The Mk III and
an SP model with three two-barrel carburetors and 330 bhp are introduced. The FF is dropped this year.

1976 Jensen goes
out of business and the last original Interceptor is built.

The forerunner of the Interceptor was the bizarre-looking CV8.

1983 A new Mk IV
Interceptor enters production, built by Jensen Parts and Service.

UNDER THE SKIN

Live rear axle

Box-section chassis

Independent front suspension

Four-wheel disc brakes

Cast-iron V8

Built to last

Carried over from the CV8, the chassis is a steel box-section frame. Double-skinned bulkheads and welded steel panels add to the body's stiffness. Suspension is typical for the era with wishbones and coil springs up front and leaf springs at the rear supporting a solid axle. A Panhard rod helps rear axle location and disc brakes are fitted all around.

THE POWER PACK

Chrysler V8 power

Original Interceptors are powered by Chrysler 383-cubic inch (6.3-liter) and 440-cubic inch (7.2-liter) V8s. Both engines are made of cast-iron with chain-driven camshafts, a five main-bearing crankshaft and two valves per cylinder. With the larger unit acceleration is phenomenal, although handling naturally suffers. Mark IV cars use a small-block 5.9-liter V8, based on the early 340-cubic inch unit. This produced improved fuel economy and slightly better handling.

Single camshaft

Two valves per cylinder

All cast-iron construction

Automatic transmission

Hi-tech FF

Standing for Ferguson Formula, the Jensen FF has four-wheel drive, rack-and-pinion steering, and anti-lock brakes. Slightly longer than the standard Interceptor, it is a complex machine and only 320 were built. Only a small number still remain today.

The Jensen FF was in production from 1966 to 1971.

Jensen INTERCEPTOR

The Jensen Interceptor, launched in 1966 at the London Motor Show, is by far the company's best-remembered product and its biggest seller. The car was so good that it was reborn in the early 1980s.

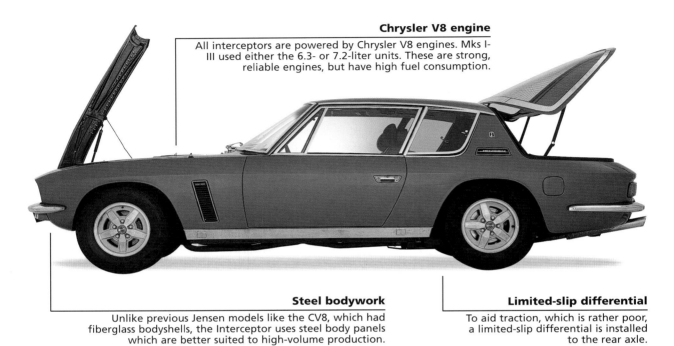

Chrysler V8 engine
All interceptors are powered by Chrysler V8 engines. Mks I-III used either the 6.3- or 7.2-liter units. These are strong, reliable engines, but have high fuel consumption.

Steel bodywork
Unlike previous Jensen models like the CV8, which had fiberglass bodyshells, the Interceptor uses steel body panels which are better suited to high-volume production.

Limited-slip differential
To aid traction, which is rather poor, a limited-slip differential is installed to the rear axle.

Glass hatchback
The bulbous back window is not only attractive, but also functional. The whole unit lifts up to provide space for luggage.

Adjustable shocks

Despite its archaic rear leaf springs, the Interceptor has adjustable telescopic shocks to help smooth out the ride.

Italian styling

The shape was originally penned by Touring of Milan and adapted by Vignale to produce the Interceptor.

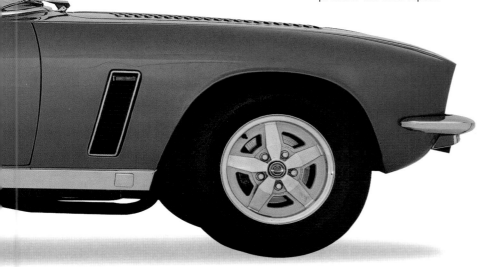

Specifications

1968 Jensen Interceptor

ENGINE

Type: V8

Construction: Cast-iron block and heads

Valve gear: Two valves per cylinder operated by hydraulic tappets, pushrods and rockers

Bore and stroke: 4.25 in. x 3.38 in.

Displacement: 6,276 cc

Compression ratio: 10.0:1

Induction system: Single Carter AFB four-barrel carburetor

Maximum power: 330 bhp at 4,600 rpm

Maximum torque: 450 lb-ft at 2,800 rpm

Top speed: 137 mph

0–60 mph: 6.4 sec.

TRANSMISSION

Chrysler TorqueFlite 727 automatic

BODY/CHASSIS

Tubular and welded sheet steel monocoque with two-door body

SPECIAL FEATURES

The Mk II Interceptor has a different front bumper with the parking lights positioned beneath it.

Fender extractor vents aid engine cooling and help to distinguish the Interceptor from the four-wheel drive FF, which has two vents per side.

RUNNING GEAR

Steering: Recirculating ball

Front suspension: Independent wishbones with coil springs and telescopic shocks

Rear suspension: Live rear axle with semi-elliptical leaf springs, telescopic shocks and a Panhard rod

Brakes: Girling discs, 11.4-in. dia. (front), 10.7-in. dia. (rear)

Wheels: Rostyle pressed steel, 15-in. dia.

Tires: Dunlop 185 x 15

DIMENSIONS

Length: 188 in.   **Width:** 70 in.

Height: 53 in.   **Wheelbase:** 105 in.

Track: 56 in. (front and rear)

Weight: 3,696 lbs.

Lamborghini COUNTACH

Ferruccio Lamborghini liked to keep Ferrari on its toes. First he beat Ferrari into production with the mid-engined Miura, then he produced one of the world's most outrageous, and fastest, supercars—the Countach. During the 1970s and 1980s, it became the supercar to have.

"...acceleration is superb."

"Once you've made your way past the wide sills, the Countach is a revelation; forward visibility is exceptionally good, even if everything behind is a mystery. Then again, no one is going to be overtaking you in a Countach. The clutch is heavier than you expect and the dog-leg first gear takes some mastering. Its acceleration is superb and matched by phenomenal grip, excellent brakes, perfect steering and handling with no hidden vices."

The cockpit is simple, clean and at your command. However, the dog-leg first gear can be a little tricky.

Milestones

1971 Bertone-styled Countach is unveiled at the Geneva Motor Show.

Early models had the purest lines of all, but still looked dramatic.

1974 Countach goes into production as the LP400 with a 375-bhp 4-liter V12 and a top speed of 190 mph.

1978 Improvements and a switch to the new low-profile Pirelli P7 tires bring a new model name: LP400S.

1982 Engine is stretched to 4.8 liters to form the LP500S.

1985 Another engine stretch, to 5.2 liters, and a switch to four valves per cylinder results in the powerful Quattrovalvole, with 455 bhp.

1988 Anniversary model, a QV with minor restyling, is the final Countach which lasts until 1991 when the Diablo comes into production.

1980s LP500S radiate power, aggression, and speed.

Old and new

The chassis is as old fashioned as the body styling was futuristic. A complicated network of round steel tubes are welded together to form a complicated, but immensely strong spaceframe chassis. Much of its strength comes from the two massive fabricated sill sections. A light steel tube superstructure holds the alloy body which is welded, riveted, or bonded in place.

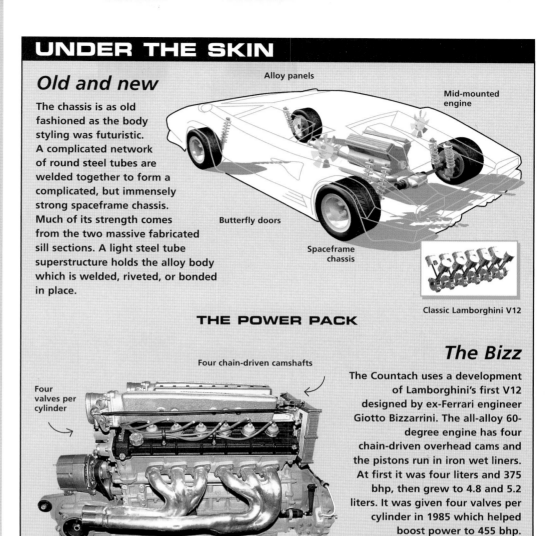

Alloy panels

Mid-mounted engine

Butterfly doors

Spaceframe chassis

Classic Lamborghini V12

THE POWER PACK

Four chain-driven camshafts

Four valves per cylinder

All-alloy construction

Iron wet cylinder liners

The Bizz

The Countach uses a development of Lamborghini's first V12 designed by ex-Ferrari engineer Giotto Bizzarrini. The all-alloy 60-degree engine has four chain-driven overhead cams and the pistons run in iron wet liners. At first it was four liters and 375 bhp, then grew to 4.8 and 5.2 liters. It was given four valves per cylinder in 1985 which helped boost power to 455 bhp. Quattrovalvoles use carburetors in Europe, but fuel injection is used on cars exported to the U.S.

Happy anniversary

The Countach's looks are very dramatic, and the most outrageous of all were the last cars, the 1988 Anniversary model. These have straked skirts and extended wheel arches, which first came with the LP400S in 1978 to cover its huge alloy wheels. Power came from the standard Quattrovalvoles engine.

Even in standard form, the Anniversary model was outrageous.

Lamborghini COUNTACH ▮▮▮

Design a car as dramatic as the Countach and you just have to make it perform the way it looks. It looked like the fastest car in the world and Lamborghini made sure it was.

Mid-mounted V12

The long V12 engine is mounted lengthwise with the transmission ahead of the engine. It was a change from Lamborghini's previous supercar, the Miura, which has its V12 engine mounted transversely.

Radiator ducts

Air flows into the huge ducts and electric fans blow the cool air across the side-mounted radiators.

Upright opening doors

Lamborghini could have made the Countach's doors open in the normal way, but that would have had nothing like the dramatic impact of doors that opened straight up, each supported on a single gas strut.

Split-rim alloy wheels

The circle of tiny bolts around each wheel shows that the Countach runs on split-rim alloys. The difference in size between front and rear wheels is enormous: the rears are 12-inches wide and the fronts 8.5 inches.

Flared wheel arches

The original Countach had no wheel-arch flares. They had to be added in 1978 when larger wheels and wider tires were fitted.

Optional rear wing

This car does without the optional rear wing which is as much for style as aerodynamic effect.

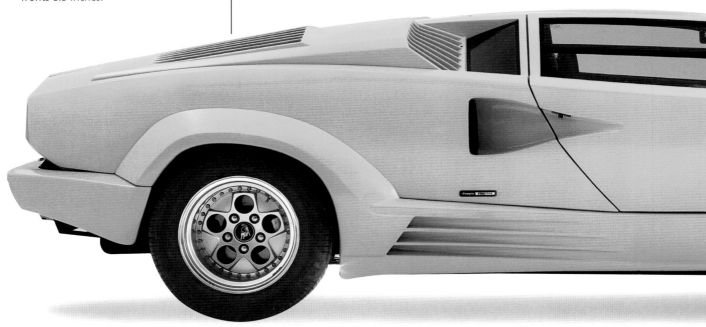

Alloy and fiberglass body

The Countach's exotic body is alloy with the exception of the fiberglass floor. None of the bodywork is structural.

Pirelli P Zero tires

The first Countachs ran on Michelin XWX tires, but in 1978 Lamborghini re-engineered the car to run on Pirelli P7s. The Anniversary model uses the latest advanced Pirelli P Zero tires.

Front spoiler

A deeper front spoiler was added in 1978 to improve high-speed stability. The front suspension geometry was altered at the same time. The two openings in the spoiler are there to keep the brakes cool.

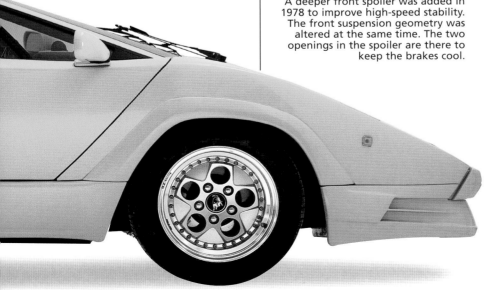

Specifications

1990 Lamborghini Countach QV Anniversary

ENGINE

Type: V12
Construction: Alloy block and heads
Valve gear: Four valves per cylinder operated by four chain-driven overhead cams
Bore and stroke: 3.38 in. x 2.95 in.
Displacement: 5,167 cc
Compression ratio: 9.5:1
Induction system: Six Weber 44 DCNF downdraft carburetors
Maximum power: 455 bhp at 7,000 rpm
Maximum torque: 369 lb-ft at 5,200 rpm
Top speed: 178 mph
0–60 mph: 5.2 sec.

TRANSMISSION

Five-speed manual

BODY/CHASSIS

Tubular steel spaceframe chassis with alloy and fiberglass two-door, two-seat body

SPECIAL FEATURES

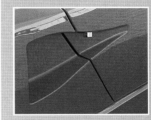

NACA-style ducts were first used in aircraft and were very efficient at channeling air in at high speed.

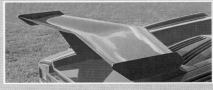

You could drive the Countach flat out without the optional rear wing, usually chosen only for dramatic effect.

RUNNING GEAR

Steering: Rack-and-pinion
Front suspension: Double wishbones, coil springs, telescopic shocks and anti-roll bar
Rear suspension: Wishbones, trailing arms, double coil springs/shocks per side, and anti-roll bar
Brakes: Vented discs 11.8 in. dia. (front), 11 in. dia. (rear)
Wheels: Split-rim alloys, 8.5 in. x 15 in. (front), 12 in. x 15 in. (rear)
Tires: Pirelli P Zero, 225/50 VR15 (front), 345/35 VR15 (rear)

DIMENSIONS

Length: 162.9 in.   **Width:** 78.7 in.
Height: 42.1 in.   **Wheelbase:** 96.5 in.
Track: 58.7 in. (front), 63.2 in. (rear)
Weight: 3,188 lbs.

Lamborghini **DIABLO**

In the 1980s, Lamborghini was faced with a big problem: what could possibly replace the legendary but dated Countach? The answer was a car that was just as outrageous and even faster—the incredible Diablo.

"...the Raging Devil."

"You hear it down the Autostrada long before you see it. And as it passes at nearly 200 mph, there is only stunned silence. Now you're behind the wheel in command of nearly 500 horses and it's a little intimidating at first. But the all-wheel drive viscous differential puts this indecent amount of power to the road and the razor-sharp steering rewards your skill. Sixty mph rushes up in just over four seconds as the V12 sings the song of the Raging Devil."

Diablo's driving position is excellent and makes it easier to concentrate on driving this high-powered supercar to its limits.

Milestones

1985 Lamborghini president

Emile Novaro asks his team to design a new car to replace the Countach. A 'super Countach' is created to evaluate parts for the forthcoming Diablo.

1990 The Diablo makes its debut

at the beginning of the year.

After 17 years, the Countach was more than ready for a replacement.

1991 A four-wheel drive

version, the Diablo VT appears. VT stands for Viscous Traction and the car has a center viscous coupling which puts up to 27 percent of drive to the front wheels.

1994 Lamborghini offers the Diablo SE

which is stripped-down and lightened to make it even quicker.

German tuner Willi Koenig dragged even more power out of the V12.

1996 Lamborghini, now owned

by Indonesian company Megatech, further increases the Diablo's appeal by launching the Diablo Roadster.

UNDER THE SKIN

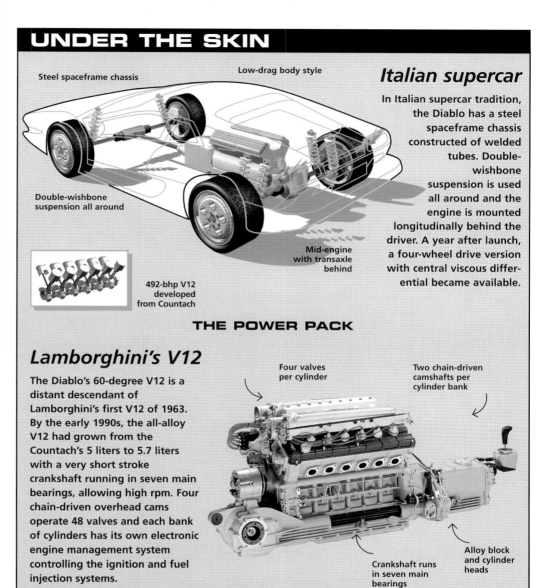

Steel spaceframe chassis

Low-drag body style

Double-wishbone suspension all around

Mid-engine with transaxle behind

492-bhp V12 developed from Countach

Italian supercar

In Italian supercar tradition, the Diablo has a steel spaceframe chassis constructed of welded tubes. Double-wishbone suspension is used all around and the engine is mounted longitudinally behind the driver. A year after launch, a four-wheel drive version with central viscous differential became available.

THE POWER PACK

Lamborghini's V12

The Diablo's 60-degree V12 is a distant descendant of Lamborghini's first V12 of 1963. By the early 1990s, the all-alloy V12 had grown from the Countach's 5 liters to 5.7 liters with a very short stroke crankshaft running in seven main bearings, allowing high rpm. Four chain-driven overhead cams operate 48 valves and each bank of cylinders has its own electronic engine management system controlling the ignition and fuel injection systems.

Four valves per cylinder

Two chain-driven camshafts per cylinder bank

Alloy block and cylinder heads

Crankshaft runs in seven main bearings

Rapid roadster

The Diablo Roadster, on sale in 1997, added one more ingredient to the 4WD Diablo—supercar performance with an open roof. The roof panel is made from carbon fiber, so it's easy for one person to lift off and stow over the engine cover.

Wind in your hair at over 180 mph!

Lamborghini DIABLO

Twelve years since the Diablo was introduced, it's still a rare and thrilling sight. One look at Marcello Gandini's masterpiece tells you it really will go way beyond 190 mph.

No spare wheel

There's no room for even a space saver spare tire. Lamborghini's explanation? "Diablo drivers do not change wheels by the side of the road."

Twin rear radiators

Two radiators are needed to cool the big V12. Mounted at the rear of the engine bay, each is assisted by a large electric fan.

Forward-hinged doors

Like the Countach before it, the Diablo has long doors with single hinges that lift up and forward, each supported on a single gas strut.

Side-mounted oil coolers

The vents on the lower side panels feed air to the two oil coolers which are mounted directly ahead of the rear wheels.

Larger rear wheels

The Diablo needs massive tires to feed its power to the road and the 1991 model was equipped with large very low-profile Pirelli P Zero 335/35 ZR17s on 13 inch x 17 inch split rim alloy wheels.

Poor rear vision

Like most mid-engined supercars, the Diablo has extremely limited rear vision through the small rear window.

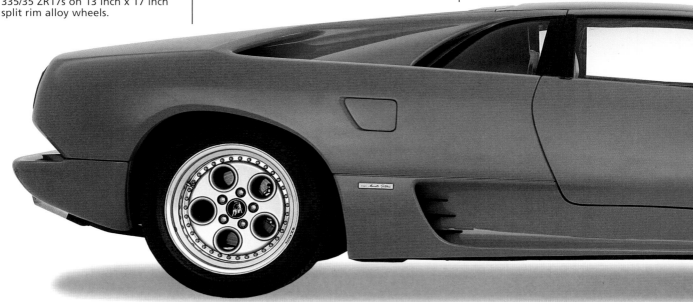

Alloy, composite and steel body

The Diablo's bodyshell is made from a mixture of materials. The roof is steel for strength, but the fenders and doors are alloy and a new composite material was used for the nose, engine cover, rockers and bumpers.

World's widest supercar

At 80.3 inches, the Diablo is wider than even Ferrari's bulky Testarossa, making it the widest supercar in the world.

Engine cooling vents

Once air has passed through the engine's twin radiators it exits through these large vents at the rear of the car.

Ventilation scoops

Cabin ventilation is provided via two small scoops in front of the windshield but, unlike the Countach, the Diablo is air conditioned.

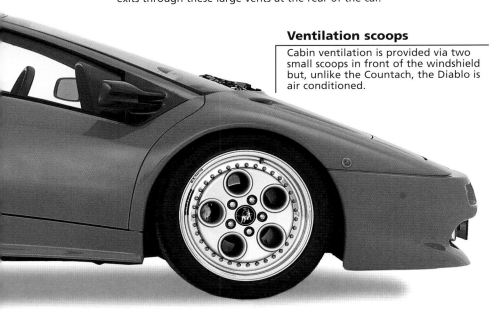

Specifications
1991 Lamborghini Diablo

ENGINE
Type: Sixty-degree V12
Construction: Light alloy block and heads
Valve gear: Four valves per cylinder operated by four chain-driven overhead camshafts
Bore and stroke: 3.43 in. x 3.15 in.
Displacement: 5,729 cc
Compression ratio: 10.0:1
Maximum power: 492 bhp at 7,000 rpm
Maximum torque: 428 lb-ft at 5,200 rpm
Top speed: 205 mph
0–60 mph: 4.3 sec.

TRANSMISSION
Five-speed manual

BODY/CHASSIS
Steel square-tube spaceframe chassis with two-door, two-seat coupe body in alloy, steel and carbon fiber

SPECIAL FEATURES

The vertically opening doors are a clever way of creating as much impact as gullwing doors, but without the same extremely difficult sealing problems.

RUNNING GEAR
Steering: Rack-and-pinion
Front suspension: Double wishbones with coil springs, telescopic shocks and anti-roll bar
Rear suspension: Double wishbones with twin coaxial spring shock units per side, and anti-roll bar
Brakes: Vented discs, 13 in. dia. (front), 11.2 in. dia. (rear)
Wheels: Multi-piece alloy, 8.5 in. x 17 in. (front), 13 in. x 17 in. (rear)
Tires: Pirelli P Zero 245/40 ZR17 (front), 335/35 ZR17 (rear)

DIMENSIONS
Length: 175.6 in.   **Width:** 80.3 in.
Height: 43.5 in.   **Wheelbase:** 104.3 in.
Track: 60.6 in. (front), 64.6 in. (rear)
Weight: 3,475 lbs.

Lamborghini **MIURA**

With one stroke, Ferruccio Lamborghini made Enzo Ferrari look foolish and his cars appear obsolete. Lamborghini beat Ferrari to the punch, building the world's first mid-engined supercar and the first with a quad-cam V12 engine.

"...sensation of the decade."

"The sensation of the 1966 Geneva Motor Show was also the sensation of the decade. Now this superb Bertone design is before you, and as you slide low into this gorgeous automobile, you realize why this is still one of the most desired cars ever built. Everything about this car is over-the-top: the colors, the sci-fi body design, the power and even the zero body roll that tempts you to push it until it suddenly breaks away."

There can be few more inviting cockpits than the Lamborghini Miura's. It's a car that truly begs to be driven hard.

Milestones

1966 Lamborghini stuns the Geneva Motor Show by unveiling the 400 GT's replacement. The Miura is styled for Bertone by a rising star in the design world, Marcello Gandini.

The beautiful Touring-bodied 400 GT was Lamborghini's second model.

1967 Miura P400 production gets under way and 475 are built before the car is updated.

1969 The Miura S is introduced with the engine tuned to produce 370 bhp and torque increases to 286 lb-ft.

1971 The S turns into the SV with even more power, 385 bhp and an improved transmission, which makes the power easier to use.

1973 The world oil crisis helps bring about the end of Miura production.

Rear slats helped the style, but did little for rear visibility.

UNDER THE SKIN

Modern monocoque

While other Italian supercar builders were still using old-fashioned spaceframes, the Miura has a modern steel monocoque structure with the strength coming from massive sills and a large center tunnel, all three joined by large bulkheads. The engine is held in a folded steel frame behind the center bulkhead.

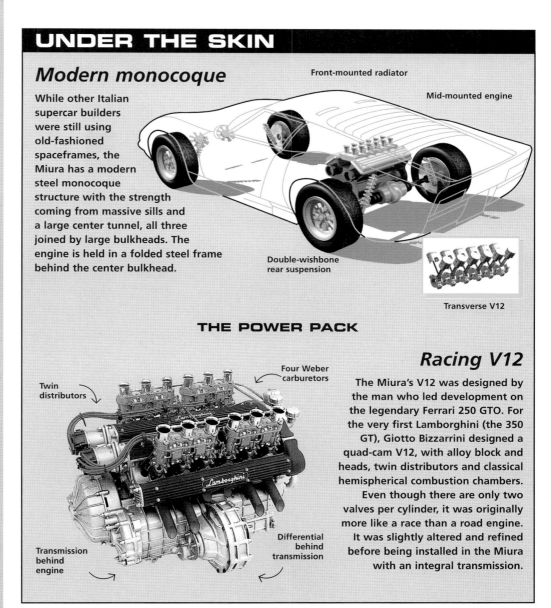

Front-mounted radiator

Mid-mounted engine

Double-wishbone rear suspension

Transverse V12

THE POWER PACK

Twin distributors

Four Weber carburetors

Transmission behind engine

Differential behind transmission

Racing V12

The Miura's V12 was designed by the man who led development on the legendary Ferrari 250 GTO. For the very first Lamborghini (the 350 GT), Giotto Bizzarrini designed a quad-cam V12, with alloy block and heads, twin distributors and classical hemispherical combustion chambers. Even though there are only two valves per cylinder, it was originally more like a race than a road engine. It was slightly altered and refined before being installed in the Miura with an integral transmission.

The Miura SV

Last and best of the Miura line is the SV, introduced in 1971. It has more power (385 bhp), enough to take the top speed to over 174 mph and drops the 0–60 mph time to 6.8 seconds. A wider track under larger wheel arches improves the Miura's handling.

The SV was the last and best of the Miuras.

Lamborghini **MIURA**

Only three years after Lamborghini started making cars, the company produced the most exotic supercar the world had ever seen. It was as advanced as it was stunning, with its 4-liter V12 engine mounted behind the driver.

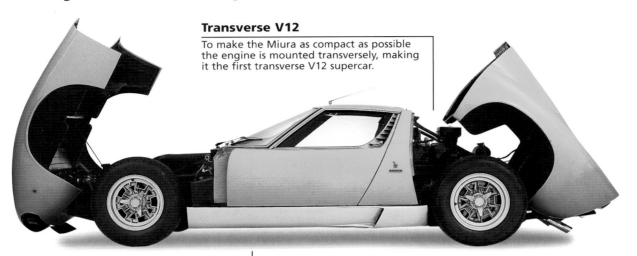

Transverse V12

To make the Miura as compact as possible the engine is mounted transversely, making it the first transverse V12 supercar.

Transmission behind engine

With a transverse engine, there is no space for the transmission to be mounted in the usual place. The Miura's transmission is behind the engine, with the transmission and engine sharing the same oil.

Slatted engine cover

The great heat generated by a large V12 running fast in a small engine bay was vented through the open slatted engine cover, which did little to improve the view through the rear-view mirror.

Alloy and steel bodywork

The main body section of the Miura is fabricated from steel for strength. Some panels, such as the engine cover and front section of the bodywork, are alloy to save weight.

Door frame air vents

One of the main styling features is the air vents—for the engine compartment—which are actually built into the door frame.

Tip forward lights

When not in use, the headlights fold back to follow the line of the bodywork, a styling feature used years later by Porsche on the 928.

Top-mounted anti-roll bar

The Miura follows racing car practice in many ways. For example, its rear anti-roll bar runs from the bottom wishbones up over the chassis.

Front-mounted radiator

Although the engine is mid-mounted, the radiator stays in the conventional place at the front where it is easier to cool with the help of two electric fans. It is angled to fit under the Miura's low sloping nose.

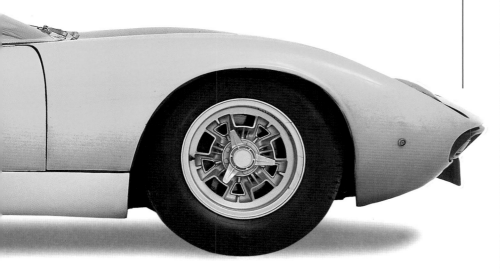

Specifications
1970 Lamborghini P400S

ENGINE
Type: V12
Construction: Light alloy block and heads
Valve gear: Two valves per cylinder operated by four chain-driven overhead camshafts
Bore and stroke: 3.23 in. x 2.44 in.
Displacement: 3,929 cc
Compression ratio: 10.7:1
Induction system: Four Weber downdraft carburetors
Maximum power: 370 bhp at 7,700 rpm
Maximum torque: 286 lb-ft at 5,500 rpm
Top speed: 172 mph
0–60 mph: 6.9 sec.

TRANSMISSION
Five-speed manual

BODY/CHASSIS
Steel monocoque platform with steel and alloy two-door, two-seat coupe body

SPECIAL FEATURES

Stylized vents behind the doors provide air to the mid-mounted engine. The door handle is cleverly shaped to blend in with the styling.

The sloping headlights have distinctive 'eyebrows'; purely a styling feature.

RUNNING GEAR
Steering: Rack-and-pinion
Front suspension: Double wishbones with coil springs, telescopic shocks and anti-roll bar
Rear suspension: Double wishbones, with coil springs, telescopic shocks and anti-roll bar
Brakes: Solid discs, 11.8 in. dia. (front),12.1 in. dia. (rear)
Wheels: Magnesium 7 in. x 15 in.
Tires: Pirelli Cinturato GT70 VR15

DIMENSIONS
Length: 171.6 in.   **Width:** 71 in.
Height: 42 in.   **Wheelbase:** 98.4 in.
Track: 55.6 in. (front and rear)
Weight: 2,850 lbs.

Lancia DELTA INTEGRALE

Although it was conceived as a homologation special for rallying, the Lancia Delta Integrale quickly became recognized as one of the all-time great road cars, thanks to its 4x4 transmission and powerful turbocharged engine.

"...glued to the ground."

"Even now there are very few road cars that can corner as fast as an Integrale. And before long you realize that this is a seriously fast car. The engine rockets the tiny car forward with a sharp whistle of the spooling turbocharger underneath the hood. It's through corners in a flat, roll-free manner, where the car really shows itself off. Its all-wheel drive and wide tires keep the Delta glued to the ground."

Bucket seats hold the driver and passenger firmly in position, even under hard cornering.

Milestones

1987 The Delta HF Turbo 4x4 is launched with
an 8-valve turbo engine. A few months later the word 'Integrale' is first seen on a new Delta with an 185-bhp powerplant.

The Delta was the most successful rally car of the late 1980s.

1989 A new 16V version is introduced with
an extra 11 bhp.

1991 An overhauled Integrale Evoluzione
gets another power boost to 210 bhp, plus revised suspension and brakes and new body modifications including a tailgate spoiler.

The Integrale gained a 16-valve engine in 1989.

1992 Lancia wins the World Rally Championship
for manufacturers and the Evoluzione 2 version is introduced.

1994 Production of this
Italian legend ends.

UNDER THE SKIN

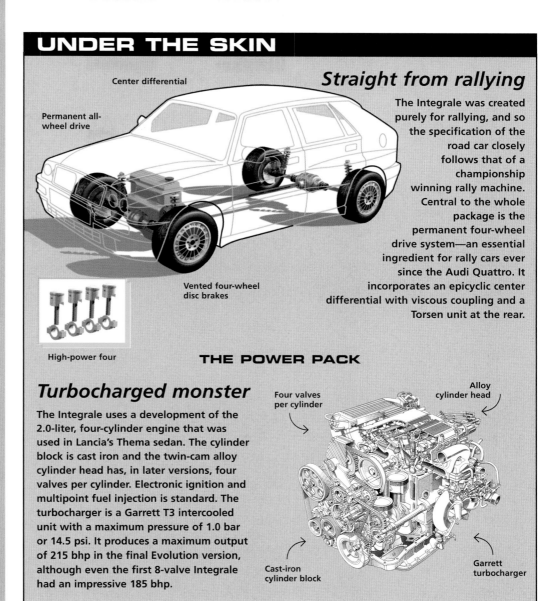

Center differential

Permanent all-wheel drive

Straight from rallying

The Integrale was created purely for rallying, and so the specification of the road car closely follows that of a championship winning rally machine. Central to the whole package is the permanent four-wheel drive system—an essential ingredient for rally cars ever since the Audi Quattro. It incorporates an epicyclic center differential with viscous coupling and a Torsen unit at the rear.

Vented four-wheel disc brakes

High-power four

THE POWER PACK

Turbocharged monster

The Integrale uses a development of the 2.0-liter, four-cylinder engine that was used in Lancia's Thema sedan. The cylinder block is cast iron and the twin-cam alloy cylinder head has, in later versions, four valves per cylinder. Electronic ignition and multipoint fuel injection is standard. The turbocharger is a Garrett T3 intercooled unit with a maximum pressure of 1.0 bar or 14.5 psi. It produces a maximum output of 215 bhp in the final Evolution version, although even the first 8-valve Integrale had an impressive 185 bhp.

Four valves per cylinder

Alloy cylinder head

Cast-iron cylinder block

Garrett turbocharger

Evolution

All Integrales are highly sought after, but the later the model the better. The ultimate Evolution versions, with their even more extreme bodywork and extra power, are most desired. If you're lucky you may come across one of the rare limited editions.

Connoisseurs of the Integrale go for the later cars.

Lancia **DELTA INTEGRALE**

Rally stars lined up to drive the Integrale. This car dominated world rallying for six years, and it comes as no surprise to discover that it is still one of the most coveted road cars of recent times.

Turbocharged power

Much of the charisma of the Integrale comes from its powerful, turbocharged 2.0-liter engine. With no less than 215 bhp on tap in its ultimate form, this car offers terrific performance.

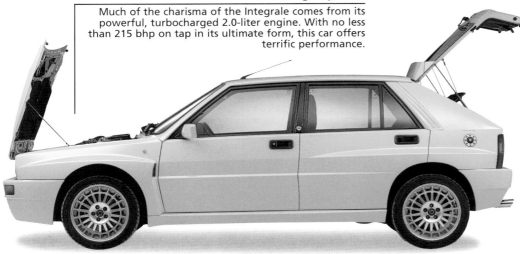

Torque-split four-wheel drive

The secret of the Integrale's pace and safety is its four-wheel drive system. This uses a torque split system with a planetary center differential incorporating a viscous coupling and a rear Torsen unit. The torque is permanently fed to all four wheels in a 47:53 percent front/rear split.

Pumped-up muscles

One of the most distinctive features of the Integrale is its very wide wheel arches. These are needed to clear the 7-inch cast-alloy wheels and wide tires. Other identifying features of the bodywork include a vented hood, small side skirts and an adjustable spoiler at the top of the tailgate.

Sporty cabin

Lancia's tradition for excellent interiors has been continued in the Integrale. The Recaro seats, Momo leather steering wheel and unique instrumentation are just right, however. Standard equipment includes power windows, mirrors and door locks, not to mention a sunroof.

Generous disc brakes

To ensure the Integrale stops as well as it accelerates, Lancia specified 11-inch vented discs up front and 10-inch solid discs at the rear.

Delta bodyshell

Because Group A rally regulations required that competition cars should be based on production car bodyshells, the Integrale uses the shell of the Delta—a rather ordinary hatchback launched in 1979. It is amazing how such an ordinary base model could be transformed into one of the best cars in the world.

Specifications

1993 Lancia Delta Integrale Evoluzione 2

ENGINE

Type: In-line four-cylinder

Construction: Cast-iron block and aluminum head

Valve gear: Four valves per cylinder operated by belt-driven double overhead camshafts

Bore and stroke: 3.3 in. x 3.54 in.

Displacement: 1,995 cc

Compression ratio: 8.0:1

Induction system: Fuel injection

Maximum power: 210 bhp at 5,750 rpm

Maximum torque: 227 lb ft at 2,500 rpm

Top speed: 137 mph

0–60 mph: 5.7 sec.

TRANSMISSION

Five-speed manual

BODY/CHASSIS

Steel monocoque five-door hatchback

SPECIAL FEATURES

Distinctive blister wheel arches cover wide wheels and tires.

The angle of the small spoiler at the top of the tailgate is adjustable.

RUNNING GEAR

Steering: Rack-and-pinion

Front suspension: MacPherson struts with lower wishbones, coil springs, shock absorbers and anti-roll bar

Rear suspension: MacPherson struts with transverse links, coil springs, shock absorbers and anti-roll bar

Brakes: Vented discs, 11-in. dia (front), solid discs, 10-in. dia. (rear)

Wheels: Alloy, 16-in. dia.

Tires: 205/45 ZR16

DIMENSIONS

Length: 153.5 in.   **Width:** 69.7 in.

Height: 53.7 in.   **Wheelbase:** 97.6 in.

Track: 59.0 in. (front and rear)

Weight: 2,954 lbs.

Lancia **RALLY 037**

Designed quickly to give Lancia a shot at the World Rally Championship before cars with four-wheel drive dominated the scene, the supercharged, mid-engined Rally 037 was a huge success, winning the title in 1983.

"...a real competition car."

"Sit in the stripped-out interior and close the flimsy doors and you know this is a real competition car. There are no rubber suspension bushings and so the ride is harsh; it's worth it though because it helps give perfectly balanced mid-engined handling. Turn-in is sharp, and there's such huge grip that it's nearly impossible to lose the back of the car on dry pavement. The steering is direct, the clutch is heavy and the ZF transmission needs a firm hand."

There are no creature comforts in the cabin of the Group B 037 rally car.

Milestones

1981 Lancia designs its new rally car using the center section of the Montecarlo Turbo which is already used for racing. The 037 name comes from Abarth's project number.

The production Montecarlo gave little more than its silhouette to the 037.

1982 The necessary 200 cars are built to satisfy homologation. The following 20 'Evolution' cars have fuel injection and some Kevlar body panels. The 037's first win comes in the Pace National rally.

Roadgoing Rally 037s are rare and desirable.

1983 Victory in the Monte Carlo Rally is the first ever win for a supercharged car. The Rally 037 goes on to win the World Rally Championship.

1984 The Evolution 2 version of the 037 is built. It has a 2,111-cc engine with 325 bhp. Lancia builds 20 of these in 1984 and 1985.

UNDER THE SKIN

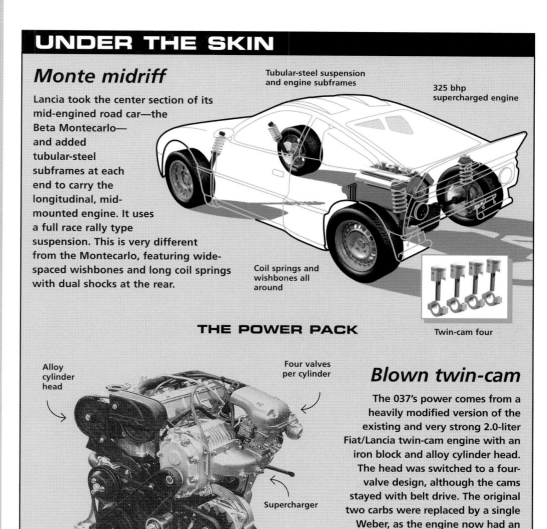

Monte midriff

Lancia took the center section of its mid-engined road car—the Beta Montecarlo—and added tubular-steel subframes at each end to carry the longitudinal, mid-mounted engine. It uses a full race rally type suspension. This is very different from the Montecarlo, featuring wide-spaced wishbones and long coil springs with dual shocks at the rear.

Tubular-steel suspension and engine subframes

325 bhp supercharged engine

Coil springs and wishbones all around

Twin-cam four

THE POWER PACK

Alloy cylinder head

Four valves per cylinder

Supercharger

Cast-iron cylinder block

Blown twin-cam

The 037's power comes from a heavily modified version of the existing and very strong 2.0-liter Fiat/Lancia twin-cam engine with an iron block and alloy cylinder head. The head was switched to a four-valve design, although the cams stayed with belt drive. The original two carbs were replaced by a single Weber, as the engine now had an Abarth Volumex mechanically-driven supercharger running up to 13 psi. of boost. This required the compression ratio to be dropped to 7.5:1.

Ultimate Evo

The ultimate Rally 037 is the Evolution 2 version, 20 of which were built in 1984 and 1985. They had the engine size increased to 2,111 cc with a larger bore and longer stroke. This helped to increase the power to 325 bhp at 8,000 rpm.

Evolution 2 037s only came in full rally trim—there were no road cars.

Lancia **RALLY 037**

The Lancia Rally 037 is one of those special breed of cars designed to compete in the exciting Group B rally championship. It is hugely effective and terrifyingly fast.

Huge rear spoiler

The huge rear spoiler had to be homologated, but it was really only necessary on the more powerful competition cars which needed to maximize their traction.

Twin-cam engine

The 037's engine is a development of the long-stroke 2-liter twin-cam which powered the successful Fiat Abarth 131 rally cars, but the iron block has a new alloy cylinder head with four valves per cylinder.

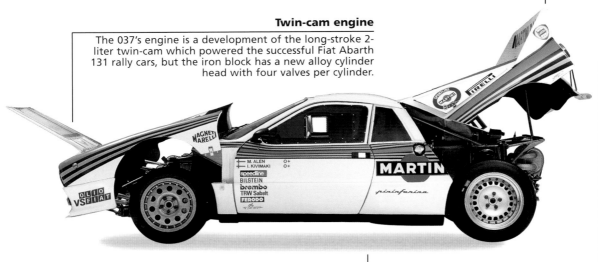

Montecarlo center section

For the sake of convenience, the center section of the Lancia Beta Montecarlo is used for the 037. Competition models required the front and rear track to be wider than that on the Montecarlo. Naturally, wider bodywork had to be grafted on.

ZF transmission

Lancia's existing transmissions were not strong enough for the supercharged engine in competition spec. The more robust German ZF five-speed was used instead.

Supercharger

Lancia chose supercharging to eliminate turbo lag and get instant throttle response. Supercharging requires similar changes to turbocharging, including reducing the compression ratio.

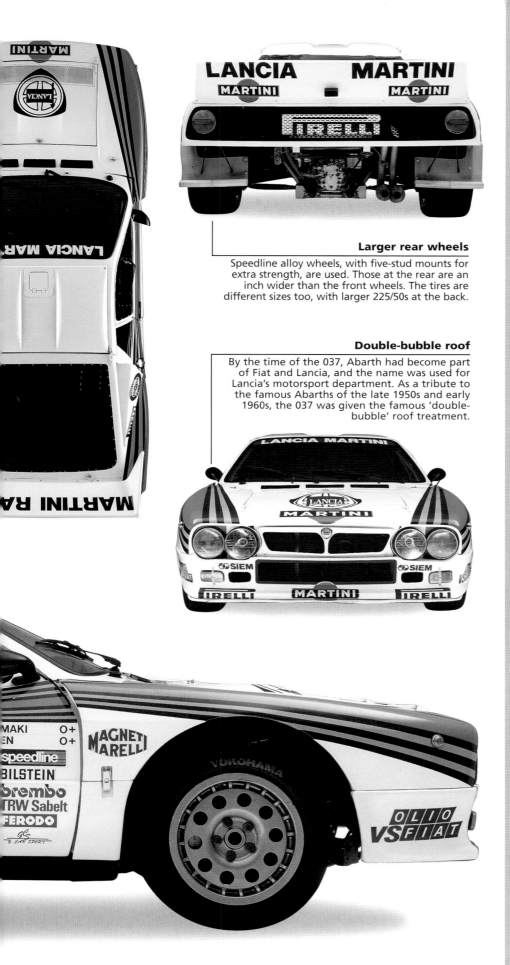

Larger rear wheels

Speedline alloy wheels, with five-stud mounts for extra strength, are used. Those at the rear are an inch wider than the front wheels. The tires are different sizes too, with larger 225/50s at the back.

Double-bubble roof

By the time of the 037, Abarth had become part of Fiat and Lancia, and the name was used for Lancia's motorsport department. As a tribute to the famous Abarths of the late 1950s and early 1960s, the 037 was given the famous 'double-bubble' roof treatment.

Specifications

1985 Lancia Rally 037 Evo 2

ENGINE

Type: In-line four

Construction: Cast-iron block and alloy cylinder head

Valve gear: Four valves per cylinder operated by twin overhead camshafts

Bore and stroke: 3.35 in. x 3.66 in.

Displacement: 2,111 cc

Compression ratio: 7.5:1

Induction system: Fuel injection with Abarth Volumex supercharger

Maximum power: 325 bhp at 8,000 rpm

Maximum torque: Not quoted

Top speed: 140 mph

0–60 mph: 6 sec.

TRANSMISSION

ZF five-speed manual

BODY/CHASSIS

Steel center section with tubular-steel subframes and steel/Kevlar body

SPECIAL FEATURES

In ultimate Evo 2 form the Fiat/Lancia twin-cam engine produces 325 bhp.

Large scoops behind the side windows provide cooling air for the engine.

RUNNING GEAR

Steering: Rack-and-pinion

Front suspension: Double wishbones with coil springs, telescopic shock absorbers and anti-roll bar

Rear suspension: Double wishbones with coil springs and dual shock absorbers

Brakes: Vented discs, 11.8-in. dia. (front and rear)

Wheels: Speedline alloy, 8 x 16 in. (front), 9 x 16 in. (rear)

Tires: Pirelli P7, 205/55 VR16 (front), 225/50 VR16 (rear)

DIMENSIONS

Length: 154.1 in.   **Width:** 72.8 in.

Height: 49.0 in.   **Wheelbase:** 96.1 in.

Track: 59.4 in. (front), 58.7 in. (rear)

Weight: 2,117 lbs.

Lancia STRATOS

The world's first purpose-built rally car was a huge success. The mid-engine Stratos won Lancia the World Rally Championship in 1974, 1975 and 1976.

"...tricky at the limit."

"You need considerable skill to drive a Stratos really fast. The gearshift is stiff, the steering light and the car twitchy thanks to the combination of its mid-engined layout and short wheelbase. Lift off suddenly through a corner and the car will snap into oversteer, which needs quick reactions to catch. If the suspension is not adjusted precisely, or the tire pressure exactly right, the car is even trickier at the limit. Although 190 bhp doesn't sound like much, in a light car it feels extremely quick."

Tight conditions and seriously off-set controls lead to an unusual driving style.

Milestones

1970 Coachbuilder
Bertone exhibits its Stratos concept car at the Turin Show in November.

1971 Bertone's next
Turin show car is the Stratos HF, inspired by the first car but one inch taller and designed to use a Ferrari V6 engine.

1973 Lancia
commissions Bertone to build the 500 cars required for race/rally homologation. The first Stratos win comes in the 1973 Spanish Firestone Rally and another car is second in the Targa Florio road race.

The Lancia Stratos won three Manufacturers' World Championships in 1974-76.

1974 Homologation
is completed and the Stratos wins the first of its three World Rally Championships.

1975/6 Stratos wins
more World Championships but production ceases in 1975.

The Stratos is a dramatic road car and a rally 'homologation special.'

UNDER THE SKIN

Reinforced occupant 'cage'   Fiberglass body

Ferrari V6

Tough chassis

To be a rally car, the Stratos had to be tremendously strong. The chassis features a center steel cage of floor, door and roof pillars and the front and rear bulkheads. Behind the rear bulkhead is an extremely strong drilled frame holding the rear-mounted engine and the strut suspension. The fiberglass bodywork has no structural role.

THE POWER PACK

Power potential

The Stratos' engine is a real thoroughbred—the V6 used in the Fiat and Ferrari Dinos, in its later iron-block Fiat form. It has four chain-driven overhead camshafts but only two valves per cylinder. For competition use, it could be tuned way beyond its standard 190 bhp, to as much as 580 bhp in one turbo-racing version. Rally versions also sometimes used four-valve cylinder heads where allowed. In standard form, it breathes through three downdraft twin-choke Weber carburetors.

Compact mid-engined layout

Four chain-driven camshafts

Iron block

Alloy sump

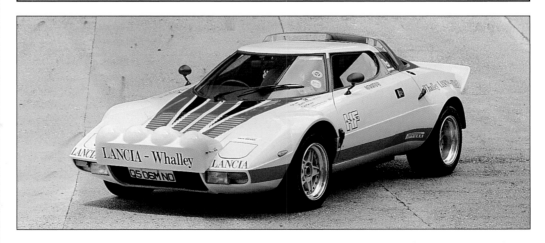

Competitive

There was little to match the Stratos and it won every major rally except the RAC and Safari, with 82 international wins in all, 16 in World Championship events. It was still surprisingly competitive in 1979 when Bernard Darniche won the Monte Carlo. It also won the Targa Florio in 1974.

The Stratos scored more than 80 international rally wins.

Lancia STRATOS

The Stratos looks almost as strange as the show car that gave it its name, yet it is extremely versatile. Not only was it a World Championship Rally-winning car, but also a successful road racer and a desirable roadgoing sports car.

Fiberglass body

None of the Stratos' body panels are load bearing, so they are made of fiberglass, keeping its weight to a minimum.

Ferrari Dino engine

By the time the Stratos was developed, Lancia had access to Ferrari engines and used its V6 'Dino' quad-cam V6 engine.

Removable bodywork

Quick and easy mechanical access is vital in a rally car, so the front and rear sections of the Stratos lifts clear for maintenance. Both panels can also be completely removed quickly.

Short wheelbase

Mid-engined cars like the Stratos are normally very nimble and maneuverable, but the Stratos is more agile than most due to its short wheelbase.

Central spoiler

The tiny central spoiler is enough to provide extra downforce, supplementing the rear wing which helps keep the back of the car firmly on the road.

Wishbone front suspension

Classic twin-wishbone suspension is used in the front. The front wheel arches are bulged at the top to allow long wheel travel required in rallying.

Vented disc brakes

Very effective brakes were required, so the Stratos has vented four-wheel discs, for improved stops.

Front-mounted radiator

The rear-mounted engine is cooled by a radiator in the front, with two electric fans, accounting for its louvered hood.

Specifications
1974 Lancia Stratos

ENGINE

Type: V6, quad cam
Construction: Cast-iron block and alloy cylinder heads
Valve gear: Two valves per cylinder operated by four chain-driven overhead camshafts
Bore and stroke: 3.64 in. x 2.36 in.
Displacement: 2,418 cc
Compression ratio: 9.0:1
Induction system: Triple Weber carburetors
Maximum power: 190 bhp at 7,000 rpm
Maximum torque: 166 lb-ft at 5,500 rpm
Top speed: 140 mph
0–60 mph: 7 sec

TRANSMISSION

Five-speed manual

BODY/CHASSIS

Fiberglass two-door, two-seat coupe body with folded sheet-steel frame

SPECIAL FEATURES

The wraparound roof spoiler provides additional downforce and also helps guide air into the engine bay.

Rear bodywork lifts up as one panel.

RUNNING GEAR

Steering: Rack-and-pinion
Front suspension: Twin wishbones with coil springs, telescopic shocks and anti-roll bar
Rear suspension: MacPherson struts and anti-roll bar
Brakes: Vented discs, 9.9 in. dia. (front and rear)
Wheels: Alloy, 14-in. dia.
Tires: 205/70 VR14

DIMENSIONS

Length: 146 in.   **Width:** 68.9 in.
Height: 68.9 in.   **Wheelbase:** 85.5 in.
Track: 56.3 in. (front), 57.5 in. (rear)
Weight: 2,161 lbs.

Lotus **ESPRIT V8**

In 1996, the Lotus Esprit finally got the engine its wonderful chassis deserved. Squeezing a twin-turbo V8 into the Esprit transformed it into a serious Ferrari-fighting supercar.

"...world class steering."

"The 349-bhp Esprit V8 shows why Lotus takes lessons from no one when it comes to making a car perform and handle. Its steering sets it apart—one of the world's best power-assisted systems tells you exactly what's going on, giving you the confidence to place the car with absolute precision. Staggering acceleration and outright performance make up for its few faults. The transmission is awkward and the twin-turbo still lacks the immediate throttle response of the best normally-aspirated engines."

Leather-trimmed cabin is far higher quality than in early Esprits. Placement of the controls and driving position are not ideal, though.

Milestones

1976 The first Esprit appears, with a 160-bhp version of the Lotus 2-liter twin-cam four.

1980 After minor changes in 1978 to produce the S2, Lotus enlarges the engine to 2.2 liters. The Turbo Esprit is launched, with 210 bhp, stronger chassis, revised suspension, wider wheels and tires.

Early Esprits had much sharper lines, but the overall shape is similar to the current car.

1987 Body is radically restyled in-house with rounded, softer lines. Turbo now has 215 bhp.

1989 SE (Special Equipment) Turbo model is the best yet, with handling improvements and power up to 264 bhp.

1993 Further improvement produces the S4 (0–60 mph in 5.0 seconds) and the lightweight Sport 300.

1995 S4S combined the best of S4 and Sport 300 with 285 bhp, dropping 0-60 mph to under five seconds.

1996 Esprit V8 is launched with a new 349-bhp twin-turbo V8 engine.

UNDER THE SKIN

Typically Lotus

The fiberglass bodywork covers an absolutely typical Lotus chassis, with a deep center backbone fabricated from sheet steel and featuring double wishbones at the front and a multi-link layout at the rear. The chassis had to be changed surprisingly little to take the V8 and the suspension is slightly upgraded to take the extra 110 lbs. of the new engine.

Double-wishbone front suspension

Mid-mounted engine

Fiberglass body

Renault-based transmission

THE POWER PACK

New V8 engine

Red cam covers—like a Ferrari

Four camshafts

Two small Garrett T25 turbochargers

Race-bred V8

Lotus designed an engine capable of 520 bhp for GT1-class racing and detuned it for the street-legal Esprit, so it's more than strong enough to cope with 349 bhp. It's all alloy and extremely compact, with four cams, 32 valves and hydraulic lifters, and it uses two small Garrett T25 turbochargers to overcome turbo lag. While outright power is impressive its torque output (295 lb-ft at 4,250 rpm) and the spread of torque from 2,250 rpm up is even more so.

GT racer

In 1996, a V8 Esprit took on the likes of the McLaren F1 and the new Porsche 911 GT1 in international GT racing and proved that the basic design was extremely competitive. A lack of funds and development slowed the car, but its career was short because Lotus intended to use its V8 in the racing Elise.

Flames spurt from the Lotus's twin turbos at Le Mans in 1996.

Lotus **ESPRIT V8**

You have to look closely to tell the difference between the Esprit S4 and the new V8 because Lotus spent all the money it could afford on doubling the car's number of cylinders and turbochargers.

Twin intercoolers

To lower the temperature of the intake air (making it denser and helping combustion and power) each turbocharger has an intercooler.

Split-rim wheels

The V8 Esprit comes equipped with OZ Racing split-rim alloys which are different sizes front and rear, the fronts being 'only' 8.5-inches wide.

New V8 engine

This is the first production Lotus V8, a 349-bhp all-alloy quad-cam design. A more powerful version powers Lotus's new racing Elise at events like the 24 Hours of Le Mans.

Upgraded ABS

One significant change between four-cylinder and V8 Esprits is the switch to Kelsey-Hayes four-channel ABS, which gives some of the most impressive braking in the world.

Kevlar reinforcement

Kevlar is used to reinforce the roof pillars to improve roll-over protection and increase their strength without making them thicker. Kevlar is also used in the sills to help make the whole structure stiffer.

Renault transmission

Lotus first used Renault parts in the Europa in the 1960s and turned to Renault once again in the Esprit. The V8 uses a transmission derived from that used in the fast GTA and A610 Renault Alpine sports cars.

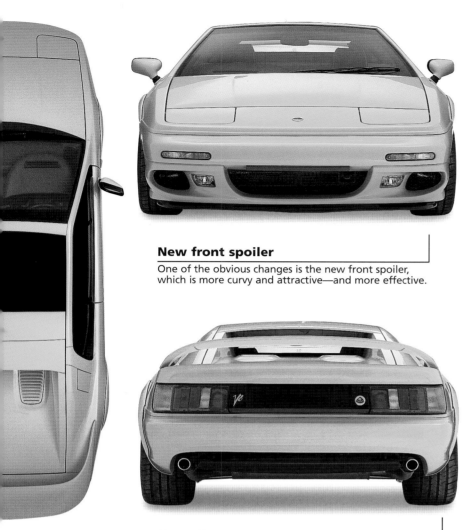

New front spoiler

One of the obvious changes is the new front spoiler, which is more curvy and attractive—and more effective.

Huge tires

The V8's tires are much larger than those used on the first Esprit over 20 years ago, particularly at the back of the car where they are 285/35 ZR18s running on wheel rims 10 inches wide.

Front radiator

Because there's no room in the engine bay for a radiator, it's mounted at the front where it cools more effectively.

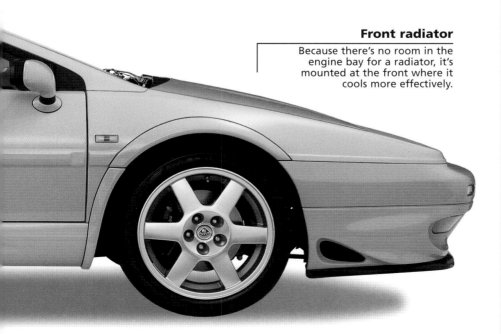

Specifications
1997 Lotus Esprit V8

ENGINE
Type: V8
Construction: Alloy block and heads
Valve gear: Four valves per cylinder operated by four overhead camshafts and hydraulic lifters
Bore and stroke: 3.19 in. x 3.27 in.
Displacement: 3,506 cc
Compression ratio: 8.0:1
Induction system: Electronic fuel injection with twin Garrett T25 turbochargers
Maximum power: 349 bhp at 6,500 rpm
Maximum torque: 295 lb-ft at 4,250 rpm
Top speed: 172 mph
0–60 mph: 4.2 sec

TRANSMISSION
Five-speed manual

BODY/CHASSIS
Sheet steel fabricated backbone chassis with fiberglass two-door coupe body

SPECIAL FEATURES
V8 uses two turbochargers, one for each bank of cylinders, to give the engine better throttle response than if it used a larger single turbo.

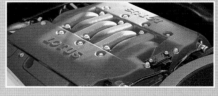

One of the easiest ways to tell the V8 apart is by its new front spoiler with its larger air intakes.

RUNNING GEAR
Steering: Rack-and-pinion
Front suspension: Double wishbones with coil springs, telescopic shocks and anti-roll bars
Rear suspension: Upper and lower links, coil springs, telescopic shocks and anti-roll bar
Brakes: Vented discs, 11.7 in. dia. (front), 11.8 in. dia. (rear); ABS
Wheels: OZ Racing split-rim alloys, 8.5 in. x 17 in. (front), 10 in. x 18 in. (rear)
Tires: 235/40 ZR17 (front), 285/35 ZR18 (rear)

DIMENSIONS
Length: 173.9 in.   **Width:** 78 in.
Height: 45.3 in.   **Wheelbase:** 95.3 in.
Track: 59.8 in. (front and rear)
Weight: 2,968 lbs.

Maserati **BIRDCAGE**

Called the Birdcage because of the incredibly complex chassis of tiny metal tubes, there is more to the Maserati than its memorable nickname. Its construction made it light and fast with excellent handling.

"...nimble and finely balanced."

"The Birdcage is as light to drive as its name suggests, nimble and finely balanced with perfectly weighted steering. Even with the rear-mounted transmission, the gear shifter is good and the close ratios make it easy to exploit all the twin cam's power. As with most early-1960s' racing cars, the emphasis is on handling rather than ultimate grip—although that is better than most—and the light rear end with the de Dion axle gives excellent traction. It really should have won more often."

There are no creature comforts in the Birdcage, just a simple instrument panel, bucket seat, and a tangle of tubular steel from the chassis.

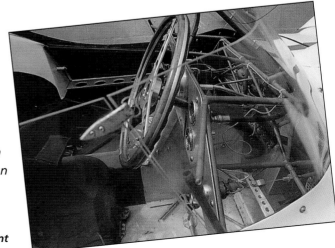

Milestones

1958 Giulio Alfieri starts to
design Maserati's new 2-liter sports racing car. Maserati's dire financial situation makes him design around some existing parts from the 200SI sports racing model and the famous 250F Grand Prix car.

Dan Gurney and Stirling Moss managed to win the 1960 Nürburgring 1000 km in a Camoradi Tipo 61.

1959 Production begins
on the Birdcage. With Stirling Moss driving, the 2-liter Tipo 60 wins its first event at Rouen, France.

1960 Lloyd Casner's Camoradi team
competes in every round of the World Sports Car Championship with the larger-engined Tipo 61. The only victory comes in Germany at the Nürburgring 1000 km with Moss and Dan Gurney sharing the driving.

1961 Again there's just the
one major win in the year. It's the Nürburgring 1000 km again, but this time Casner and Masten Gregory are driving. Now, rival companies are producing mid-engined cars and the front-engined Birdcage has become uncompetitive.

UNDER THE SKIN

Complicated

More than 200 pieces of high-grade steel tubing are welded together to form a very light but very strong structure. Diameter of the tubing varies according to its place in the chassis, and thinner tubes are used to triangulate joints for extra stiffness. Double-wishbone front suspension that came from the Grand Prix 250F and the de Dion rear axle is similar to the 250F's, with a transverse leaf spring. This allowed the transmission to be mounted at the back.

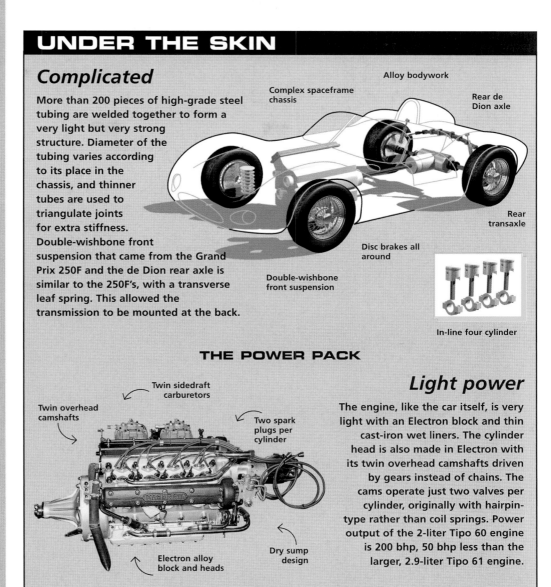

Complex spaceframe chassis

Alloy bodywork

Rear de Dion axle

Rear transaxle

Disc brakes all around

Double-wishbone front suspension

In-line four cylinder

THE POWER PACK

Twin overhead camshafts

Twin sidedraft carburetors

Two spark plugs per cylinder

Electron alloy block and heads

Dry sump design

Light power

The engine, like the car itself, is very light with an Electron block and thin cast-iron wet liners. The cylinder head is also made in Electron with its twin overhead camshafts driven by gears instead of chains. The cams operate just two valves per cylinder, originally with hairpin-type rather than coil springs. Power output of the 2-liter Tipo 60 engine is 200 bhp, 50 bhp less than the larger, 2.9-liter Tipo 61 engine.

Bigger engine

The Tipo 60 was the first Birdcage, but it was the bigger-engined Tipo 61 which was a more competitive racing car. It led every round of the 1960 World Sports Car Championship, including the 24 Hours of Le Mans and the Targa Florio.

Maserati only produced five of the Tipo 60 racers.

Maserati BIRDCAGE

The Birdcage was the ultimate front-engined spaceframe racing car. Despite its clever design, progress left the car behind and the opportunities it had for winning races—before it became obsolete—were almost all wasted.

Four-cylinder twin-cam

The lightweight four-cylinder features two overhead gear-driven camshafts, Electron block and heads and was produced in two displacements, 2.0 and 2.9 liters. It is canted at a 45-degree angle to fit under the low hood.

Transverse rear spring

Although coil springs are fitted at the front, Maserati chose to use a transverse semi-elliptic spring at the rear for the de Dion axle.

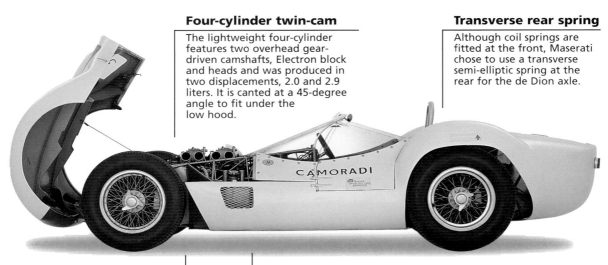

Disc brakes

The Birdcage was the first Maserati racer to use disc brakes. By the time the Tipo 60 and 61 were built, every top-ranked European racing car was using disc rather than drum brakes.

Alloy bodywork

Maserati had great experience in producing alloy bodywork over a separate chassis and there was never any question of the Birdcage having anything but an alloy body.

Spaceframe chassis

Maserati used a complicated network of small tubes welded together and triangulated wherever possible to produce a light but very strong structure.

Rear transaxle

To help make the weight distribution as equal as possible the five-speed transmission is mounted at the back, along with the differential in an alloy-cased transaxle.

Wishbone front suspension

The classic system of double wishbones, coil springs, telescopic shocks and anti-roll bar was the standard form of front suspension for racing cars in the late 1950s and 1960s.

Cockpit cooling scoop

This particular Birdcage has a scoop added to channel cooling air to the cockpit, even though it's an open car.

De Dion rear axle

The de Dion axle—where the axle tube connects both wheels but curves around the transaxle which is fixed to the chassis—reduces unsprung weight compared to an old-fashioned live axle.

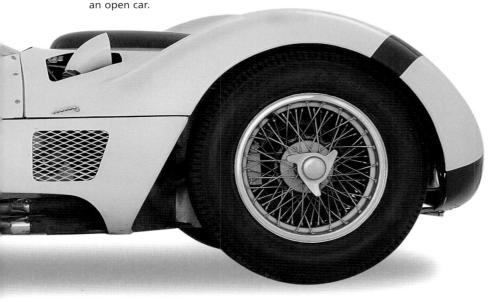

Specifications
1960 Maserati Birdcage Tipo 61

ENGINE
Type: In-line four cylinder
Construction: Electron alloy block and head with cast-iron wet liners
Valve gear: Two inclined valves per cylinder operated by twin gear-driven overhead camshafts
Bore and stroke: 3.94 in. x 3.62 in.
Displacement: 2,890 cc
Compression ratio: 9.0:1
Induction system: Two Weber 52 DCOE sidedraft carburetors
Maximum power: 250 bhp at 7,000 rpm
Maximum torque: Not quoted
Top speed: 165 mph
0–60 mph: Not quoted

TRANSMISSION
Five-speed rear-mounted transaxle

BODY/CHASSIS
Tubular steel spaceframe chassis with open alloy sports racing bodywork

SPECIAL FEATURES

Metal gear shifter gate has a lock to prevent the inadvertent selection of reverse.

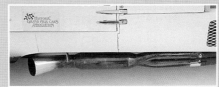

The four-into-one exhaust header design is ideal for maximum power.

RUNNING GEAR
Steering: Rack-and-pinion
Front suspension: Double wishbones, coil springs, telescopic shocks and anti-roll bar
Rear suspension: De Dion axle, twin parallel trailing arms per side, transverse leaf spring and telescopic shocks
Brakes: Four-wheel discs
Wheels: Borrani wire spoke 16-in. dia.
Tires: Crossply, 4.5 in. x 16 in. (front), 6.5 in. x 16 in. (rear)

DIMENSIONS
Length: 149.6 in.   **Width:** 59.1 in.
Height: 39.4 in.   **Wheelbase:** 86.6 in.
Track: 49.2 in. (front), 47.2 in. (rear)
Weight: 1,649 lbs.

Maserati BORA

The Bora marked Maserati's move into the modern world in the early 1970s. It was the company's first mid-engined supercar and was designed to compete with exotic mid-engined rivals from Ferrari and Lamborghini.

"...mid-engined V8 performer."

"Almost an Italian muscle car rather than a supercar, the Bora has a lot in common with the De Tomaso, employing a big V8 engine instead of a high-revving 12 cylinder engine. The V8 has masses of torque and powers the Bora to 100 mph in just 15 seconds. The car cruises comfortably at high speeds, but its stiff springing results in a hard ride. Although it has very responsive steering, it takes a brave driver to throw the Bora around."

The Bora's interior is comfortable, but unfortunately it has hard-to-read instruments.

Milestones

1968 Citroën becomes Maserati's major shareholder and gives the firm financial strength to consider exciting new models. Maserati agrees to build two mid-engined cars, the V6 Merak and V8 Bora.

1971 The Bora makes its world debut at the Geneva Show in March, and enters production soon after.

Maserati's 4.7-liter V8 also powers the beautiful Ghibli.

1974 Long after being sold in Europe, the Bora is finally made suitable for the American market. The larger 4.9-liter V8 satisfies the more stringent emissions and safety requirements.

Smaller than the Bora, the Merak features V6 power.

1980 Production of the Bora finally comes to an end.

UNDER THE SKIN

Old and new

Chassis construction is a mix of monocoque and a separate body-on-the-frame. The center and front sections are a folded steel monocoque, but the rear is a tubular steel structure carrying the longitudinally mid-mounted engine, transmission, and suspension. The entire rear of the car can be detached for maintenance.

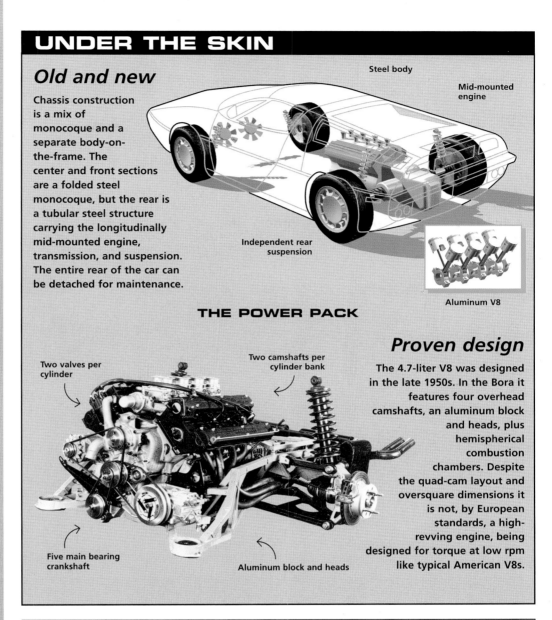

Steel body

Mid-mounted engine

Independent rear suspension

Aluminum V8

THE POWER PACK

Proven design

The 4.7-liter V8 was designed in the late 1950s. In the Bora it features four overhead camshafts, an aluminum block and heads, plus hemispherical combustion chambers. Despite the quad-cam layout and oversquare dimensions it is not, by European standards, a high-revving engine, being designed for torque at low rpm like typical American V8s.

Two valves per cylinder

Two camshafts per cylinder bank

Five main bearing crankshaft

Aluminum block and heads

Bigger engine

In 1974 a bigger, 4.9-liter version of the V8 was used in Boras destined for the U.S. The larger engine was required to satisfy economy and emissions laws. Available in European trim from 1976, it produces 10 bhp extra and naturally offers more performance.

Although it had a long production run, only 570 Boras were built.

Maserati BORA

The Bora, which is the Italian name for a strong wind, has a slippery shape and slices through the air at speeds of up to 160 mph thanks to its 310 bhp quad-cam V8 engine.

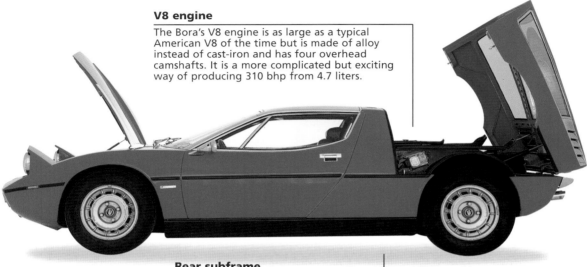

V8 engine

The Bora's V8 engine is as large as a typical American V8 of the time but is made of alloy instead of cast-iron and has four overhead camshafts. It is a more complicated but exciting way of producing 310 bhp from 4.7 liters.

Rear subframe

At the rear, a welded-up square tube structure is used to support the engine, transmission and rear suspension.

Early alloy bodies

The very first Boras were produced with hand-crafted alloy bodies, a skill Maserati was well versed in. Standard production Boras, however, have steel bodies.

Transmission behind engine

German manufacturers ZF supplied the transmission, which is mounted behind the engine toward the tail of the car. This requires a longer and more complicated gear linkage.

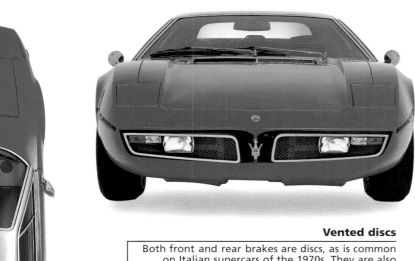

Vented discs
Both front and rear brakes are discs, as is common on Italian supercars of the 1970s. They are also vented to improve cooling and to prevent fade.

Aerodynamic shape
Even though the Bora never went anywhere near a wind tunnel, designer Giorgetto Giugiaro achieved a drag coefficient of just 0.30.

Front-mounted radiator
Unlike later mid-engined cars, the Bora has a front-mounted radiator with electric fans.

Specifications
1973 Maserati Bora

ENGINE
Type: V8

Construction: Light alloy block and heads

Valve gear: Two inclined valves per cylinder operated by four chain-driven overhead camshafts via bucket tappets

Bore and stroke: 3.69 in. x 3.35 in.

Displacement: 4,719 cc

Compression ratio: 8.5:1

Induction system: Four Weber DCNF/14 downdraft carburetors

Maximum power: 310 bhp at 6,000 rpm

Maximum torque: 325 lb-ft at 4,200 rpm

Top speed: 160 mph

0–60 mph: 6.5 sec

TRANSMISSION
Five-speed ZF manual

BODY/CHASSIS
Steel unitary construction front sections with square-tube rear frame; steel two-door coupe body

SPECIAL FEATURES

The flat rear end or 'Kamm tail' was a popular feature on 1970s supercars.

The Bora was an early Giorgetto Giugiaro design.

RUNNING GEAR
Steering: Rack-and-pinion

Front suspension: Double wishbones with coil springs, telescopic shocks and anti-roll bar

Rear suspension: Double wishbones with coil springs, telescopic shocks and anti-roll bar

Brakes: Vented discs (front and rear), with Citroën high-pressure hydraulics

Wheels: Alloy, 7.5 in. x 15 in.

Tires: Michelin 215/70 VR15

DIMENSIONS
Length: 170.4 in.   **Width:** 68.1 in.

Height: 44.6 in.   **Wheelbase:** 102 in.

Track: 58 in. (front), 57 in. (rear)

Weight: 3,570 lbs.

Maserati **GHIBLI**

Beautiful, extremely powerful and very quick, the Ghibli is close to the top of the supercar league. It was one of the last of the great front-engined equipped supercars.

"unrivaled power and torque."

"With the Ghibli, you first notice its unrivaled power and torque from the quad-cam V8. The engine is happy to trickle through traffic or punch the car effortlessly to 60 mph in under seven seconds and on towards 155 mph. It's easy to exploit the power, too, because the clutch and five-speed gearshift are light, while the steering and brakes are excellent. Although the chassis and suspension design seems simple, it works perfectly well. The Ghibli handles great and has a nice comfortable ride—two difficult things to combine."

Unlike some supercars, the Ghibli is as happy to tackle traffic as it is on the open road.

Milestones

1966 The Maserati Ghibli appears at the Turin Show. The shape is designed by Ghia, for whom Giorgetto Giugiaro is already chief designer.

1967 Production of the Ghibli starts, in coupe form only.

Maserati first used the four-cam V8 in the 1959 5000GT.

1969 Open Spyder version is introduced, with optional hardtop, automatic transmission, and wire wheels.

The Ghibli name survives on a later Maserati model.

1970 More power is needed. The result is the Ghibli SS with a larger, 4,930-cc engine. Power only increases 5 bhp due to the effect of new emissions controls.

1973 Ghibli production ends after 1,149 coupes and 125 Spyders have been built.

UNDER THE SKIN

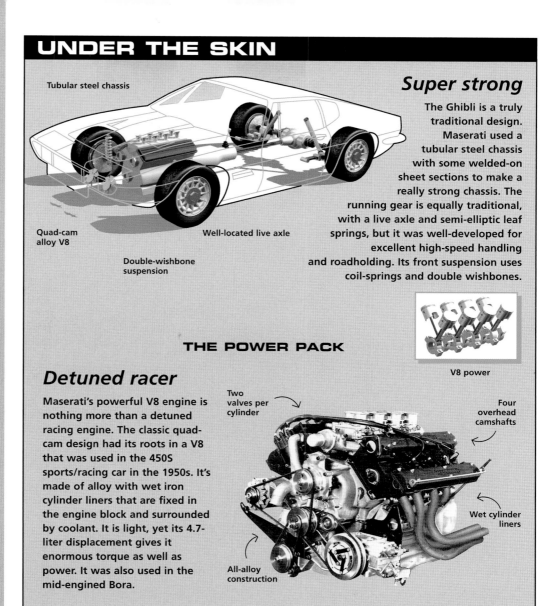

Tubular steel chassis

Quad-cam alloy V8

Double-wishbone suspension

Well-located live axle

Super strong

The Ghibli is a truly traditional design. Maserati used a tubular steel chassis with some welded-on sheet sections to make a really strong chassis. The running gear is equally traditional, with a live axle and semi-elliptic leaf springs, but it was well-developed for excellent high-speed handling and roadholding. Its front suspension uses coil-springs and double wishbones.

V8 power

THE POWER PACK

Detuned racer

Maserati's powerful V8 engine is nothing more than a detuned racing engine. The classic quad-cam design had its roots in a V8 that was used in the 450S sports/racing car in the 1950s. It's made of alloy with wet iron cylinder liners that are fixed in the engine block and surrounded by coolant. It is light, yet its 4.7-liter displacement gives it enormous torque as well as power. It was also used in the mid-engined Bora.

Two valves per cylinder

Four overhead camshafts

Wet cylinder liners

All-alloy construction

Open style

Most desirable of all the Ghiblis is the Spyder, which went on sale two years after the coupe. It was more expensive than the coupe and had optional wire wheels. The bodyshell retained much of its stiffness so the handling was hardly affected.

The highly desirable Spyder is the ultimate Maserati Ghibli.

Maserati GHIBLI

Maserati claimed the Ghibli could reach 174 mph, the same as the more famous Ferrari Daytona, but no one ever quite reached that speed in magazine road testing.

Dry sump lubrication

The V8 engine does not have a conventional oil pan under the engine. The oil is held in a separate tank and pumped around the engine. This had two advantages; the engine could be lower and there was no oil surge under hard cornering.

Quad-cam V8

The most advanced feature of the Ghibli is the quad-cam engine. It is all alloy with four chain-driven overhead camshafts and four Weber carburetors.

Pop-up headlights

These are common today but few cars had pop-up lights in the 1960s. They helped to lower the car's noseline.

Twin-caliper disc brakes

The Ghibli has effective brakes because the front discs are vented and have two calipers which give a larger pad area than single calipers would.

Reinforced tubular-steel chassis

Like all Italian supercars of the era, the Ghibli has a tubular-steel chassis reinforced with welded-on sheet steel to make some sections even stronger.

Steel body

Maserati was not really interested in saving weight with the Ghibli because it had plenty of power, so the body is steel instead of alloy.

Wishbone front suspension

Maserati had made great racing cars so it's no surprise that racing-type twin-wishbone front suspension with an anti-roll bar is used on the Ghibli.

Live rear axle

Despite its exotic looks and performance, Maserati persisted with an old-fashioned live rear axle supported on simple leaf springs for the Ghibli.

Ghia styling

Ghia is now a part of Ford, but was an independent coachbuilder in the 1960s. Giugiaro was chief designer before he moved on to greater fame with Ital Design.

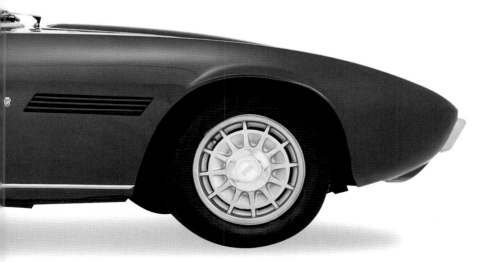

ENGINE

Type: V8, quad cam
Construction: Alloy block with wet liners and alloy cylinder heads
Valve gear: Two valves per cylinder operated by four chain-driven overhead cams
Bore and stroke: 369 in. x 3.35 in.
Displacement: 4,719 cc
Compression ratio: 8.5:1
Induction system: Four Weber 42 DCNF carburetors
Maximum power: 370 bhp at 5,500 rpm
Maximum torque: 326 lb-ft at 4,000 rpm
Top speed: 154 mph
0–60 mph: 6.8 sec.

TRANSMISSION

Five-speed manual

BODY/CHASSIS

Steel two-door 2+2 coupe with tubular-steel chassis

SPECIAL FEATURES

The side vents cool the engine and keep the Ghibli from looking too slab sided.

Lockable fuel filler flaps were built into the Ghibli's rear quarters on both sides to fill the car's twin tanks.

RUNNING GEAR

Steering: Recirculating ball
Front suspension: Twin wishbones with coil springs, shocks and anti-roll bar
Rear suspension: Live axle with semi-elliptic leaf springs, radius arms, Panhard rod and telescopic shocks
Brakes: Vented discs (front), solid discs (rear)
Wheels: Alloy 7.5 in. x 15 in.
Tires: Crossply 205 x 15 in.

DIMENSIONS

Length: 180.7 in.   **Width:** 70.9 in.
Wheelbase: 100.4 in.   **Height:** 46.6 in.
Track: 56.7 in. (front), 55.4 in. (rear)
Weight: 3,745 lbs.

Maserati SEBRING

The Sebring was Maserati's way of giving a new lease on life to its popular 3500GT. With modern bodywork, more powerful engines and a five-speed transmission, the customers loved the Sebring.

"...high speed stability."

"A shorter wheelbase gives the Sebring better handling than the outgoing 3500GT. It has a well-balanced, neutral tendency, and it needs a heavy right foot to cause oversteer. High-speed stability is impressive, as is the ride at all speeds. The springs are very stiff and give it exceptionally good body control. Four-wheel discs provide excellent braking—essential when you can hit 120 mph in only 30 seconds and the top speed is nearly 140 mph."

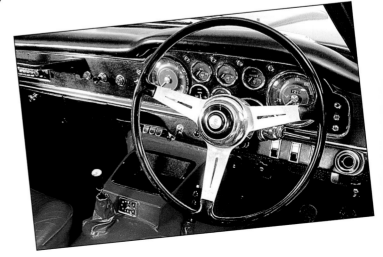

A classic three-spoke steering wheel sets off the well-stocked dashboard.

Milestones

1957 Maserati introduces the 3500GT
as its first real mass-production sports coupe.

The 3500GT catapulted Maserati into the supercar league.

1961 The 3500GT is
improved with a standard five-speed transmission and Lucas fuel injection in place of carburetors.

Styled by Frua, the Mistral used the Sebring's straight-six engine.

1963 New Vignale bodywork
is different enough to call for a name change. Maserati chooses Sebring after the Florida race circuit. Power comes from 3.5-, 3.7- and 4.0-liter straight-six units.

1966 Sebring production
ends after 438 cars have been built. By this time the more glamourous Ghibli has taken over.

UNDER THE SKIN

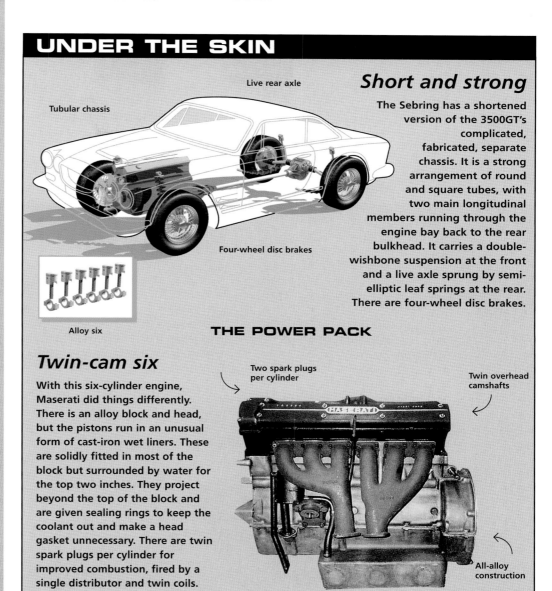

Live rear axle

Tubular chassis

Four-wheel disc brakes

Alloy six

Short and strong

The Sebring has a shortened version of the 3500GT's complicated, fabricated, separate chassis. It is a strong arrangement of round and square tubes, with two main longitudinal members running through the engine bay back to the rear bulkhead. It carries a double-wishbone suspension at the front and a live axle sprung by semi-elliptic leaf springs at the rear. There are four-wheel disc brakes.

THE POWER PACK

Twin-cam six

With this six-cylinder engine, Maserati did things differently. There is an alloy block and head, but the pistons run in an unusual form of cast-iron wet liners. These are solidly fitted in most of the block but surrounded by water for the top two inches. They project beyond the top of the block and are given sealing rings to keep the coolant out and make a head gasket unnecessary. There are twin spark plugs per cylinder for improved combustion, fired by a single distributor and twin coils.

Two spark plugs per cylinder

Twin overhead camshafts

All-alloy construction

Full bore

The most exciting Sebrings are the later versions with stretched six-cylinder, twin-cam engines that displace 4.0 liters. This gives it 255 bhp, which is enough to take the top speed to 146 mph in an attempt to match rivals Ferrari and Lamborghini.

The biggest 4.0-liter Sebring is by far the fastest of the entire range.

Maserati SEBRING

Vignale's compact body made the Sebring look much more modern than the 3500GT thanks to features like its four-headlight front end and its sharper, more distinct lines.

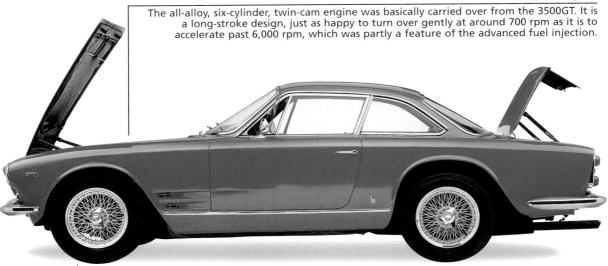

Twin-cam engine

The all-alloy, six-cylinder, twin-cam engine was basically carried over from the 3500GT. It is a long-stroke design, just as happy to turn over gently at around 700 rpm as it is to accelerate past 6,000 rpm, which was partly a feature of the advanced fuel injection.

Steel and alloy wheels

Sebrings could be ordered with either Borrani wire-spoke, knock-on wheels or discs. Like the Borranis the steel disc wheels actually had steel centers with alloy rims for lightness.

Recirculating ball steering

It was not until the 1970s that Maserati saw the benefit of using rack-and-pinion steering. It claimed that perfectly good results could be achieved with the theoretically inferior recirculating ball arrangement.

Live axle

The rear suspension is a simple live axle suspended on semi-elliptic leaf springs, but Maserati made sure it is well located with a torque reaction arm as well as an anti-roll bar and shock absorbers angled inward toward the differential.

Shorter wheelbase

The Sebring is built on a chassis similar to the 3500GT but with a 3.9-inch shorter wheelbase. This helped to make it slightly more agile.

Specifications

1964 Maserati Sebring

ENGINE
Type: Inline six-cylinder
Construction: Alloy block and head
Valve gear: Two valves per cylinder operated by twin overhead camshafts
Bore and stroke: 3.38 in. x 3.94 in.
Displacement: 3,485 cc
Compression ratio: 8.8:1
Induction system: Lucas mechanical fuel injection
Maximum power: 235 bhp at 5,500 rpm
Maximum torque: 232 lb-ft at 4,000 rpm
Top speed: 137 mph
0–60 mph: 8.5 sec.

TRANSMISSION
ZF five-speed manual

BODY/CHASSIS
Separate fabricated steel-tube chassis with steel coupe bodywork by Vignale

SPECIAL FEATURES

Fender vents behind the front wheels vent hot air from the disc brakes.

The subtle hood scoop gives the Sebring a more muscular look.

RUNNING GEAR
Steering: Recirculating ball
Front suspension: Double wishbones with coil springs, telescopic shock absorbers and anti-roll bar
Rear suspension: Live axle with semi-elliptic leaf springs, torque arm, telescopic shock absorbers and anti-roll bar
Brakes: Girling discs (front and rear)
Wheels: Borrani wires, 6.5 x 16 in.
Tires: Pirelli Cinturato, 185 x 16

DIMENSIONS
Length: 176.0 in. **Width:** 65.3 in.
Height: 52.0 in. **Wheelbase:** 98.5 in.
Track: 54.7 in. (front), 53.5 in (rear)
Weight: 3,335 lbs.

Mazda **RX-7**

After its 1991 Le Mans win, Mazda unveiled the third-generation RX-7. Lighter and faster than ever, its twin turbochargers gave 255 bhp and a top speed of over 155 mph. The RX-7 had gone from a sports car to a junior league supercar in one leap.

"...the RX-7 has it all."

"Power, performance, handling; the RX-7 has it all. There's no turbo lag and the engine runs quickly to 4,000 rpm: With both turbos spinning furiously, it really takes off as it soars to its 6,500 rpm power peak. The steering is razor sharp and the RX-7 responds instantly to every driver input. You can place the Mazda exactly where you want it, and then adjust its cornering line with the throttle. There's only one (acceptable) penalty—the rock hard ride."

Stark, black plastic interior is typically Japanese, but the RX-7 is more about performance and driver enjoyment than luxury.

Milestones

1967 Mazda introduces the Cosmo, its first real sports car, pioneering a twin-rotor Wankel engine.

1978 With experience gained from the Cosmo, Mazda designs the first RX-7, again with a twin-rotor engine but with a simple live rear axle.

Racing experience helped in the development of the road car.

1985 The second-generation RX-7 appears, still with a rotary engine of course, but now bigger, with hints of Porsche styling and a more advanced independent rear suspension.

1991 Mazda finally wins the 24 Hours of Le Mans outright after years of participation with rotary cars. Later this year, the third-generation RX-7 appears. It is in a different class from the previous car and one of the best handling sports cars ever made.

1996 With Mazda looking at a smaller version of their frontline rotary sports car, the RX-01 show car, the days of the twin-turbo RX-7 are numbered and the decision is made to end production.

UNDER THE SKIN

Lightweight

The RX-7 was designed to be light and as fast as possible. The shell is steel but all the advanced double-wishbone suspension components are alloy, daringly bolted directly to the body without rubber bushes to help give more precise handling. For the same reason, alloy cross braces are featured to help make the body as stiff as possible and a frame joins the transmission to the final drive.

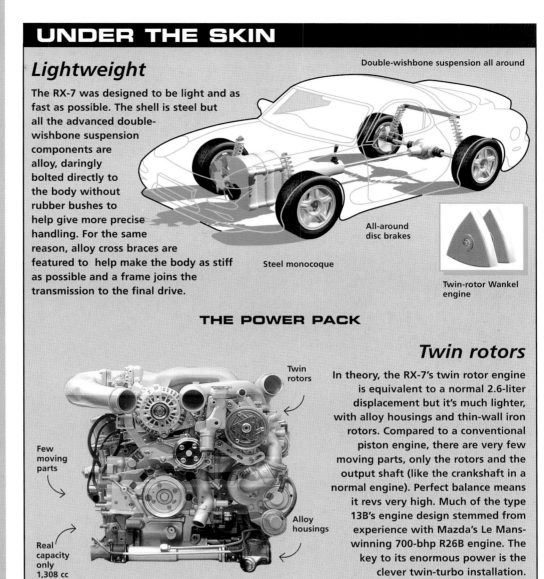

Double-wishbone suspension all around

All-around disc brakes

Steel monocoque

Twin-rotor Wankel engine

THE POWER PACK

Twin rotors

Few moving parts

Real capacity only 1,308 cc

Alloy housings

Twin rotors

In theory, the RX-7's twin rotor engine is equivalent to a normal 2.6-liter displacement but it's much lighter, with alloy housings and thin-wall iron rotors. Compared to a conventional piston engine, there are very few moving parts, only the rotors and the output shaft (like the crankshaft in a normal engine). Perfect balance means it revs very high. Much of the type 13B's engine design stemmed from experience with Mazda's Le Mans-winning 700-bhp R26B engine. The key to its enormous power is the clever twin-turbo installation.

Curvaceous

With the RX-7, Mazda cleverly combined the best of oriental and western styling. The Japanese influence comes in the number and form of scoops and vents which are functional and add interest to the shape. Western influence shows in the simple but elegant lines.

The third generation RX-7 has the power to match its stunning looks.

Mazda **RX-7**

The RX-7 shows just how much progress Mazda has made since 1978, when the RX-7 had less than half the power of the 1997 model. Even the second-generation car was nearly 100-bhp less powerful.

Comprehensive equipment

Although the RX-7 was designed to be as light as possible, it went on sale in some markets with a long list of standard equipment, such as leather seats, cruise control and air conditioning—all of which made the car heavier.

Twin-rotor engine

There are no conventional reciprocating valves in a twin-rotor Wankel engine. The turbos force the fuel mixture through ports uncovered in the rotor housing as the rotors sweep around.

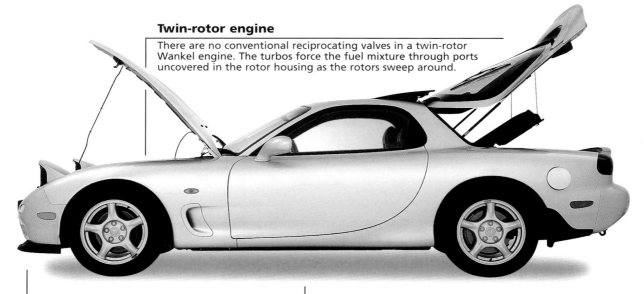

Pop-up lights

Mazda had no choice but to use pop-up lights—the car was so low it was the only way to get the headlamps up to the required legal height.

Limited slip differential

To avoid power-wasting wheelspin in corners, a limited slip differential was installed. The efficient worm-drive Torsen (standing for 'torque sensing') type was used.

'Powerplant frame'

A light but strong cast-alloy beam is used to connect the transmission and the final drive. It eliminates movement in the drivetrain and makes the car's structure stiffer.

Vented discs

The RX-7's high performance was matched by its braking. Four-wheel 11.6 inch dia., vented discs are used with standard anti-lock braking.

Oil cooler ducts

Oil coolers supplement the normal radiator. Air is ducted to the coolers via vents on either side of the radiator opening.

Rear wing

Mazda installed a rear wing to increase high-speed stability at the expense of aerodynamic drag, thus reducing the car's top speed.

Equal size tires

It's not unusual for cars with this much power to have larger rear tires, but they are all 225/50 ZR16s on the RX-7.

Specifications
1993 Mazda RX-7

ENGINE
Type: Twin-rotor Wankel
Construction: Alloy housing with cast-iron rotors and end plates
Valve gear: Circumferential porting
Bore and stroke: N/A
Displacement: 1,308 cc (nominal)
Compression ratio: 9.0:1
Induction system: Bosch electronic fuel injection with twin Hitachi HT 12 turbochargers
Maximum power: 255 bhp at 6,500 rpm
Maximum torque: 217 lb-ft at 5,000 rpm
Top speed: 156 mph
0–60 mph: not quoted

TRANSMISSION
Five-speed manual transmission

BODY/CHASSIS
Unitary construction steel two-door coupe body with supplementary light-alloy 'powerplant frame'

SPECIAL FEATURES

An alloy beam connecting the transmission and final drive stiffens the car's structure, improving handling and reducing snatch in the drivetrain.

With a short, curved roof, the RX-7's sunroof cannot slide back inside the headlining.

RUNNING GEAR
Steering: Rack-and-pinion
Front and rear suspension: Double unequal-length wishbones, coil springs, telescopic shocks and anti-roll bar
Brakes: Four-wheel vented discs, 11.6 in. dia. with anti-lock system
Wheels: Cast-alloy 8 in. x 16 in.
Tires: Bridgestone Expedia 225/50 ZR16

DIMENSIONS
Length: 168.5 in.   **Width:** 68.9 in.
Height: 48.4 in.   **Wheelbase:** 95.5 in.
Track: 57.5 in. (front and rear)
Weight: 2,800 lbs.

McLaren **F1**

When the seven-time Formula One world champions at McLaren decided to build their first road car, they created the world's most exotic and most expensive supercar, the 627-bhp F1.

"...nothing even comes close."

"The F1's central seating layout allows the driver perfect visibility over the small, neat instrument pod and a comfortable driving position without the compromises of lesser supercars. The F1 is not a difficult car to drive. It is as civilized as it is fast and with over 600 bhp there's none faster—it accelerates faster than a Formula 1 car. Steering response is instant, but like a race car, it needs expert hands to really get it to perform to its limits."

The driver's seat is in the center of the car, with passenger's seats set slightly back, to improve driver vision and comfort.

Milestones

1992 The McLaren F1

appears on May 28 at the Monaco GP. Production starts the following year.

1995 McLaren produces the GTR

version for international GT racing. Power is increased to 636 bhp with different cam profiles and remapped engine management. The GTR wins its first race and goes on to win Le Mans.

McLaren's F1 is one of the easiest supercars to drive.

1996 In celebration of the

Le Mans win, McLaren introduces the LM version with 668 bhp and an extra 41 lb-ft of torque. Changes are made to the floor shape (for aerodynamics), bumpers, rear suspension and steering. 0-60 mph time falls to 3.2 seconds.

F1's striking lines were penned by designer Peter Stevens.

1997 McLaren brings

out the new GTR racer, heavily revised and much lighter with a smaller, 600-bhp 6-liter engine and improved aerodynamics.

UNDER THE SKIN

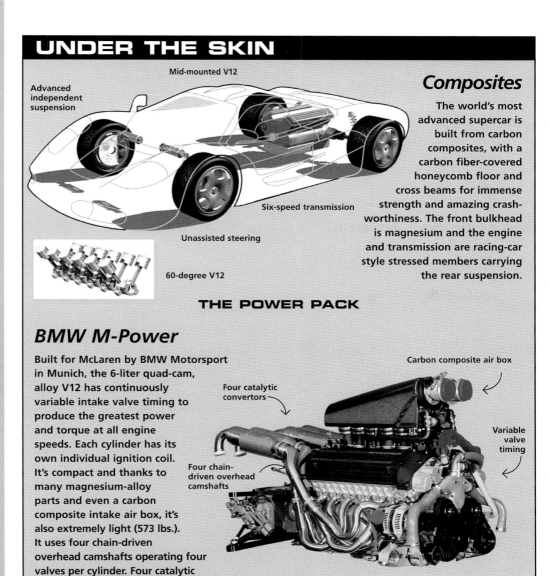

Advanced independent suspension

Mid-mounted V12

Six-speed transmission

Unassisted steering

60-degree V12

Composites

The world's most advanced supercar is built from carbon composites, with a carbon fiber-covered honeycomb floor and cross beams for immense strength and amazing crash-worthiness. The front bulkhead is magnesium and the engine and transmission are racing-car style stressed members carrying the rear suspension.

THE POWER PACK

BMW M-Power

Built for McLaren by BMW Motorsport in Munich, the 6-liter quad-cam, alloy V12 has continuously variable intake valve timing to produce the greatest power and torque at all engine speeds. Each cylinder has its own individual ignition coil. It's compact and thanks to many magnesium-alloy parts and even a carbon composite intake air box, it's also extremely light (573 lbs.). It uses four chain-driven overhead camshafts operating four valves per cylinder. Four catalytic convertors ensure emissions are clean.

Carbon composite air box

Four catalytic convertors

Variable valve timing

Four chain-driven overhead camshafts

Le Mans winner

The most expensive F1, the LM version, was built to celebrate McLaren's win at Le Mans in 1995. Based on the F1 GTR, it produces 668 bhp, is 132 lbs. lighter and has a claimed top speed of 225 mph. It's slower than the standard car due to drag from the large spoiler.

1997's GTR was significantly revised, especially from an aerodynamic standpoint.

McLaren F1 🇬🇧

McLaren managed to build the world's best supercar in its very first attempt with the Gordon Murray-designed F1. Unlike most other street-legal supercars, it was good enough to win Le Mans.

Plasma-coated glass

Plasma sprayed onto the inside of the outer glass laminate provides a tint and a heating element to defrost or defog the windshield extremely fast.

'Brake and balance' spoiler

Under heavy braking the spoiler rises at an angle of 30 degrees, generating rear downforce and overcoming the usual pitching.

Luggage storage

Because space in the front luggage compartment is limited, there are other clever compartments, such as those ahead of the rear wheels, to increase total luggage space.

BMW V12 engine

McLaren commissioned the quad-cam V12 engine from BMW. Light, compact and powerful, its output rose from 550 bhp in 1994 to 668 bhp, all without turbochargers.

Formula 1 brakes

The F1's huge vented brakes made by Brembo are as effective as Formula 1 brakes before they were made of carbon fiber.

Six-speed transmission

Six speeds allow the McLaren to have the first five ratios close together and a high 'overdrive' sixth for relaxed high-speed travel.

Survival cell

If the F1 crashes at very high speeds, the occupants are protected by a survival cell; an extremely strong cockpit made of carbon fiber.

Ground effects

Air passing through the venturi tunnels under the F1 drops in pressure, generating 'ground effect' and sucking the car firmly down on the road at high speeds.

Central driver's seat

The driver sits in the center to get the best view and control and also the best weight distribution. Passengers sit on either side, and slightly behind him.

Impact absorbing muffler

The muffler is huge, with a capacity of 65 liters and it has a dual purpose, also acting as a crumple zone in the case of a rear impact.

Specifications
1995 McLaren F1

ENGINE

Type: V12 quad cam by BMW
Construction: Alloy block and heads
Valve gear: Four valves per cylinder operated by four chain-driven overhead cams with variable intake timing
Bore and stroke: 3.39 in. x 3.43 in.
Displacement: 6,064 cc
Compression ratio: 10.5:1
Maximum power: 627 bhp at 7,300 rpm
Maximum torque: 479 lb-ft at 4,000 rpm
Top speed: 231 mph
0–60 mph: 3.2 sec.

TRANSMISSION

Six-speed manual

BODY/CHASSIS

Carbon fiber two-door, three-seat coupe with carbon fiber and Nomex/alloy honeycomb monocoque chassis

SPECIAL FEATURES

The rear spoiler rises under heavy braking, increasing rear downforce and stopping the nose diving.

The driver sits in the center of the car, with a full racing harness rather than a normal seat belt.

RUNNING GEAR

Steering: Rack-and-pinion
Front suspension: Twin wishbones, coil springs, shocks and anti-roll bar
Rear suspension: Twin wishbones with coil springs and shocks
Brakes: Brembo discs, 13.1 in. dia. (front), 12 in. (rear)
Wheels: Magnesium 9 in. x 17 in. (front), 11.5 in. x 17 in. (rear)
Tires: 235/45 ZR17 (front) and 315/40 ZR17 (rear)

DIMENSIONS

Length: 169 in.　**Width:** 72 in.
Height: 45 in.　**Wheelbase:** 107 in.
Track: 62 in. (front), 58 in. (rear)
Weight: 2,245 lbs.

Mercedes 300SL

Created from Mercedes-Benz's first Le Mans-winning racing car, the 300SL 'Gullwing' was a race car built for the road. In the mid-1950s, it gave a few lucky drivers 1990s levels of performance.

"...spectacular and rare."

"Few have ever seen, let alone driven, one of the most coveted cars Mercedes Benz ever produced. Those lucky souls don't think about the astronomical price this 300SL would bring, they just enjoy this spectacular and rare automobile. It's actually fast enough to keep up with many modern sports cars. The transmission has synchros on all four gears and is easy to use, although the clutch is heavy. The ride is firm, like a sports cars should be, but definitely not old fashioned."

The cabin of the Gullwing was not a nice place to be on a hot day— it didn't have opening windows. Owners opened their doors in traffic for fresh air.

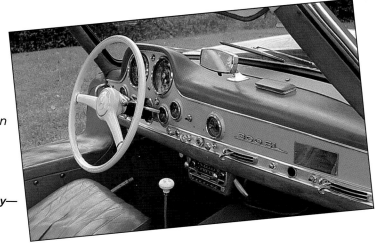

Milestones

1952 Mercedes builds its first postwar racer, the 300SL coupe. With a spaceframe chassis, Gullwing doors and 172 bhp from its six-cylinder engine, it leads its first event, the 1952 Mille Miglia, but finishes second before winning Le Mans and the Carrera Panamericana.

The 300SL: successful in racing.

1954 The street-legal version of the 300SL is introduced at the New York Motor Show.

1955 Production gets fully underway and the 300SL—with fuel injection replacing carburetors—is faster than the racer. It is also more than twice as expensive as a Chevrolet Corvette in the U.S.

1957 The Gullwing is discontinued after 1,400 have been built and the open Roadster appears at the Geneva Show. The chassis has been redesigned to allow conventional doors and the swing-axle rear suspension has been improved. Its top speed is up to 150 mph.

1961 Disc brakes with servo assistance are added to the car, vastly increasing stopping power. Production ends in 1963.

UNDER THE SKIN

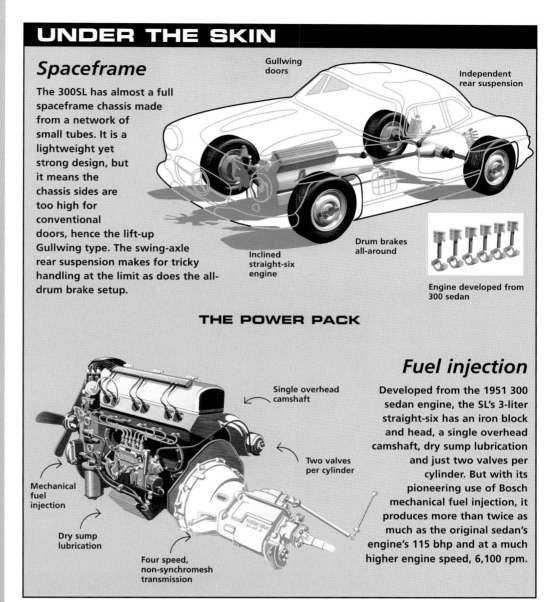

Spaceframe

The 300SL has almost a full spaceframe chassis made from a network of small tubes. It is a lightweight yet strong design, but it means the chassis sides are too high for conventional doors, hence the lift-up Gullwing type. The swing-axle rear suspension makes for tricky handling at the limit as does the all-drum brake setup.

Gullwing doors

Independent rear suspension

Drum brakes all-around

Inclined straight-six engine

Engine developed from 300 sedan

THE POWER PACK

Single overhead camshaft

Two valves per cylinder

Mechanical fuel injection

Dry sump lubrication

Four speed, non-synchromesh transmission

Fuel injection

Developed from the 1951 300 sedan engine, the SL's 3-liter straight-six has an iron block and head, a single overhead camshaft, dry sump lubrication and just two valves per cylinder. But with its pioneering use of Bosch mechanical fuel injection, it produces more than twice as much as the original sedan's engine's 115 bhp and at a much higher engine speed, 6,100 rpm.

Open top fun

Although the Gullwing is more highly valued, the Roadster is by far the nicer car to drive. It had much more power, revised rear suspension for more predictable handling and a much less claustrophobic cabin than the cramped Gullwing.

Although not as desirable, the 300SL Roadster is an easier car to live with.

Mercedes 300SL

The dramatic looks of the world's first postwar supercar were dictated by the racing car chassis under the body which made the Gullwing doors essential.

Hood bulges
Only one bulge is required, to clear the injection system—the other is there to balance the design.

Tilting steering wheel
Getting in and out of the 300SL could be difficult because of the high sills, so the steering wheel tilts to make room.

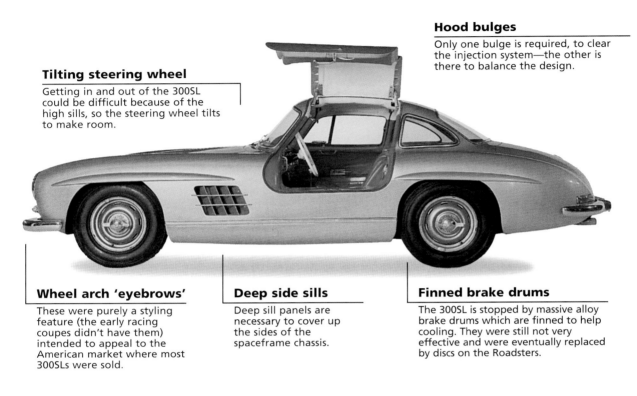

Wheel arch 'eyebrows'
These were purely a styling feature (the early racing coupes didn't have them) intended to appeal to the American market where most 300SLs were sold.

Deep side sills
Deep sill panels are necessary to cover up the sides of the spaceframe chassis.

Finned brake drums
The 300SL is stopped by massive alloy brake drums which are finned to help cooling. They were still not very effective and were eventually replaced by discs on the Roadsters.

Air extractors
To get a good flow of air through the cabin, twin extractors are incorporated into the rear of the roof.

Alloy doors

To ease the strain on the roof-mounted hinges, the doors are made from alloy rather than steel. It also helps save weight overall, as do the alloy hood and trunk lid.

Flush fitting door handles

The door handles are almost too small to notice. The end is pushed in to reveal the whole handle. Handles like these inspired the designers of the Fiat Barchetta in the 1990s.

Sedan engine

Apart from its pioneering use of fuel injection, the specification of the 300SL's engine was quite ordinary due to its sedan origins.

Specifications
1955 Mercedes 300SL

ENGINE

Type: Straight-six
Construction: Cast-iron block and head
Valve gear: Two valves per cylinder operated by single overhead camshaft
Bore and stroke: 3.35 in. x 3.46 in.
Displacement: 2,996 cc
Compression ratio: 8.5:1
Induction system: Bosch mechanical fuel injection
Maximum power: 240 bhp at 6,100 rpm
Maximum torque: 216 lb-ft at 4,800 rpm
Top speed: 165 mph
0–60 mph: 9 sec.

TRANSMISSION

Four-speed manual

BODY/CHASSIS

Steel and alloy two-door coupe with steel spaceframe chassis

SPECIAL FEATURES

Engines in early cars tended to overheat so these large vents were added to allow hot engine-bay air to escape.

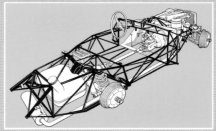

Spaceframe chassis was made light and strong, and was based on that of SL racers.

RUNNING GEAR

Steering: Recirculating ball
Front suspension: Twin wishbones with coil springs and telescopic shocks
Rear suspension: Swinging half axles with coil springs and telescopic shocks
Brakes: Drums all around
Wheels: Steel discs 5 in. x 15 in.
Tires: Crossply 6.7 in. x 15 in.

DIMENSIONS

Length: 178 in. **Width:** 70 in.
Height: 49.7 in. **Wheelbase:** 94 in.
Track: 54.5 in. (front), 56.5 in. (rear)
Weight: 2,850 lbs.

Mercedes E55 AMG

Any collaboration between Mercedes and its famous tuning partners, AMG, produces an outstanding car. With a V8 engine stretched to 5.4 liters and 354 bhp, the E55 is currently one of the fastest and most exclusive sport sedans on the market.

"...amazingly agile."

"Enormous V8 torque sends the bulky E55 through the ¼-mile in 14 seconds at well over 100 mph. More surprising is the accurate, well-weighted steering, which, combined with the lowered, stiffened suspension, results in amazingly agile handling for such a giant. The price to pay is a very harsh ride, particularly at low speeds, and lots of tire noise. Road holding is incredible and the massive brakes are easily among the world's best."

Luxury abounds inside the E55 with power everything and two-tone upholstery.

Milestones

1995 Mercedes introduces
its new E-Class, which fits in the range below the huge S-Class cars. The range includes the base 136-bhp, 2.0-liter E200, the 220-bhp, 3.2-liter six-cylinder E320, and the E420 with its 275-bhp, 4.2-liter V8.

A new, larger Mercedes E-Class went on sale in 1995.

1996 AMG and Mercedes
introduce the E50. It has an uprated 5.0-liter 32-valve V8 from the 500SL in the E-Class body distinguished by body extensions and 18-inch wheels. With its 347 bhp, it can rocket to 60 mph in 6.4 seconds.

Smaller brother to the E55 AMG is the C43 with a 4.3-liter V8.

1997 A new flagship for the
E-Class is introduced with the E55 AMG. Although fitted with a 5.4-liter 24-valve V8 developed from the existing E420 motor, power is up 7 bhp, but economy and emissions are better.

UNDER THE SKIN

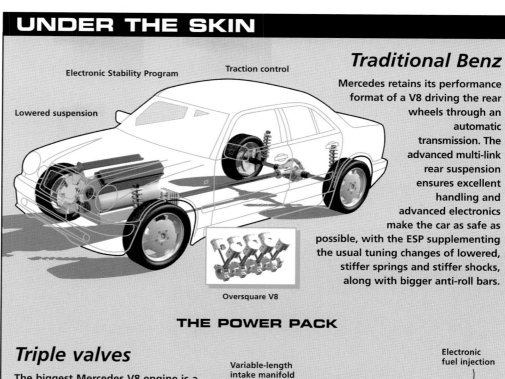

Electronic Stability Program

Traction control

Lowered suspension

Oversquare V8

Traditional Benz

Mercedes retains its performance format of a V8 driving the rear wheels through an automatic transmission. The advanced multi-link rear suspension ensures excellent handling and advanced electronics make the car as safe as possible, with the ESP supplementing the usual tuning changes of lowered, stiffer springs and stiffer shocks, along with bigger anti-roll bars.

THE POWER PACK

Triple valves

The biggest Mercedes V8 engine is a modular design, but with bore and stroke increased from the base 4.3 liter to an oversquare 5.4 liters. Alloy heads carry three valves per cylinder, with two inlets to maximize the fuel/air mixture fed into the engine. All are opened by a single camshaft for each bank of cylinders, and twin spark plugs fitted to each cylinder fire in quick succession to produce complete combustion. A variable-length intake manifold broadens the engine's torque curve.

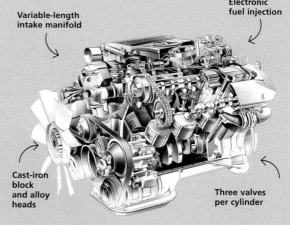

Variable-length intake manifold

Electronic fuel injection

Cast-iron block and alloy heads

Three valves per cylinder

Top Wagon

Incredibly, you can have virtually the same power and performance of the E55 AMG sedan in wagon form. The power and top speed are the same, but the extra weight and bulkier body mean the 0-60 and ¼-mile times are just 0.2 second slower.

A station wagon version of the E55 AMG is also offered.

Mercedes **E55 AMG**

The flagship of the E-Class range, the E55 AMG has it all. Plastic headlight lenses, ultrasonic parking, stability and traction control, plus outstanding performance—traditionally a hallmark of AMG tuned Mercedes.

Window airbags

E-Class Mercedes can have up to eight airbags. The most recent introductions are bags in the roof rail, which inflate to cover the side windows and protect against impact and broken glass.

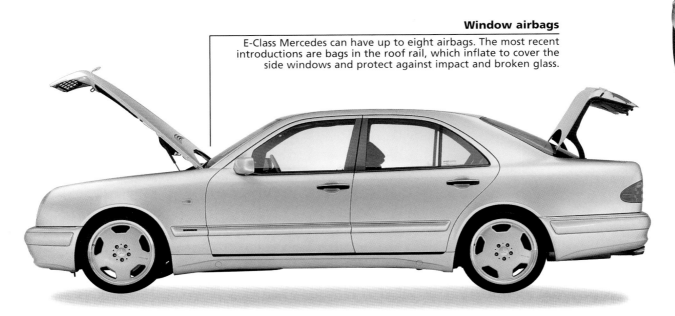

Electronic Stability Program

The Electronic Stability Program (ESP) sensors detect when a driven wheel is spinning and signal the engine management to reduce power. If that doesn't work immediately, just enough braking is applied to the wheel to restore control.

Parktronic assistance

Six sensors in the front bumper and four in the rear send ultrasonic signals that bounce off obstacles and illuminate a warning display on the dashboard.

Oval-shaped headlights

The distinctive oval-shaped and angled headlights have polycarbonate lenses, powerful gas diffusion bulbs and a high-pressure wash system.

Performance suspension

The suspension of the AMG has shorter, stiffer springs, uprated adjustable gas-pressurized shocks, and thicker anti-roll bars.

Three-valve engine

Mercedes has sacrificed one exhaust valve to make room for twin spark plugs, ensuring complete combustion and reduced emissions.

Specifications

1998 Mercedes-Benz E55 AMG

ENGINE

Type: V8

Construction: Cast-iron block and alloy heads

Valve gear: Three valves per cylinder (two inlet, one exhaust) operated by a single overhead camshaft per bank of cylinders

Bore and stroke: 3.82 in. x 3.62 in.

Displacement: 5,439 cc

Compression ratio: 10.5:1

Induction system: Electronic fuel injection

Maximum power: 354 bhp at 5,500 rpm

Maximum torque: 391 lb-ft at 3,000 rpm

Top speed: 155 mph

0–60 mph: 5.4 sec.

TRANSMISSION

Five-speed automatic

BODY/CHASSIS

Steel monocoque with four-door sedan body

SPECIAL FEATURES

Mercedes took a gamble with the E-Class by giving it these distinctive headlights.

Both front and rear wheels are a very large 18 inches in diameter.

RUNNING GEAR

Steering: Rack-and-pinion

Front suspension: Double wishbones with coil springs, telescopic shock absorbers and anti-roll bar

Rear suspension: Coil springs with telescopic shock absorbers and anti-roll bar

Brakes: Vented discs, 13.1-in. dia. (front), 11.8-in. dia. (rear)

Wheels: Alloy, 8 x 18 in. (front), 9 x 18 in. (rear)

Tires: 235/40 (front), 265/35 (rear)

DIMENSIONS

Length: 188.8 in.   **Width:** 78.5 in.

Height: 55.5 in.   **Wheelbase:** 111.5 in.

Track: 61.4 in. (front), 60.7 in. (rear)

Weight: 3,600 lbs.

Mercury COUGAR ELIMINATOR

A true performance Cougar emerged in 1969 and continued through 1970. Available with a long list of sports options, it posed a considerable threat to the established muscle cars both on the street and at the drag strip. Despite its potential, the Eliminator is often overlooked by enthusiasts today.

"...a gentleman's muscle car."

"With its wood-rimmed steering wheel and full instrumentation, the Cougar appears to be a gentleman's muscle car. Starting up the monster 428 engine reveals a totally different character. The big engine demands high-octane fuel and concentration on the open road. Its greatest asset is the huge amount of mid-range torque. A drag racer's dream, it is enough to humble any would-be challenger. It's quick enough to run the ¼ mile in 14.1 seconds."

This Eliminator has base model trim and is fitted with vinyl seats instead of leather ones.

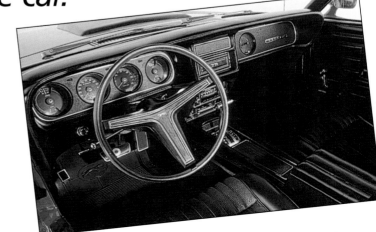

Milestones

1967 Two years after

Mustang, Mercury launches its own pony car, the Cougar. It features a distinctive front end with a razor-style grill and hidden headlights. Initially it is offered only as a hardtop.

Mercury's other 1969 muscle car was the Cyclone. This one is a Spoiler II.

1969 After minor updates

for 1968, the Cougar is restyled the following year and a convertible is now offered. A high performance model, the Eliminator, is launched mid-year and is available with a host of extra performance options, and was painted with 'high impact' exterior colors such as yellow blue, and orange.

The Cougar shares the 302 and 428 engines with the Mustang.

1970 The Eliminator

returns for its second and final season. Its body restyling is more refined than the 1969 model. Just over 2,000 cars are sold and the model is dropped after only two years of production.

UNDER THE SKIN

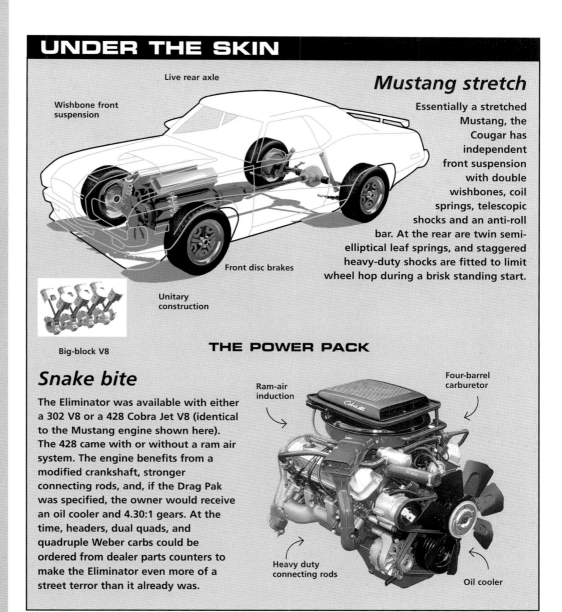

Live rear axle

Wishbone front suspension

Front disc brakes

Unitary construction

Big-block V8

Mustang stretch

Essentially a stretched Mustang, the Cougar has independent front suspension with double wishbones, coil springs, telescopic shocks and an anti-roll bar. At the rear are twin semi-elliptical leaf springs, and staggered heavy-duty shocks are fitted to limit wheel hop during a brisk standing start.

THE POWER PACK

Snake bite

The Eliminator was available with either a 302 V8 or a 428 Cobra Jet V8 (identical to the Mustang engine shown here). The 428 came with or without a ram air system. The engine benefits from a modified crankshaft, stronger connecting rods, and, if the Drag Pak was specified, the owner would receive an oil cooler and 4.30:1 gears. At the time, headers, dual quads, and quadruple Weber carbs could be ordered from dealer parts counters to make the Eliminator even more of a street terror than it already was.

Ram-air induction

Four-barrel carburetor

Heavy duty connecting rods

Oil cooler

Street racer

Since the Eliminator is longer and heavier than the Mustang, it is able get more grip and harness the power from the mighty 428 V8. Though the engine had a factory rating of 335 bhp it actually made closer to 410. The lower rating was to fool insurance companies.

The 1970 Eliminator is offers more refined body panels than the 1969 car.

Mercury **COUGAR ELIMINATOR**

This is Mercury's version of the high-performance Mustang. More refined than its baby brother, it still keeps the Ford heritage with bright paint, side stripes, spoilers, a hood scoop, and big block power.

'High Impact' paintwork

'High Impact' exterior colors was the order of the day in 1970. The Cougar was available in bright blue, yellow and Competition Orange as seen here.

Staggered shocks

Axle tramp can be a serious problem with smaller-sized performance Fords from this era, especially those with big engines. The Cougar Eliminator has staggered rear shock absorbers to help overcome this problem.

Cobra Jet engine

The Eliminator is available with either the 290-bhp Boss 302 or the more stout 428 Cobra Jet with a conservatively rated 335 bhp. This example is powered by the larger 428, often thought of as one of the finest muscle car engines ever produced.

Interior trim

Although more luxurious than the Mustang, the Eliminator is a base model Cougar and has vinyl upholstery. Full instrumentation is standard and includes a tachometer.

Drag Pak

This Eliminator is garnished with the legendary 'Drag Pak' option, which includes the 428 Super Cobra Jet engine, an oil cooler, and ultra-low rear-end gearing (3.91:1 or 4.30:1). This makes the Cougar one of the fastest accelerating muscle cars.

Restyled front

For 1970 the Cougar received a revised front grill with vertical bars and a more pronounced nose. The tail panel was also slightly altered.

Sequential turn indicators

The rear indicators, which are also combined with the brake lights, flash in sequence when the driver flicks the lever. These are also found on contemporary Shelby Mustangs.

Specifications
1970 Mercury Cougar Eliminator

ENGINE

Type: V8

Construction: Cast-iron block and heads

Valve gear: Two valves per cylinder operated by pushrods and rockers

Bore and stroke: 4.0 in. x 3.5 in.

Displacement: 428 c.i.

Compression ratio: 10.6:1

Induction system: Four-barrel carburetor

Maximum power: 335 bhp at 5,200 rpm

Maximum torque: 440 lb-ft at 3,400 rpm

Top speed: 106 mph

0–60 mph: 5.6 sec.

TRANSMISSION

C-6 Cruise-O-Matic

BODY/CHASSIS

Steel monocoque two-door coupe body

SPECIAL FEATURES

The headlights are concealed behind special 'flip-up' panels.

A rear Cougar spoiler is standard Eliminator equipment.

RUNNING GEAR

Steering: Recirculating ball

Front suspension: Unequal length wishbones with coil springs, telescopic shocks and anti-roll bar

Rear suspension: Semi-elliptical multi-leaf springs with staggered rear telescopic shocks

Brakes: Discs (front), drums (rear)

Wheels: Styled steel, 5 x 14 in.

Tires: F60-14 Goodyear Polyglas GT

DIMENSIONS

Length: 191.6 in.   **Width:** 77.6 in.

Height: 52.8 in.   **Wheelbase:** 111 in.

Track: 60 in. (front), 60 in. (rear)

Weight: 3,780 lbs.

MG METRO 6R4

Like Ford with its RS200, Austin-Rover tried to create the perfect Group B rally car, producing it just in time for the end of international Group B racing. With a mid-mounted V6, it is far removed from the standard Metro.

"...phenomenal traction."

"Austin-Rover made no attempt to turn the 6R4 into a road car. Even so, it is impressively flexible and has phenomenal traction. Unless the road is unbelievably slippery, it is almost impossible to generate wheelspin. The hard suspension, direct steering and short wheelbase mean the car is very agile. Once strapped into the 6R4, you will notice that it is incredibly noisy. Also, the heat from the engine and lack of insulation makes the cabin get uncomfortably warm inside."

Despite the stripped-out interior, the dash and door panels are identical to stock Metros.

Milestones

1981 Williams Grand Prix engineering begins
work on a new Group B mid-engined rally car for Austin-Rover.

Standard MG Metros were offered in normally-aspirated and turbo form.

1982 The first Rover V6-engined (a V8 with
two cylinders shaved off) car is completed at the end of the year.

1984 An interim car is unveiled in March,
and within months it goes on to win its first rally.

After Group B was banned, some 6R4s were used in track events.

1985 The last of the 200 cars needed to
homologate the 6R4 for Group B are built in November. The works cars debut in the Lombard RAC rally. One finishes third overall.

1986 Group B is
banned after many near fatal automobile accidents.

UNDER THE SKIN

Pure racer

Like many race cars, the 6R4 bears only a skin-deep resemblance to the stock Metro. The 6R4 is a full competition prototype. It has a tubular chassis with front and rear subframes and an integral roll cage. The suspension is comprised of coil springs and MacPherson struts in all four corners. Huge vented discs handle the braking chores, and all of the wheels are driven through a viscous-coupling center differential.

Vented discs front and rear

Tubular spaceframe chassis

All-wheel drive with center viscous coupling

24-valve V6

THE POWER PACK

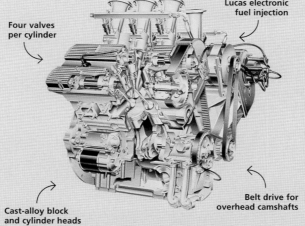

Four valves per cylinder

Lucas electronic fuel injection

Cast-alloy block and cylinder heads

Belt drive for overhead camshafts

Totally new V6

Although a Rover V8, chopped down to form a V6, was used in the prototype, production 6R4s have a bespoke V6. Dubbed the V6 4V—denoting a four-valve-per-cylinder V6 layout—the 2,991-cc engine has twin belt-driven camshafts per cylinder bank and is strongly reminiscent of the 1970s Cosworth DFV V8. Fuel is supplied through a Lucas electronic fuel injection system. Standard 6R4s produce 250 bhp, but later Evolution models have up to 410 bhp.

Evolution

After the initial 200 cars were finished, an additional 20 'Evolution' models were produced. Compared to the 250-bhp cars, the Evolution 6R4 produces 410 bhp, has a dog-leg gear shift, composite body material and several other options.

Evolution 6R4s have tweaked V6s and weigh less than the road-going Metro.

MG **METRO 6R4**

The Metro 6R4 is one of those unique supercars that was specifically created for racing in the now-defunct Group B rally championship. It was Leyland's last attempt to dominate world-class motorsports.

V6 engine

The engine is a 90-degree 3.0-liter quad-cam V6. The basic design was strong enough to be tweaked to produce more than 600 bhp in later, modified rallycross cars.

Built-in roll cage

The Metro 6R4 has an immensely strong structure, which is further strengthened by a full roll cage.

All-wheel drive

Power is fed to all four wheels through a five-speed transmission. The all-wheel drive has no fewer than three torque-splitting differentials. The rear differential is located within the engine oil pan.

Aerodynamic package

While the 6R4 was developed, a number of additional bits of bodywork were added. With the 'snowplow' front and tail styling, in addition to the roof-mounted rear spoiler, it earned itself the nickname '400-bhp shopping cart.'

Extended short wheelbase

Originally the 6R4 had an even shorter wheelbase. This made the car tricky to drive and thus it was extended as far as possible, giving very short front and rear overhangs.

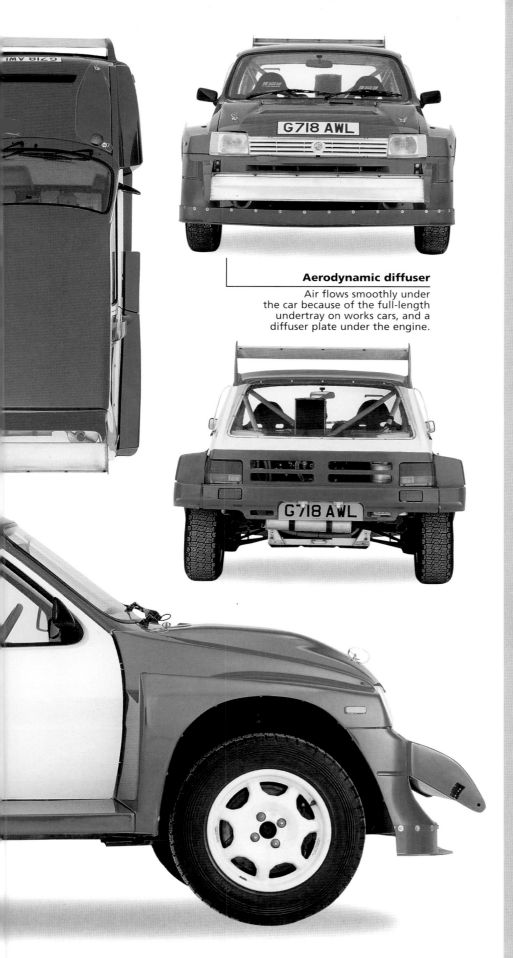

Aerodynamic diffuser

Air flows smoothly under the car because of the full-length undertray on works cars, and a diffuser plate under the engine.

Specifications

1985 MG Metro 6R4 Evolution*

ENGINE
Type: V6

Construction: Cast-alloy block and heads

Valve gear: Four valves per cylinder operated by two overhead camshafts per cylinder bank

Bore and stroke: 3.62 in. x 2.95 in.

Displacement: 2,991 cc

Compression ratio: 12.0:1

Induction system: Lucas electronic fuel injection

Maximum power: 410 bhp at 9,000 rpm

Maximum torque: 270 lb-ft at 6,500 rpm

Top speed: 140 mph

0–60 mph: 4.5 sec.

TRANSMISSION
Five-speed manual

BODY/CHASSIS
Chassis-less construction with multi-tubed underframe, suspension subframes and integral roll cage and carbonfiber and Kevlar body panels.

SPECIAL FEATURES

The huge side extensions contain the twin radiators to keep the engine cool.

Like most Group B cars, the whole rear panel can be removed for engine access.

RUNNING GEAR
Steering: Rack-and-pinion

Front suspension: Macpherson struts with lower wishbones, coil springs and anti-roll bar

Rear suspension: Macpherson struts with lower wishbones, coil springs and anti-roll bar

Brakes: Vented discs (front and rear)

Wheels: Magnesium alloy, 16-in. dia.

Tires: Michelin, 16-in. dia

DIMENSIONS
Length: 131.9 in.   **Width:** 74.0 in.

Height: 59.1 in.   **Wheelbase:** 94.1 in.

Track: 59.5 in. (front), 59.7 in. (rear)

Weight: 2,266 lbs.

*Details apply to 6R4 race version Evolution.

Mitsubishi 3000 GT

The Mitsubishi 3000GT is equipped with every high-tech performance extra available: a 281-bhp multi-cam V6, four-wheel steering, four-wheel drive and active aerodynamics. It is capable of challenging the best European cars.

"...amazing acceleration."

"As well as performance, the 3000GT offers comfort. The air conditioning can be accurately controlled to maintain a set temperature and the firm seats are infinitely adjustable. A full throttle take-off can be accomplished with little or no wheel spin and acceleration is amazing, with the car reaching 100 mph in just over 16.1 seconds. Four-wheel drive, four-wheel steering and four-wheel disc brakes ensure safe grip, handling and stopping."

The 3000GT combines supercar performance with luxury and comfort.

Milestones

1991 A Mitsubishi GT,
the 3000GT, is launched. The top-of-the-line twin-turbo VR-4 model offers supercar performance at around half the price. A Dodge-badged version, the Stealth, is also available.

Mitsubishi adopted the four-wheel-drive system for the 3000GT from the Gallant VR-4.

1995 The car is revamped
with a six-speed transmission, fixed headlights and other minor styling changes. The VR-4, with its 281-bhp twin-turbo V6 and four-wheel drive, remains the top of the range.

Mitsubishi's junior performance car is the Eclipse GSX.

1996 Dodge drops
the slow-selling Stealth, although the successful Mitsubishi 3000GT, with newly styled aluminum wheels, returns. Internally, the twin-turbo V6 is boosted to 320 bhp. Mitsubishi claims the 3000GT is "the most effective way to suspend the ageing process".

UNDER THE SKIN

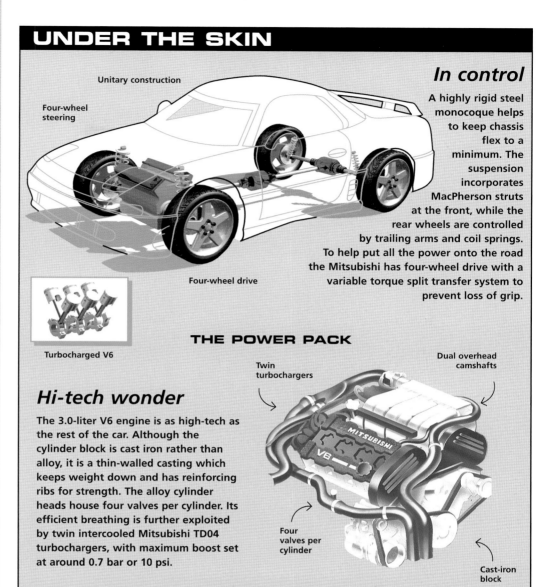

Unitary construction
Four-wheel steering
Four-wheel drive
Turbocharged V6

In control

A highly rigid steel monocoque helps to keep chassis flex to a minimum. The suspension incorporates MacPherson struts at the front, while the rear wheels are controlled by trailing arms and coil springs. To help put all the power onto the road the Mitsubishi has four-wheel drive with a variable torque split transfer system to prevent loss of grip.

THE POWER PACK

Twin turbochargers
Dual overhead camshafts
Four valves per cylinder
Cast-iron block

Hi-tech wonder

The 3.0-liter V6 engine is as high-tech as the rest of the car. Although the cylinder block is cast iron rather than alloy, it is a thin-walled casting which keeps weight down and has reinforcing ribs for strength. The alloy cylinder heads house four valves per cylinder. Its efficient breathing is further exploited by twin intercooled Mitsubishi TD04 turbochargers, with maximum boost set at around 0.7 bar or 10 psi.

Updated

After 1995, 3000GTs differ only in detail from earlier models. The biggest change is a six-speed transmission in place of the five-speed. In addition, dramatic-looking fixed headlights replace the 'pop-up' units and the tail lights are slightly altered.

Post-1994 models have slightly different styling.

Mitsubishi **3000 GT**

Introduced in 1991, the Mitsubishi 3000GT bristled with the highest technology. Few cars are able to offer comparable performance at a similar price.

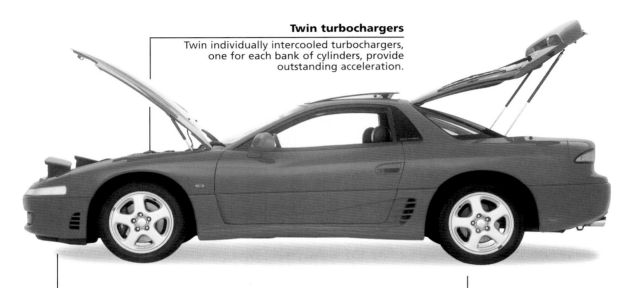

Twin turbochargers

Twin individually intercooled turbochargers, one for each bank of cylinders, provide outstanding acceleration.

Active aerodynamics

Above 50 mph a motorized spoiler lip extends down from the front bumper to form a smooth plane over the bottom of the car, that provides ground effect.

Four-wheel drive

The 3000GT's permanent four-wheel drive system features a viscous coupling between the front and rear wheels.

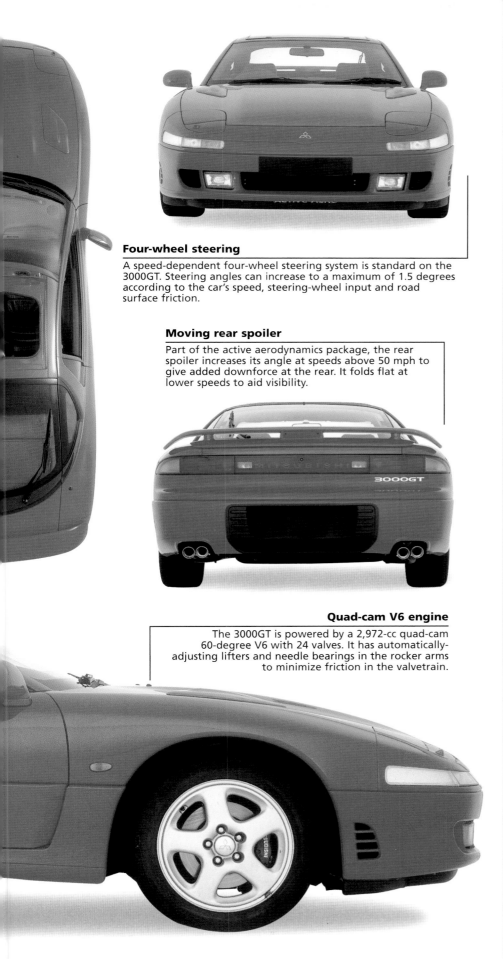

Four-wheel steering

A speed-dependent four-wheel steering system is standard on the 3000GT. Steering angles can increase to a maximum of 1.5 degrees according to the car's speed, steering-wheel input and road surface friction.

Moving rear spoiler

Part of the active aerodynamics package, the rear spoiler increases its angle at speeds above 50 mph to give added downforce at the rear. It folds flat at lower speeds to aid visibility.

Quad-cam V6 engine

The 3000GT is powered by a 2,972-cc quad-cam 60-degree V6 with 24 valves. It has automatically-adjusting lifters and needle bearings in the rocker arms to minimize friction in the valvetrain.

Specifications

1991 Mitsubishi 3000GT

ENGINE

Type: V6

Construction: Cast-iron thin-walled block and alloy cylinder heads

Valve gear: Four valves per cylinder operated by twin overhead camshafts per cylinder bank

Bore and stroke: 3.59 in. x 3 in.

Displacement: 2,972 cc

Compression ratio: 8.0:1

Induction system: Electronic multipoint fuel injection and twin turbochargers

Maximum power: 281 bhp at 6,000 rpm

Maximum torque: 300 lb-ft at 3,000 rpm

Top speed: 152 mph

0–60 mph: 6.0 sec.

TRANSMISSION

Five-speed manual with four-wheel drive

BODY/CHASSIS

Steel monocoque two-door coupe body

SPECIAL FEATURES

The rear spoiler can be raised and lowered. It's part of the active aerodynamics package.

A state-of-the-art video screen shows variations in temperature control settings.

RUNNING GEAR

Steering: Power-assisted rack-and-pinion

Front suspension: MacPherson struts with electronically-adjustable telescopic shocks and anti-roll bar

Rear suspension: Double wishbones with trailing arms, coil springs, electronically-adjustable shocks and anti-roll bar

Brakes: Vented discs, 12.3-in. dia. (front), 11.8-in. dia. (rear)

Wheels: Alloy, 7.5 x 17 in.

Tires: Dunlop Sports 225/50 ZR17

DIMENSIONS

Length: 179.5 in.   **Width:** 72.4 in.

Height: 50.6 in.   **Wheelbase:** 97.2 in.

Track: 61.4 in. (front), 61.4 in. (rear)

Weight: 3,990 lbs.

JAPAN 1998

Mitsubishi **LANCER EVO V**

Tommi Makinen, driving Mitsubishi's Lancer, won the World Rally Championship in 1996, 1997 and 1998. The roadgoing version of this car is the very rare four-wheel drive Evo V, which boasts a 276-bhp turbocharged engine and stunning acceleration.

"...balanced perfection."

"There are more powerful cars, but none will hurl you to 30 mph like the Evo V with its perfect four-wheel drive traction. But it's not just the turbo surge past 3,000 rpm that is so impressive. Phenomenal grip makes the Evo feel glued to the road, whatever the conditions. The handling represents balanced perfection, and if you do reach a corner too quickly, you can take comfort that the brakes are among the best in the world."

White-faced instruments and steering wheel hint at the Evo's performance character.

Milestones

1993 Mitsubishi launches the GSR

Evolution version of the Lancer. This retains the 1,997-cc engine and evolves steadily, gaining more power and speed.

The Evo is quickly carving a niche as an all-time rally great.

1998 Although teammate Richard Burns

wins in the Safari Rally in Africa, Tommi Makinen draws a blank there but wins in Argentina.

1998 Driven by Makinen, the Mitsubishi

wins in Finland, followed by further wins in San Remo and Australia.

The Mitsubishi Eclipse uses a version of the Lancer's engine.

1998 Although Makinen unluckily

goes out early in the final round of the championship in Britain, teammate Burns wins with the Lancer and Makinen becomes champion again.

UNDER THE SKIN

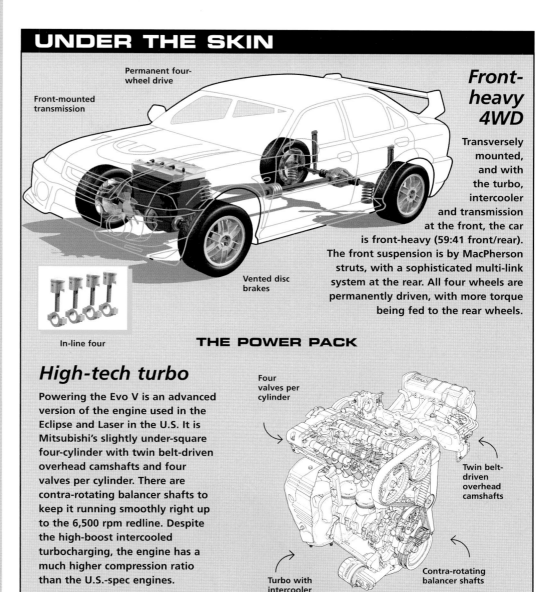

Permanent four-wheel drive

Front-mounted transmission

Vented disc brakes

In-line four

Front-heavy 4WD

Transversely mounted, and with the turbo, intercooler and transmission at the front, the car is front-heavy (59:41 front/rear). The front suspension is by MacPherson struts, with a sophisticated multi-link system at the rear. All four wheels are permanently driven, with more torque being fed to the rear wheels.

THE POWER PACK

High-tech turbo

Powering the Evo V is an advanced version of the engine used in the Eclipse and Laser in the U.S. It is Mitsubishi's slightly under-square four-cylinder with twin belt-driven overhead camshafts and four valves per cylinder. There are contra-rotating balancer shafts to keep it running smoothly right up to the 6,500 rpm redline. Despite the high-boost intercooled turbocharging, the engine has a much higher compression ratio than the U.S.-spec engines.

Four valves per cylinder

Twin belt-driven overhead camshafts

Contra-rotating balancer shafts

Turbo with intercooler

Title winner

For a collector, the car to have is one of Mitsubishi's World Rally Championship winners, ideally the car that took Tommi Makinen to his third straight title win for Mitsubishi. With more than 300 bhp it has much more power than the road car.

The rally version has a higher power-to-weight ratio than the road car.

Mitsubishi **LANCER EVO V**

The Evo V looks fantastic, but none of it is just cosmetic. All the features that make it look so stunning, such as the vast front air dam, big wheels, rear spoiler and hood scoops, are all there for performance.

Intercooled turbocharger

Mitsubishi uses its own turbocharger, which pumps in air at a high maximum boost of 16 psi. Such a high boost is partly made possible by the massive intercooler.

Twin-cam engine

In the U.S. market—in the Eclipse—the Evo's four-cylinder 16-valve twin-cam engine has 66 bhp less, at just 210 bhp, as well as 60 lb-ft of torque less than the Evo V's 274 lb-ft.

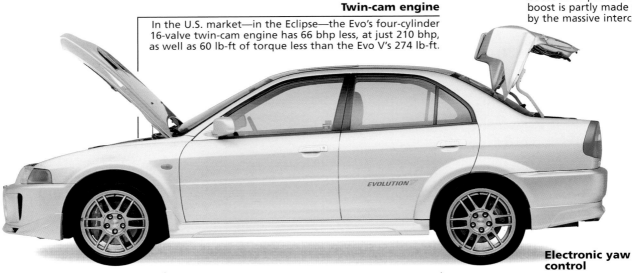

Tall wheels

The alloy wheels fitted to the Evo V are very tall, at 17 inches in diameter. One reason is to allow room for the extremely large disc brakes.

Multi-link rear

A complex multi-link rear suspension system with twin angled transverse links per side keeps the wheels on the road.

Electronic yaw control

The rear differential detects excessive under- or oversteer and varies the torque split to the two rear wheels to restore balance.

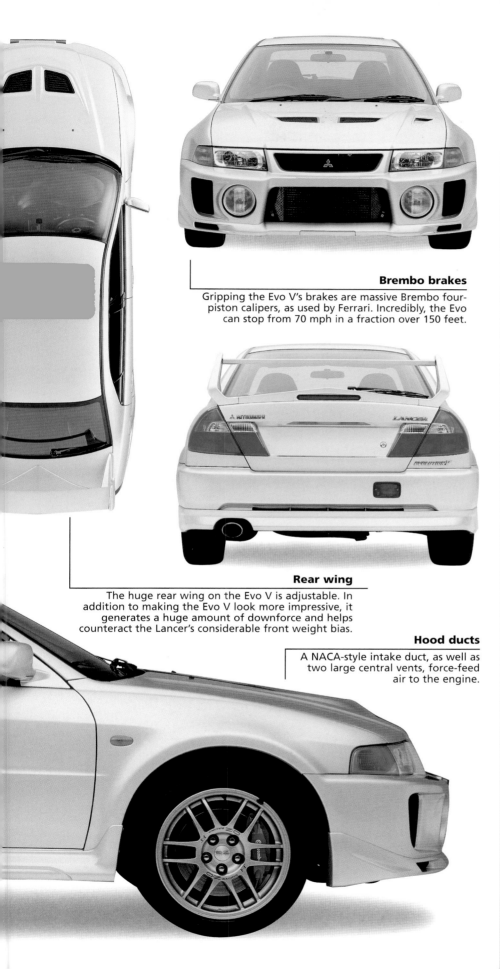

Brembo brakes

Gripping the Evo V's brakes are massive Brembo four-piston calipers, as used by Ferrari. Incredibly, the Evo can stop from 70 mph in a fraction over 150 feet.

Rear wing

The huge rear wing on the Evo V is adjustable. In addition to making the Evo V look more impressive, it generates a huge amount of downforce and helps counteract the Lancer's considerable front weight bias.

Hood ducts

A NACA-style intake duct, as well as two large central vents, force-feed air to the engine.

Specifications

1998 Mitsubishi Lancer Evo V

ENGINE

Type: In-line four-cylinder

Construction: Alloy block and head

Valve gear: Four valves per cylinder operated by twin overhead camshafts

Bore and stroke: 3.35 in. x 3.46 in.

Displacement: 1,997 cc

Compression ratio: 8.8:1

Induction system: Electronic fuel injection with intercooled turbocharger

Maximum power: 276 bhp at 6,500 rpm

Maximum torque: 274 lb-ft at 3,000 rpm

Top speed: 147 mph

0–60 mph: 4.7 sec.

TRANSMISSION

Five-speed manual

BODY/CHASSIS

Unitary monocoque construction with steel sedan body

SPECIAL FEATURES

Massive Brembo calipers are fitted to the Evo's vented disc brakes.

Rear wings usually play a cosmetic role, but the Evo's maximizes downforce.

RUNNING GEAR

Steering: Rack-and-pinion

Front suspension: MacPherson struts with lower wishbones, coil springs, telescopic shock absorbers and anti-roll bar

Rear suspension: Multi-link with coil springs, telescopic shock absorbers and anti-roll bar

Brakes: Vented discs, 12.6-in. dia. (front), 12-in. dia. (rear).

Wheels: Alloy, 7.5 x 17 in.

Tires: Bridgestone Potenza SO-1, 225/45 ZR17

DIMENSIONS

Length: 171.3 in.   **Width:** 73.8 in.

Height: 55.9 in.   **Wheelbase:** 98.8 in.

Track: 59.4 in. (front), 59.3 in. (rear)

Weight: 3,160 lbs.

Nissan **300ZX TURBO**

Using the Porsche 944 Turbo as its target, Japanese giant Nissan set to transform the image of its cumbersome 300ZX—a task in which it succeeded. The new model was one of the fastest and best-handling sports cars of its day.

"...smooth, luxurious and fast."

"It's 1969, and you're driving the original 240ZX, a pure, hard-edged sports car that will inspire thousands of enthusiasts and produce a highly collectible classic. By 1984, the Z car is suffering from middle-age bloat, so a new team of experts cooks up a leaner, meaner, tastier dish. Now it's 1990, and the cult of the Z car has been recaptured with the 300ZX. You've got advanced four-wheel steering, twin intercooled turbos, plus a 20 percent stiffer 'box. It's smooth, luxurious and fast—but not as pure as the original."

Often described as the "Japanese Corvette," the feel of 300ZX cockpit is purposeful and refined.

Milestones

1984 The line that started with the original 240Z in 1969 culminates in the bloated and ugly 300ZX—it was time for a fundamental change. Nissan creates a new project team to go back to basics and design a world-beating Z car for the 1990s.

Nissan's new 300ZX Turbo was blisteringly fast, and had the braking to match.

1989 New 300ZX is launched on the vital American market after making its world debut in February at the Chicago Motor Show.

At last Nissan's Z car had a chassis to match its great performance.

1990 The 300ZX becomes available in Europe.

1992 To broaden the car's appeal a two-seater convertible is introduced, unveiled at the Detroit Motor Show, showing how important the North American market continues to be for Nissan.

UNDER THE SKIN

Computer designed

The suspension sets the Nissan apart. With the help of two huge Cray supercomputers, double-wishbone suspension was developed to complement the four-wheel steering system which comes into operation at high speed. Such precise suspension also required an extremely stiff bodyshell and the 300ZX's is 20 percent stiffer than the previous ZX.

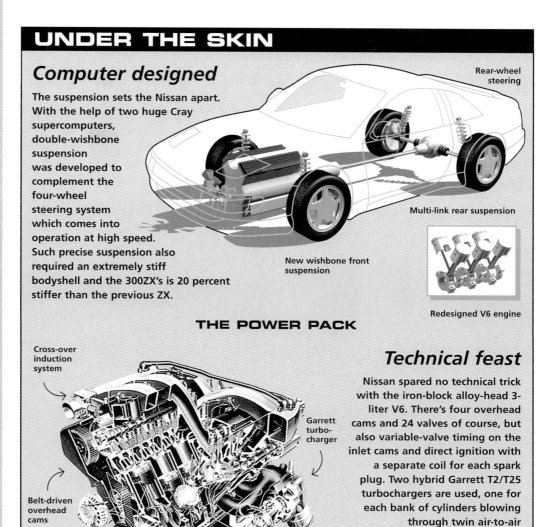

Rear-wheel steering

Multi-link rear suspension

New wishbone front suspension

Redesigned V6 engine

THE POWER PACK

Cross-over induction system

Garrett turbo-charger

Belt-driven overhead cams

Cast-iron block

Technical feast

Nissan spared no technical trick with the iron-block alloy-head 3-liter V6. There's four overhead cams and 24 valves of course, but also variable-valve timing on the inlet cams and direct ignition with a separate coil for each spark plug. Two hybrid Garrett T2/T25 turbochargers are used, one for each bank of cylinders blowing through twin air-to-air intercoolers. For engine tuning, the induction pipes from each turbo are very long, each running across the engine.

Less is more

The pick of the bunch for the real enthusiast is the two-seater. It's shorter by around 15 inches, so it's lighter and, with a 5-inch shorter wheelbase, even more agile. Better still is the two-seater convertible available in 1992; Nissan's first fully open Z car.

Shorter wheelbase makes the two-seater more compact and desirable.

Nissan **300ZX TURBO**

In 1990, the 300ZX was the most advanced and complicated sports car Nissan had ever built. It was gimmicky, but all the advanced technology was there for a good reason—to enable it to compete on equal terms with the best in the world.

Multi-link front suspension

The 300ZX's variation on front wishbone suspension is a curious design, with the upper arms almost level with the top of the coil springs, and actually projecting out over the top of each wheel.

Quad-cam V6

The V6 engine is a redesign of the V6 used in the previous 300ZX, with four cams and four valves per cylinder plus variable-valve timing. A 222-bhp normally aspirated version was available as well as the powerful turbo.

Twin turbos

Twin turbochargers give a quicker response than a single larger turbo does and they also reduce turbo lag.

Multi-link rear suspension

Not only does a multi-link system give good wheel control on the 300ZX, it's designed to give a small amount of toe-in under both braking and acceleration to keep the car stable.

Removable roof panels

The 300ZX's sunroof does not slide in the conventional way— the panels are removed manually and then stowed in a vinyl pouch in the trunk.

Four-wheel steering

Some four-wheel steering systems are designed to make the car more maneuverable at low speeds, for easy parking, for example. The 300ZX's was designed to operate only at high speeds to improve cornering and lane changing.

Intercooler vents

The vents below the square spotlights feed air to the engine's two intercoolers. An oil cooler is also mounted to the front.

Direct ignition

Each of the six cylinders has a spark plug with its own coil. Signals from the crankshaft-angle sensor determine when each coil fires. It's an absolutely precise system.

Flush-fitting glass

Nissan followed Audi's lead in equipping the 300ZX with flush-fitting side glass which looks more stylish and is also more aerodynamically efficient.

Specifications
1990 Nissan 300ZX Turbo

ENGINE
Type: V6
Construction: Cast-iron block and alloy cylinder heads
Valve gear: Four valves per cylinder operated by four overhead camshafts; variable timing on inlet cams
Bore and stroke: 3.4 in. x 3.3 in.
Displacement: 2,960 cc
Compression ratio: 8.5:1
Induction system: Electronic fuel injection with twin Garrett T2/25 intercooled turbochargers
Maximum power: 300 bhp at 6,400 rpm
Maximum torque: 273 lb-ft at 3,600 rpm
Top speed: 155 mph
0–60 mph: 5.8 sec.

TRANSMISSION
Five-speed manual

BODY/CHASSIS
Steel monocoque with two-door coupe, two-seater or 2+2 body

SPECIAL FEATURES

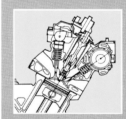

Twin cams on each bank of cylinders operate angled valves, with variable intake timing. Only one bank of cylinders is shown here.

Nissan's headlight supplier, Ichiko Kogyo, made a new glass pressing process for body-contoured headlights.

RUNNING GEAR
Steering: Rack-and-pinion
Front suspension: Multi-link with lower wishbones, coil springs, telescopic shocks and anti-roll bar
Rear suspension: Multi-link with coil springs, shocks and anti-roll bar
Brakes: Vented discs with ABS
Wheels: Cast-alloy 16 in.
Tires: 225/50 ZR16 (front), 245/45 ZR16 (rear)

DIMENSIONS
Length: 178.2 in. **Width:** 70.9 in.
Height: 49.4 in. **Wheelbase:** 101.2 in.
Track: 58.9 in. (front), 60.4 in. (rear)
Weight: 3,485 lbs.

Nissan SKYLINE TURBO

The Skyline may be Nissan's oldest nameplate, dating back to 1955, but the GT-R is part of the modern supercar era. An ultra-high-performance machine crammed with high technology, it is one of the fastest four seaters in the world.

"...maximum boosted power"

"It may have a huge rear spoiler and fat alloy wheels but, otherwise, the two-door GT-R doesn't look that special. Underneath, however, Nissan has created one of the most memorable driving machines ever. Keep the revs up to maintain maximum boosted power to enjoy all the performance you'll need. The steering is full of feel and the huge brakes are massively powerful. This is one of the world's quickest cars on winding roads."

The Skyline boasts a functional interior with excellent contoured bucket seats.

Milestones

1989 The first Skyline GT-R

is unveiled as an ultra-high-performance version of the new, smoother-looking eighth-generation Skyline model.

The last real high performance sports car that Nissan made was the 300ZX.

1994 A new ninth-generation

Skyline is launched, together with an improved GT-R V-Spec model. The car is sold in only right-hand-drive Far Eastern markets — mainly Japan and Australia.

The next fastest car in the current Nissan line-up is the 200SX.

1997 Having astounded

the motoring press the world over, the GT-R makes its debut on the British market. As a very limited volume model just 100 are available in the first year. It becomes the quickest production car to lap the famous 14-mile Nürburgring circuit.

UNDER THE SKIN

High technology

Underneath, the Skyline GT-R is a haven of technological excellence. The shell itself is stiffened with tie-bars in the engine bay and trunk. State-of-the-art multi-link suspension provides excellent handling, and traction is aided by a split-torque system to the front and rear wheels. An active rear-wheel steer set-up eliminates understeer, and braking is provided by large-diameter vented discs.

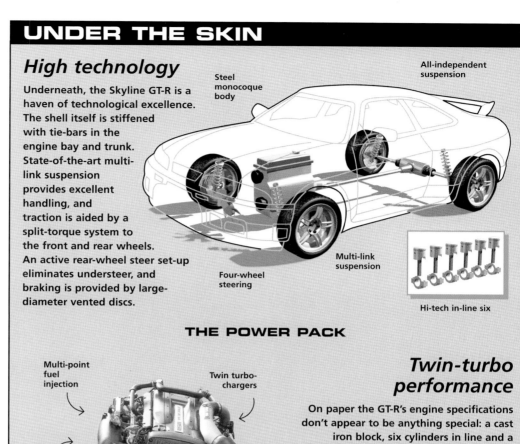

Steel monocoque body

All-independent suspension

Multi-link suspension

Four-wheel steering

Hi-tech in-line six

THE POWER PACK

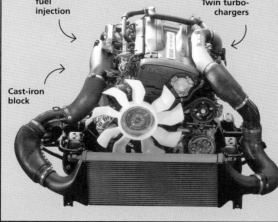

Multi-point fuel injection

Twin turbo-chargers

Cast-iron block

Twin-turbo performance

On paper the GT-R's engine specifications don't appear to be anything special: a cast iron block, six cylinders in line and a maximum output of 277 bhp. However, the GT-R powerplant should not be underestimated. With sequential multi-point fuel injection, four valves per cylinder, twin overhead cams, twin Garrett T3 hybrid ceramic turbochargers, and individual throttle bodies for each cylinder, it wouldn't be out of place competing on the racetrack. The GT-R's power output can easily be boosted to nearly 500 bhp.

Awesome

The GT-R is an awesome machine in any form. It is offered as a two-door coupe or limited edition four-door sedan. For even more exclusivity and much more power, try the Autech-modified version, developed by Nissan's performance car division.

The GT-R offers outrageous performance by any standards.

Nissan SKYLINE GTR

This car holds the record for the fastest lap by a production car at the famous Nürburgring circuit in Germany. The GT-R is a true performance machine for the keenest drivers.

Highly-tunable engine

The in-line six-cylinder engine is capable of delivering much more than it does in standard tune, since the GT-R's top speed is limited electronically to 135 mph. Most owners upgrade the engine's electronic management system to yield an extra 80 bhp.

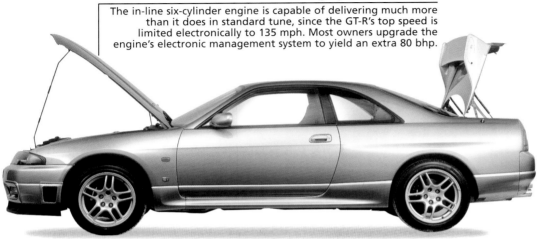

Active limited-slip differential

To prevent the rear tires from scrabbling under heavy acceleration, sensors on each rear wheel detect tire slip and automatically transfer more power to another wheel. Each wheel has its own multi-plate clutch so that the torque is infinitely variable between the wheels. Computer adjustments are made every 100th of a second.

Torque-split four-wheel drive

A computer-controlled four-wheel drive system provides optimum traction. Normally, 100 percent of drive is directed to the rear axle. Sensors analyze the car's traction and stability every 100th of a second. Up to 50 percent of the engine's torque can be directed to the front wheels.

Four-wheel steering

The Super HICAS four-wheel steering system has multiple sensors which detect steering input, turning rate, the car's speed, its yaw rate, and the lateral g-forces. It then calculates the amount of rear-wheel steer to be applied via an electric motor.

Adjustable rear spoiler

The body-colored rear spoiler mounted on the trunk lid is adjustable. It forms part of the GT-R body package, which also includes flared wheel arches, side skirts, an inset mesh grill and a deep front bumper/air dam.

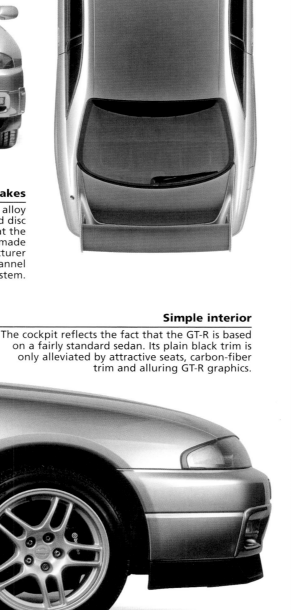

Racing brakes

Behind the double five-spoke alloy wheels are very large vented disc brakes. They are 12.8 inch across at the front (with four-piston calipers made by Italian racing brake manufacturer Brembo). There is also a four-channel ABS anti-lock braking system.

Simple interior

The cockpit reflects the fact that the GT-R is based on a fairly standard sedan. Its plain black trim is only alleviated by attractive seats, carbon-fiber trim and alluring GT-R graphics.

Specifications

1998 Nissan Skyline GT-R

ENGINE

Type: In-line six-cylinder

Construction: Cast-iron cylinder block and aluminum cylinder head

Valve gear: Four valves per cylinder operated by double overhead camshafts

Bore and stroke: 3.38 in. x 2.91 in.

Displacement: 2,568 cc

Compression ratio: 8.5:1

Induction system: Sequential multi-point fuel injection

Maximum power: 277 bhp at 6,800 rpm

Maximum torque: 271 lb-ft at 4,400 rpm

Top speed: 155 mph

0–60 mph: 5.6 sec.

TRANSMISSION

Five-speed manual

BODY/CHASSIS

Integral with two-door steel and aluminum coupe body

SPECIAL FEATURES

The rear spoiler is adjustable for rake to give varying amounts of down force.

Ferrari-style circular tail lights evoke a thoroughbred, racing flavor.

RUNNING GEAR

Steering: Rack-and-pinion

Front suspension: Multi-link with coil springs, telescopic shocks, and anti-roll bar

Rear suspension: Multi-link with coil springs telescopic shocks, and anti-roll bar

Brakes: Vented discs, 12.8-in. dia. (front), 11.8-in. dia. (rear)

Wheels: Alloy, 17-in. dia.

Tires: 245/45 ZR17

DIMENSIONS

Length: 184 in.   **Width:** 70.1 in.

Height: 53.5 in.   **Wheelbase:** 107.1 in.

Track: 58.3 in. (front), 57.9 in. (rear)

Weight: 3,530 lbs.

Oldsmobile 4-4-2 W30

While the 1968 4-4-2 had plenty of power with its 400-cubic inch V8 engine, this stock-looking Oldsmobile street machine has been modified with a massive 455 V8 that makes the kind of power found only in the limited edition Hurst-modified cars.

"...fast and fun street machine."

"The 1968 Oldsmobile 4-4-2 came with a W-30 360-bhp 400-cubic inch engine with the new, forced-air option. This custom example, however, has a full-size 455-cubic inch Rocket motor with added performance parts, similar to the Hurst/Olds introduced that same year. With a 410 bhp under the hood and a convertible top, this 4-4-2 is a fast and fun street machine. It accelerates like a rocket and handles better than most cars of its era."

The interior remains relatively stock, but the engine under the hood is a different story.

Milestones

1964 The 4-4-2
nameplate debuts as a package option on the mid-size F-85™.

1965 The standard
4-4-2 engine is a destroked and debored 425 V8 creating the new 400-cubic inch V8.

Early 4-4-2s have more square bodywork than the later cars.

1967 Tri-power
induction is offered for one year and the engine makes 360 bhp.

1968 A restyled body
gives the 4-4-2 a more elegant look. 3,000 modified versions known as the Hurst/Olds are offered with 455 engines.

The 1970 W-30 came with a big 455 V8 and fiberglass hood.

1970 A 455-cubic
inch engine becomes available with Oldsmobile's "select fit" parts. The W-30 455 makes 370 bhp, but its 14.3 quarter mile time suggests this car made more power. These cars had fiberglass hoods and plastic fender liners.

UNDER THE SKIN

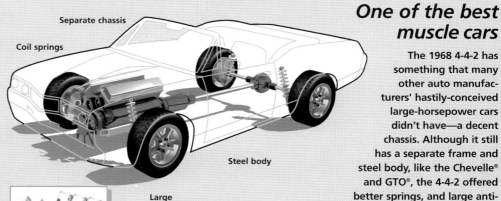

Separate chassis

Coil springs

Steel body

Large displacement engine

Toronado™ V8

One of the best muscle cars

The 1968 4-4-2 has something that many other auto manufacturers' hastily-conceived large-horsepower cars didn't have—a decent chassis. Although it still has a separate frame and steel body, like the Chevelle® and GTO®, the 4-4-2 offered better springs, and large anti-sway bars for an improved ride and handling.

THE POWER PACK

Full-size V8

After 1965 the first '4' in 4-4-2 stood for the size of the standard 400-cubic inch engine. Oldsmobile destroked and debored its full-size 425 V8 engine just for the 4-4-2. For 1966, Olds™ offered a tri-carburetors boosting power to 360 bhp (right). In 1970, its size was increased again to 455. It was the biggest and most powerful engine Olds ever offered. The owner of the model featured here has replaced the factory 400 V8 engine with a 455-cubic inch Rocket motor that makes 410 bhp thanks to special modifications.

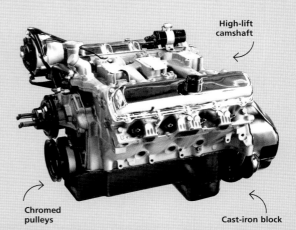

High-lift camshaft

Chromed pulleys

Cast-iron block

Convertible

The new 1968 range of 4-4-2 models updated the earlier cars. At the top of the new range, above the hardtop coupe, was the convertible. It offered incredible value for this type of car, not to mention loads of fun with the top down in the summer.

The convertible top and stock wheels give this 4-4-2 a stealth-like look.

Oldsmobile **4-4-2 W30**

The 4-4-2 was one of the best muscle cars of the 1960s. It has incredible performance and, unlike many of its rivals, it also has the agility and braking to match the speed.

4-4-2 badging

By 1968 the 4-4-2 nameplate had become familiar and sought-after property. Badging in the grill announced that you were driving something special.

Custom paint

The bodywork has been sprayed with a base coat of Infinity White paint, followed by a clear coat to give a deep, high gloss finish.

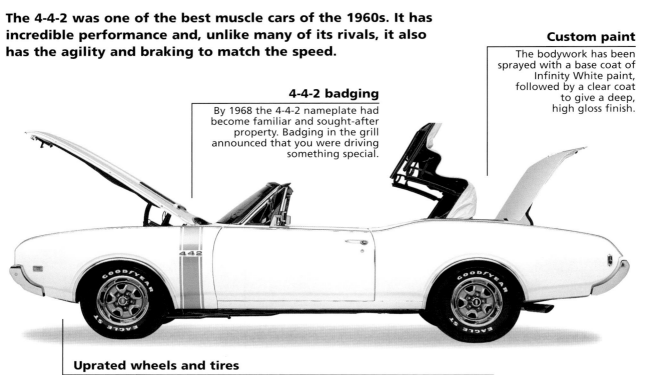

Uprated wheels and tires

The 1968 4-4-2 had 14-inch diameter wheels, but the owner of this car has chosen to upgrade to 15-inch Super Stock II rims, shod with Goodyear Eagle ST tires.

Improved cabin

As well as 1970 Gold Madrid interior, this particular car features full GM and AutoGauge instruments and a 'Rallye' steering wheel.

Heavy-duty suspension

The rear end has been beefed up by replacing the stock coil springs with heavy-duty springs from a station wagon. Modern polyurethane bushings and 1⁷/₈-inch thick front and rear anti-roll bars have also been added to tighten the suspension further.

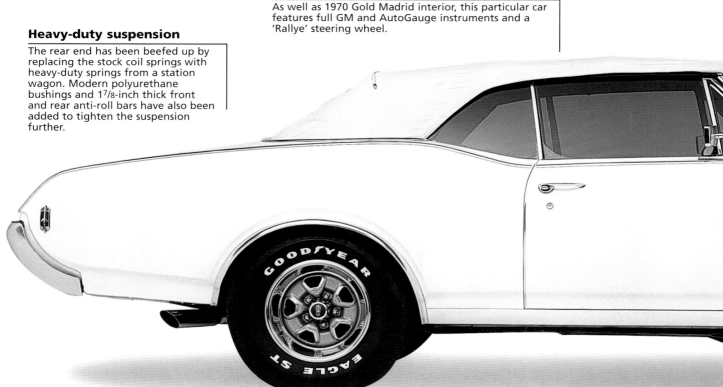

Sharp steering

To improve handling, the owner installed a quick-ratio steering box. This means the wheel has to be turned less when cornering.

Big 455 V8

Although the 455 V8 engine was not offered in the 1968 4-4-2, it was available in a special edition called the Hurst/Olds. It became standard for all 4-4-2 models in 1970.

Specifications

Oldsmobile 4-4-2 Convertible

ENGINE

Type: V8

Construction: Cast-iron cylinder block and cylinder heads

Valve gear: Two valves per cylinder operated by a single camshaft

Bore and stroke: 4.12 in. x 4.25 in.

Displacement: 455 c.i.

Compression ratio: 10.5:1

Induction system: Four-barrel carburetor

Maximum power: 410 bhp at 5,500 rpm

Maximum torque: 517 lb-ft at 3,500 rpm

Top speed: 154 mph

0–60 mph: 6.8 sec.

TRANSMISSION

Turbo HydraMatic 350 three-speed automatic

BODY/CHASSIS

Separate chassis with two-door convertible steel body

SPECIAL FEATURES

The interior has been taken from a 1970 Oldsmobile and features Gold Madrid vinyl upholstery.

On this modified car, the exhaust tips exit behind the rear tires rather than out of the back as on the standard 4-4-2s.

RUNNING GEAR

Steering: Recirculating ball

Front suspension: Wishbones with coil springs, shocks, and anti-roll bar

Rear suspension: Rigid axle with coil springs, shocks, and anti-roll bar

Brakes: Discs front, drums rear

Wheels: Super Stock II, 15-in. dia.

Tires: Goodyear Eagle ST

DIMENSIONS

Length: 201.6 in.   **Width:** 76.2 in.

Height: 52.8 in.   **Wheelbase:** 112 in.

Track: 59.1 in. (front), 59.1 in. (rear)

Curb weight: 3,890 lbs.

Plymouth **HEMI 'CUDA**

As a muscle car legend, there are few cars to rival a 1970 Hemi 'Cuda. It has classic, well-proportioned good looks and an engine that is just as famous as the car itself. Despite its relative rarity, some owners feel the need to build themselves a better Hemi 'Cuda.

"...the definitive Plymouth."

"The Hemi 'Cuda is the definitive Plymouth muscle car. It combines a great looking body style with the fearsome Hemi powerplant. Slip behind the steering wheel of this modified 'Cuda and prepare for an adventure. Off the line it is obvious that this engine has been modified. Next you notice that the huge modern tires grip fantastically. Power-shifting into second causing the rear tires to screach reveals this Hemi 'Cuda's explosive acceleration."

This 'Cuda retains a stock interior including a pistol grip shifter and multiple gauges.

Milestones

1964 The Barracuda is launched
as Plymouth's retaliation to Ford's successful Mustang. It is built on the Valiant platform and has fastback coupe styling. Top engine option is the 273-cubic inch V8.

The 1967 GTX was just one of Plymouth's many Hemi powered muscle cars.

1967 A more powerful
383-cubic inch V8 gives the Barracuda more performance.

1968 The Hemi engine
is finally fitted to a small number of 'Cudas.

The Duster was Plymouth's entry level muscle car for 1970.

1970 The 'Cuda is restyled
with Chrysler's new E-body. The Hemi is now a real production option, and 652 hardtops and 14 convertibles are manufactured.

1971 The Hemi engine
is retained for one final year. Power remains at 425 bhp and 490 lb-ft of torque.

UNDER THE SKIN

Solid as a rock

Based on Chrysler's E-body, the 'Cuda uses a steel monocoque. The front suspension uses double wishbones with torsion bar springing. The rear is more conventional with a semi-elliptic leaf-sprung live rear axle. This car has Koni adjustable shock absorbers in place of the standard Chrysler units. Disc brakes are in the front, while drums are in the rear.

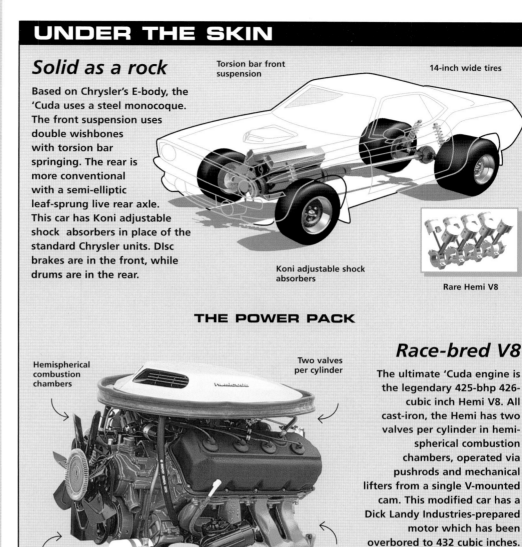

Torsion bar front suspension

14-inch wide tires

Koni adjustable shock absorbers

Rare Hemi V8

THE POWER PACK

Hemispherical combustion chambers

Two valves per cylinder

Forged steel crankshaft

All cast-iron construction

Race-bred V8

The ultimate 'Cuda engine is the legendary 425-bhp 426-cubic inch Hemi V8. All cast-iron, the Hemi has two valves per cylinder in hemispherical combustion chambers, operated via pushrods and mechanical lifters from a single V-mounted cam. This modified car has a Dick Landy Industries-prepared motor which has been overbored to 432 cubic inches. A 3-inch exhaust system helps make even more power.

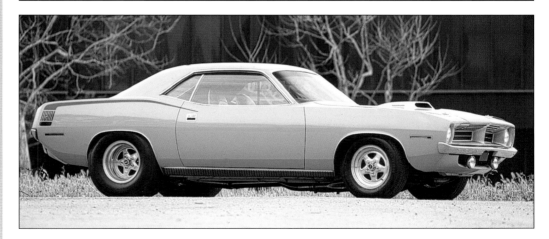

King 'Cuda

Of all the Barracuda range, the 1970 Hemi 'Cuda is the pick of the bunch. Its race-bred engine and rarity make it a real collector's piece, popular with purists and performance freaks alike. Not many are modified as they command higher prices in stock condition.

This car is finished in the original factory color of Lime Light.

Plymouth HEMI 'CUDA

Lime Light green was only one of the factory optioned 'High Impact' colors available for the 1970 'Cuda. If you have an engine as powerful as this one, why not have a paint scheme that's equally outrageous?

Hemi V8
The Hemi V8 was so called because of its hemispherical combustion chambers. These promote more efficient combustion of the air/fuel mixture. It was one of the most powerful engines ever put in any muscle car.

Low ratio back axle
The lowest standard axle ratio available was 4.10:1. This car has an even lower 4.56:1 ratio axle for more urgent acceleration.

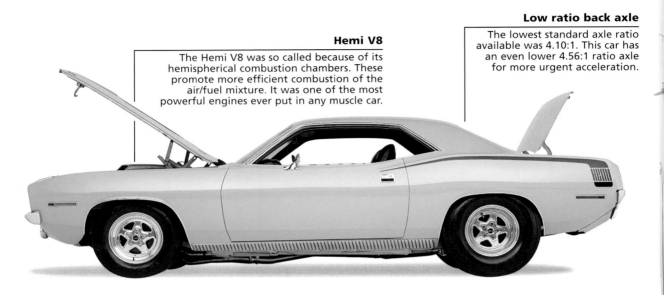

Torsion bar front suspension
The 'Cuda uses double wishbone front suspension sprung by longitudinally-mounted torsion bars. Adjustable Koni shock absorbers are used on this car.

Drag racing tires and wheels
For looks and performance, huge 14-inch wide Weld Racing Pro-Star alloy wheels and super-sticky Mickey Thompson tires have been added to this wild Hemi 'Cuda.

Hardtop body
This, like most Hemi 'Cudas, has a two-door hardtop body. There were only 14 Hemi convertibles made in 1970.

Hood-retaining pins

These race-style hood-retaining pins were actually factory fitted with the shaker hood which came as standard equipment on the Hemi 'Cuda.

Custom tail pipes

Even with the free-flow system fitted to this car, the owner has managed to retain the neat feature of having the twin tail pipes exiting through the rear valance.

Limited-slip differential

The 'Cuda has a Chrysler 'Sure-Grip' limited-slip differential as standard equipment.

Specifications

1971 Plymouth Hemi 'Cuda

ENGINE

Type: V8

Construction: Cast-iron block and heads

Valve gear: Two valves per cylinder actuated by a single camshaft via mechanical lifters and pushrods

Bore and stroke: 4.25 in. x 3.75 in.

Displacement: 432 c.i.

Compression ratio: 10.25:1

Induction system: Twin Carter AFB four-barrel carburetors

Maximum power: 620 bhp at 6,500 rpm

Maximum torque: 655 lb-ft at 5,100 rpm

Top speed: 137 mph

0–60 mph: 4.3 sec.

TRANSMISSION

Chrysler A-833 four-speed manual

BODY/CHASSIS

Steel monocoque two-door coupe body

SPECIAL FEATURES

This Hemi 'Cuda has the popular shaker hood. The Shaker was often a different color from the bodywork.

The most obvious change from stock on this car is the enormous rear wheels and tires.

RUNNING GEAR

Steering: Recirculating ball

Front suspension: Double wishbones with longitudinal torsion bars, Koni adjustable telescopic shock absorbers and anti-roll bar

Rear suspension: Live axle with semi-elliptic leaf springs, Koni adjustable shock absorbers

Brakes: Discs (front), drums (rear)

Wheels: Weld Racing Pro-Star, 15 x 7 (front), 15 x 14 (rear)

Tires: P225/70R-15 General (front), 18.5-31 Mickey Thompson (rear)

DIMENSIONS

Length: 186.7 in. **Width:** 74.9 in.

Height: 50.9 in. **Wheelbase:** 108 in.

Track: 59.7 in. (front), 60.7 in. (rear)

Weight: 3,945 lbs.

Plymouth SUPERBIRD

Developed from the budget Road Runner coupe, the Superbird was designed to defeat Ford's Talladegas in NASCAR superspeedway races. Shortly after Plymouth's powerful rocket appeared, NASCAR had changed the rules, and Superbirds were only allowed to race the 1970 season.

"…NASCAR racing warrior."

"Plymouth built more than 1,935 Superbirds as a follow up to Dodge's less-than-victorious 1969 Daytonas that were designed to slaughter Ford's Talladegas. The strikingly similar looking Superbird proved to be a NASCAR racing warrior. The aluminum wing, flush mounted rear window, Hemi engine, and 18-inch metal nose cone all added up to victory in 1970. In race trim at speeds in excess of 190 mph, the Superbird's nose cone actually added more weight to the front wheels, while the rear wing had to be properly adjusted or the rear tires would wear prematurely."

Stock Superbirds had typical Plymouth interiors with only the necessary gauges, console and shifter.

Milestones

1963 Chrysler decides to take on Ford in NASCAR. As owners of Plymouth and Dodge, they had the 426-cubic inch Hemi V8 engine, whose power should have been enough to guarantee supremacy.

1964–68 Power alone is not enough. On stock car ovals, Ford's supremacy continues because their cars have better aerodynamics.

1969 Dodge Charger Daytona appears with a rear wing giving downforce to keep the car on the track at 200 mph speeds. They win 18 NASCAR races this year. Unfortunately, Ford takes home more than 30.

The Superbirds proved their worth on the superspeedways.

1970 Superbird has better aerodynamics than the Dodge Charger and wins 21 races (including the Daytona 500) and beating Ford. Not very many people liked its unusual styling, so many were stripped of their wings and nose cones and turned back into Road Runners just so Plymouth could sell them.

1971 NASCAR rules, designed to keep racing equal, impose a 25 percent engine volume restriction on rear-winged cars, which spells the end of the Superbird in competition.

UNDER THE SKIN

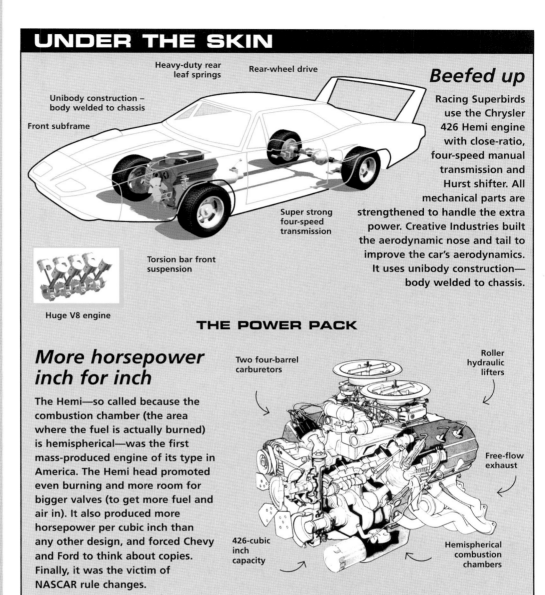

Heavy-duty rear leaf springs

Rear-wheel drive

Unibody construction – body welded to chassis

Front subframe

Super strong four-speed transmission

Torsion bar front suspension

Huge V8 engine

Beefed up

Racing Superbirds use the Chrysler 426 Hemi engine with close-ratio, four-speed manual transmission and Hurst shifter. All mechanical parts are strengthened to handle the extra power. Creative Industries built the aerodynamic nose and tail to improve the car's aerodynamics. It uses unibody construction— body welded to chassis.

THE POWER PACK

More horsepower inch for inch

The Hemi—so called because the combustion chamber (the area where the fuel is actually burned) is hemispherical—was the first mass-produced engine of its type in America. The Hemi head promoted even burning and more room for bigger valves (to get more fuel and air in). It also produced more horsepower per cubic inch than any other design, and forced Chevy and Ford to think about copies. Finally, it was the victim of NASCAR rule changes.

Two four-barrel carburetors

Roller hydraulic lifters

Free-flow exhaust

426-cubic inch capacity

Hemispherical combustion chambers

Vinyl Top

Did you ever notice that all Superbirds had vinyl tops? Plymouth was in a hurry to homologate these cars for NASCAR racing. Instead of properly doing the body work around the flush mounted rear window, it just hid the rough body work with a vinyl top.

The fender scoops cover a cut out giving better tire clearance at high speeds.

Plymouth SUPERBIRD

The Superbird could achieve over 200 mph on the race track using the vital downforce generated by the huge rear wing. Even the tamer street version could easily reach 140 mph.

Rear suspension

Asymmetric rear leaf springs (the front third was stiffer than the rear two-thirds) helped locate the rear axle.

Roll cage

The NASCAR version used a tubular roll cage welded to the frame that stiffened it tremendously as well as protected the driver at 200 mph.

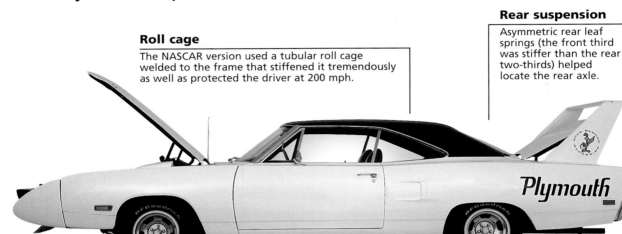

Four-speed transmission

Heavy-duty four-speed Chrysler model 883 was the strongest transmission available at the time.

Standard steel wheels

Steel wheels are still standard in NASCAR—wider 9.5 inch x 15 inch are used now, 15 inch x 7 inch when the Superbird ran. All NASCAR tires then were bias ply with inner tubes.

Live rear axle

Dana-built rear axle was originally intended for a medium-duty truck. Even in drag racing, the mighty Hemi could break it.

High-mounted rear wing

The rear wing provided downforce at the rear. Its angle was adjustable—too much and the increased force would shred the tires.

Front suspension

Front torsion bars resulted in better front suspension than competitors.

Cowl induction

Carburetor intake air was picked up from the high-pressure area at the base of the windshield—called cowl induction.

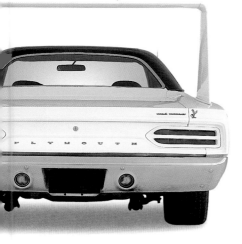

Aerodynamic nose

The nose was designed to lower drag and increase top speed while adding downforce—it actually put more weight on the front as speed increased.

Specifications
1970 Plymouth Superbird

ENGINE
Type: Hemi V8
Construction: Cast-iron block and heads; hemispherical combustion chambers
Valve gear: Two valves per cylinder operated by single block-mounted camshaft
Bore and stroke: 4.25 in. x 3.74 in.
Displacement: 426 c.i.
Compression ratio: 12:1
Induction system: Two four-barrel carbs, aluminum manifold
Maximum power: 425 bhp at 5,000 rpm
Maximum torque: 490 lb-ft at 4,000 rpm
Top speed: 140 mph
0–60 mph: 6.1 sec.

TRANSMISSION
Torqueflite three-speed auto plus torque converter or Mopar 883 four-speed manual

BODY/CHASSIS
Steel channel chassis welded to body with bolted front subframe

SPECIAL FEATURES

Front spoiler overcomes front-end lift.

The rear wing's height means it operates in less-disturbed airflow.

RUNNING GEAR
Steering: Recirculating ball steering, power-assisted on road cars
Front suspension: Double wishbones with torsion bars and telescopic shocks
Rear suspension: Live axle with asymmetric leaf springs and telescopic shocks
Brakes: Vented discs 11 in. dia. (front), drums 11 in. dia. (rear)
Wheels: Steel disc, 7 in. x 15 in.
Tires: Goodyear 7.00/15

DIMENSIONS
Length: 218 in.　　　**Width:** 76.4 in.
Wheelbase: 116 in.
Height: 1159.4 in. (including rear wing)
Track: 59.7 in. (front), 58.7 in. (rear)
Weight: 3,841 lbs.

Pontiac GTO JUDGE

Looking to boost sales of its muscle cars, Pontiac created The Judge option package for its 1969 model lineup and made it available on the tire-incinerating GTO. With its attention-getting paint scheme and outrageous graphics, a Ram Air-powered GTO Judge was a street-wise combination of flamboyance and force.

"...All rise for the GTO Judge."

"With its legendary Ram Air engines, the GTO is the quintessential muscle car. In 1969, a new option gave this powerful Poncho a new image—all rise for the GTO Judge. The Judge makes a statement even when it stands still. On the move its true intentions become evident. Push down on the throttle and feel its torque as your body sinks into its bucket seat. Bang second gear and listen to the tires chirp—now that's power. This honorable hot rod gives a very judicious jaunt."

A firm bucket seat, Hurst shifter and a hood mounted tach—what more do you need?

Milestones

1969 Although originally conceived as a single-color, bare-bones GTO at a low price, the Judge debuts as an option package on the Goat. It is equipped with the standard Ram III or optional Ram Air IV engines. The first 2,000 cars are painted Carousel Red, but later variants are available in any factory GTO color.

This 1968 GTO was one of the first cars to use a plastic Endura front bumper.

1970 GM A-bodies undergo a major restyle, and the GTO has more bulging lower sheet metal, plus new front and rear styling. Power-train choices on the Judge are unchanged, but there are new colors, and spring and suspension settings are altered. Late in the model year, a 455-cubic inch V8 becomes available.

The final, 1971 incarnation of the Judge is noticeably different from its predecessors.

1971 The Judge is retired due to a lack of consumer interest.

UNDER THE SKIN

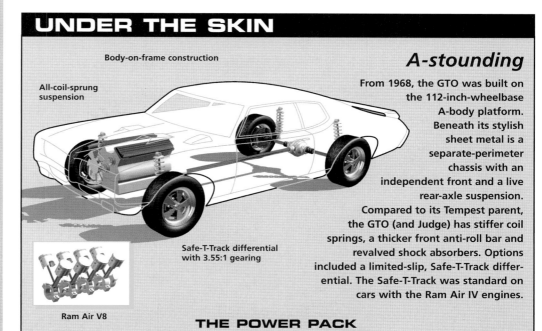

Body-on-frame construction

All-coil-sprung suspension

Safe-T-Track differential with 3.55:1 gearing

Ram Air V8

A-stounding

From 1968, the GTO was built on the 112-inch-wheelbase A-body platform. Beneath its stylish sheet metal is a separate-perimeter chassis with an independent front and a live rear-axle suspension. Compared to its Tempest parent, the GTO (and Judge) has stiffer coil springs, a thicker front anti-roll bar and revalved shock absorbers. Options included a limited-slip, Safe-T-Track differential. The Safe-T-Track was standard on cars with the Ram Air IV engines.

THE POWER PACK

Ramming air—III or IV

With outrageous styling, The Judge had to have the power to match. Its standard engine was a 400-cubic inch, Ram Air III, V8. This engine had D-port cylinder heads, a hydraulic camshaft, free-flowing exhaust manifolds and a Rochester Quadrajet 4-barrel carburetor. It made 366 bhp. Three is keen but with four you definitely get more. Owners who wanted to maximize performance ordered their Judge with the barely streetable Ram Air IV 400. It came with forged pistons, round-port cylinder heads and 1.65:1 rocker arms. According to the factory, this engine only made 4 more bhp than the III, but this figure was grossly underrated.

In session

Offered for sale for only three model years, the Judge has long been coveted by collectors. 1969 models boast cleaner styling, and Carousel Red is the definitive color. Due to high demand, buyers should be aware of GTO Judge imitations.

A Carousel Red Judge with the Ram Air IV is a highly desirable car.

Pontiac GTO JUDGE

Despite taking its name from the popular *Laugh-In* TV show, the Judge was no joke. Fitted with the Ram Air IV, it was one of the most respected muscle cars on the street.

III or IV for the road

Whereas regular GTOs came with a 350-bhp 400 as the standard V8, Judges got the 366-bhp Ram Air III. The hot setup, however, was the $389.68 Ram Air IV engine option with a 4-speed transmission. It was endowed with an aluminum intake manifold, 4-bolt mains and, of course, oval-port heads with 67cc combustion chambers. Only 34 buyers ordered their GTO Judges with the RA IV/4-speed option.

Standard Ram Air IV equipment

If you ordered your GTO with the Ram Air IV engine, you automatically received a heavy-duty cooling system. The standard gear ratio with this engine was a set of 3.90:1s and a Safe-T-Track limited slip differential. If these gears weren't steep enough, a set of 4.33:1s could be specified.

Eye-catching paint scheme

By 1969, image was everything in the muscle car stakes. The Judge was launched with one of the loudest schemes around, Carousel Red, set off by blue stripes outlined in yellow and with Judge logos on the front fenders and decklid spoiler.

Heavy-duty suspension

Judges came with heavy-duty suspension, which includes stiff springs and shocks. Drum brakes were standard, but front discs were optional—and at a mere $64.25, highly advisable.

Endura nose

One of the first cars to have energy-absorbing bumpers, the GTO's optional Endura nose could withstand parking lot shunts of up to four mph. Hidden headlights were a very popular option, however this GTO retains the fixed headlights.

Well-laid-out interior

The second-generation GTO had one of the best interiors of all its peers. All of the gauges were clearly visible, front bucket seats were very supportive and the floor-mounted Hurst shifter never missed a gear.

Specifications

1969 Pontiac GTO Judge

ENGINE

Type: V8

Construction: Cast-iron block and heads

Valve gear: Two valves per cylinder operated by a single camshaft with pushrods and rockers

Bore and stroke: 4.12 in. x 3.75 in.

Displacement: 400 c.i. (R/A III)

Compression ratio: 10.75:1

Induction system: GM Rochester Quadrajet four-barrel carburetor

Maximum power: 366 bhp at 5,400 rpm

Maximum torque: 445 lb-ft at 3,600 rpm

Top speed: 123 mph

0–60 mph: 6.2 sec.

TRANSMISSION

Muncie M-21 four-speed manual

BODY/CHASSIS

Separate steel chassis with two-door coupe body

SPECIAL FEATURES

'The Judge' decals are prominently displayed all around the car.

The hood-mounted tachometer was not only stylish but very useful, too.

RUNNING GEAR

Steering: Recirculating ball

Front suspension: Unequal-length A-arms with coil springs, telescopic shock absorbers and anti-roll bar

Rear suspension: Live axle with coil springs, trailing arms and telescopic shock absorbers

Brakes: Discs (front), drums (rear)

Wheels: Steel Rally II, 14-in. dia.

Tires: Goodyear Polyglas, G-60 14

DIMENSIONS

Length: 195.0 in.   **Width:** 75.0 in.

Height: 52.0 in.   **Wheelbase:** 112.0 in.

Track: 64.0 in. (front and rear)

Weight: 3,503 lbs.

Pontiac **TRANS AM SD**

By 1974, only GM could offer anything even vaguely approaching the performance machines of the late 1960s and early 1970s, with the Chevrolet Corvette and the more powerful Pontiac Trans Am SD-455.

"...raucous takeoffs."

"The 1974 Trans Am was strictly 'old school' American muscle in the performance and handling departments. Like its predecessors a decade earlier, it was great in a straight line. The massive 455-cubic inch engine plays a part in the car's front-heavy handling, although it gives fantastic midrange acceleration. Standard disc brakes up front and a limited-slip differential for raucous takeoffs are major plus points."

There is a comfortable feel to the interior, which is unmistakably 1970s.

Milestones

1967 Pontiac introduces
the Firebird, it shares its basic shell with the Chevrolet Camaro, which debuted a few months earlier. Both are aimed at the 'pony market' created by the Mustang.

Chevrolet dropped the Camaro in 1975, leaving the Trans Am as GM's only muscle car.

1969 The Trans Am is offered
for the first time in the Firebird lineup as the top-of-the-line performance Firebird. Standard was the Ram Air III, 335 bhp 400 HO engine.

The Trans Am had a bold redesign for 1979.

1974 First major body
and engineering restyle for the Firebird/Trans Am series.

1976 Last year of the
Pontiac 455-c.i. engine, only available in the Trans Am as a limited edition.

UNDER THE SKIN

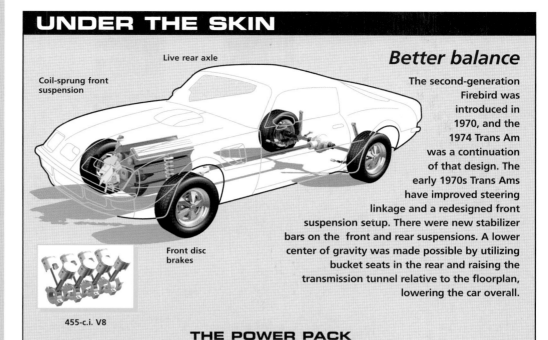

Coil-sprung front suspension

Live rear axle

Front disc brakes

455-c.i. V8

Better balance

The second-generation Firebird was introduced in 1970, and the 1974 Trans Am was a continuation of that design. The early 1970s Trans Ams have improved steering linkage and a redesigned front suspension setup. There were new stabilizer bars on the front and rear suspensions. A lower center of gravity was made possible by utilizing bucket seats in the rear and raising the transmission tunnel relative to the floorplan, lowering the car overall.

THE POWER PACK

Super-Duty punch

Pontiac's Super Duty 455 was the last bastion of big-cube power for the performance enthusiast. With a compression ratio of 8.4:1, output was down as the first of the mandatory emissions controls began to sap power. Nonetheless, the engine still sported all the performance features of the soon-to-be-gone muscle car era. This includes a lot of displacement, four-bolt mains, forged-aluminum pistons and an 800-cfm Quadrajet carb. There was even built-in provision for dry-sump lubrication. Earlier 1974 cars make use of the Ram IV camshaft and are capable of 310 bhp; later 1974 cars do not and are rated at 290 bhp.

Last of its kind

If you wanted a muscle car in 1974, there was only one choice: the Trans Am SD-455. Big-block Camaros had been discontinued and MOPAR, the purveyor of some of the hot muscle car property, had pulled the plug on performance.

For 1974, Pontiac gave the Trans Am new front-end treatment.

Pontiac **TRANS AM SD**

Pontiac Firebirds were offered in four series for 1974: Firebird, Esprit, Formula and Trans Am. The 455-SD engine could be ordered only in the Formula and the Trans Am. Super-Duty equipped Formulas are the rarest.

Special dash

Trans Ams featured a special steering wheel, a faux metal dash and a rally gauge cluster, which included a clock and dash-mounted tachometer. As a sign of the times, a new 'fuel economy' gauge was introduced later in the year.

New tires

For 1974, all General Motors cars had to use steel-belted radials. Hence, the old Firestone Wide-Oval F60-15 bias-belted tires were replaced with new Firestone 500 F60 x 15 steel-belted radials.

LSD

Standard on the Trans Am was a limited-slip differential, ensuring minimal wheelspin and consistent launches.

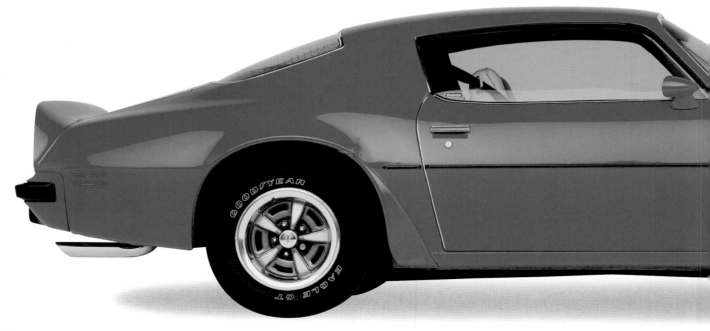

'Soft' bumpers

New for 1974 was a soft bumper treatment front and rear, utilizing molded urethane foam. These were faced with black rubber front bars to absorb parking bumps.

Scoops galore

Pontiac made sure that the Trans Am looked aggressive and powerful with flared wheel arches and front fender air extractors. The menacing-looking, rear-facing Shaker hood scoop finishes off the whole effect with SD-455 decals on the side.

Restyled rear end

The rear-end treatment includes a full-width rear spoiler. Taillights are wider, in a horizontal casing, giving a more integrated appearance.

Specifications

1974 Trans Am SD455

ENGINE

Type: V8

Construction: Cast-iron cylinder block and cylinder head

Valve gear: Two valves per cylinder

Bore and stroke: 4.15 in. x 4.21 in.

Displacement: 455 c.i.

Compression ratio: 8.4:1

Induction system: 800-cfm Quadrajet four-barrel carburetor

Maximum power: 310 bhp at 4,000 rpm

Maximum torque: 390 lb-ft at 3,600 rpm

Top speed: 132 mph

0–60 mph: 5.4 sec.

TRANSMISSION

Three-speed automatic M40 Turbo Hydramatic

BODY/CHASSIS

Steel unibody construction

SPECIAL FEATURES

The SD-455 logos are seen only on Trans Ams and Formulas.

A holographic applique on the dash perfectly reflects mid-1970s style.

RUNNING GEAR

Steering: Variable-ratio, ball-nut

Front suspension: A-arms with coil springs and telescopic shock absorbers

Rear suspension: Live rear axle with leaf springs and telescopic shock absorbers

Brakes: Discs (front), drums (rear)

Wheels: Steel, 15-in. Rally II

Tires: F60 x 15 (raised white letters) Firestone steel belted

DIMENSIONS

Length: 196.0 in.   **Width:** 73.4 in.

Height: 50.4 in.   **Wheelbase:** 108.0 in.

Track: 61.6 in. (front), 60.3 in. (rear)

Weight: 3,655 lbs.

Porsche **911 2.7 CARRERA**

The Carrera RS 2.7 is still rated by many as the best 911 of all. Just 500 were supposed to be built for homologation purposes, but because of the model's popularity the final tally was more than 1,500 cars.

"...an unmatched thoroughbred."

"Light weight and loads of power make the RS one of the most nimble-feeling 911s ever built. The flat-six engine will rev high without a hint of strain. At low speeds, it's easily controllable and its sharp throttle response is matched by a stiff chassis, precise steering and large brakes. Although the ride is firm it never feels uncomfortable. In all respects, the RS, though an unmatched thoroughbred, is just as usable as any other 911."

The dash is stock 911, but much has been deleted from the interior to reduce weight.

Milestones

1956 Porsche names its flagship
four-cam 356 models Carrera in honor of the company's class victory in the famous Carrera Panamericana.

The Carrera RS 3.0 liter succeeded the 2.7 in late 1973.

1963 The Porsche 911 is revealed
at the Frankfurt Motor Show as a successor to the 356.

Porsche built more specialized racers in the form of the 935.

1973 The 911 RS 2.7 Carrera is
announced at the end of 1972 for production in 1973. A homologation special is offered as the ultra-lightweight RSH, the slightly less basic RS Sport, the fully race-modified RSR and the road-going RS Touring with extra luxury trimmings.

1974 An RS 3.0 is introduced.
They are mainly racers, but 49 road cars out of a total of 109 are built. They produce 230 bhp in road form and 315 bhp for racing.

UNDER THE SKIN

Fighting flab

To make the most of the extra power, Porsche went to great lengths to lighten the RS. The resulting car was so different from the normal 911 that it had to be built on a separate production line. All the sound-proofing was removed, rubber mats replaced the floor carpeting, the glovebox door and even the coat hooks were removed. The rear engine cover is made of fiberglass and secured by rubber straps.

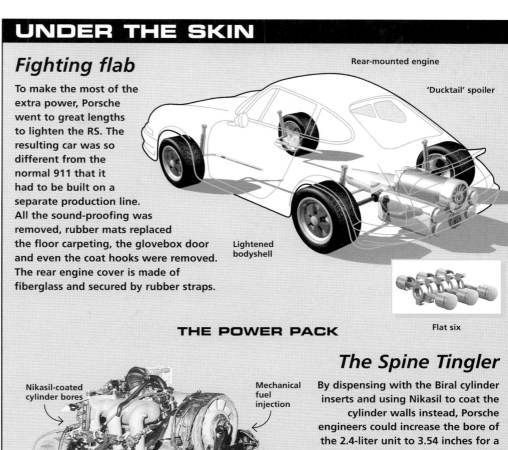

Rear-mounted engine

'Ducktail' spoiler

Lightened bodyshell

Flat six

THE POWER PACK

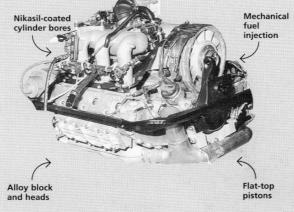

Nikasil-coated cylinder bores

Mechanical fuel injection

Alloy block and heads

Flat-top pistons

The Spine Tingler

By dispensing with the Biral cylinder inserts and using Nikasil to coat the cylinder walls instead, Porsche engineers could increase the bore of the 2.4-liter unit to 3.54 inches for a total capacity of 2,687 cc. Power went up to 210 bhp and torque was increased by 18 percent. There are flat-top pistons and uprated mechanical fuel injection. With these exceptions, the injected air-cooled flat-six is identical to the 911S with the same single-cam heads, mated to a close-ratio five-speed transmission.

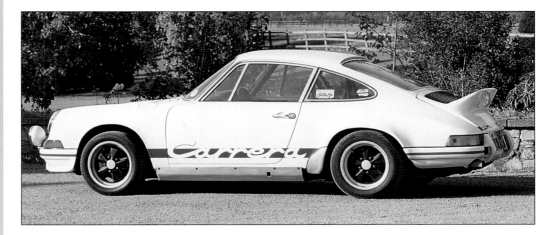

Honored name

The Carrera name was first used by Porsche for the most powerful model in the 356 range, recalling class victory in the Carrera Panamericana race in 1954. It wasn't until the introduction of the RS 2.7 that the name appeared on a 911. It has been used on and off ever since.

Unfortunately, Porsche's finest, the RS 2.7 was never available in the U.S.

Porsche **911 2.7 CARRERA**

The classic Carrera RS 2.7 has cult status among Porsche fans. Many consider it to be the most satisfying of the breed to drive. Thinner steel and fewer creature comforts give the car true lightweight status.

Uprated engine
The classic flat six looks similar on the outside but features flat-top pistons and improved mechanical fuel injection to produce extra power. It revs strongly to over 7,000 rpm.

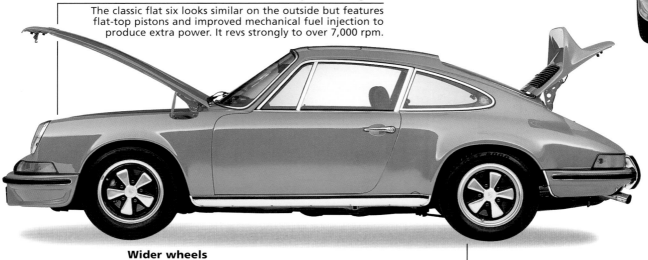

Wider wheels
To fill the flared wheel arches, the RS has wider wheels than standard (6 inches at the front, 7 inches at the rear).

Rear spoiler
The engine cover of the RS features a Burzel fiberglass rear spoiler designed to reduce tail-end lift at high speeds. A front spoiler is also used, which greatly improving stability.

Stripped interior
The cabin of the RS is stripped to the bare essentials for fast road driving, although touring road versions are a little more comfortable. All the trim is matte black.

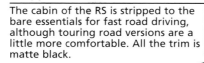

Weight paring

The RS has thinner steel and window glass and GRP bumpers; it weighs at least 150 lbs. less than a standard 911.

Improved suspension

Thicker anti-roll bars are fitted at both ends, together with Bilstein gas-filled shock absorbers.

Specifications

1973 Porsche 911 Carrera RS 2.7

ENGINE

Type: Flat-six

Construction: Aluminum-alloy block and cylinder heads

Valve gear: Two valves per cylinder operated by a single overhead camshaft per cylinder bank

Bore and stroke: 3.54 in. x 2.77 in.

Displacement: 2,687 cc

Compression ratio: 8.5:1

Induction system: Mechanical injection

Maximum power: 210 bhp at 6,300 rpm

Maximum torque: 188 lb-ft at 5,100 rpm

Top speed: 148 mph

0–60 mph: 5.9 sec.

TRANSMISSION

Five-speed manual

BODY/CHASSIS

Steel monocoque two-door coupe

SPECIAL FEATURES

The fiberglass engine cover carries this distinctive 'duck-tail' spoiler.

As with all 911s, the fuel filler cap is located on the front fender.

RUNNING GEAR

Steering: Rack-and-pinion

Front suspension: MacPherson struts with longitudinal torsion bars, lower wishbones, shock absorbers and anti-roll bar

Rear suspension: Semi-trailing arms with transverse torsion bars, shock absorbers and anti-roll bar

Brakes: Vented discs, 11.1-in. dia. (front), 11.4-in. dia. (rear)

Wheels: Fuchs alloys, 6 x 15 in. (front), 7 x 15 in. (rear)

Tires: 185/70 VR15 (front), 215 VR15 (rear)

DIMENSIONS

Length: 163.3 in.   **Width:** 63.4 in.

Height: 52.0 in.   **Wheelbase:** 89.4 in

Track: 54.0 in. (front), 54.3 in. (rear)

Weight: 2,160 lbs.

Porsche **911 RUF**

Alois Ruf has been modifying Porsches since 1977, turning them into some of the fastest cars on the road. The Turbo R is the latest expression of this tradition—a twin-turbocharged, 200-mph uprated Porsche 911.

"...a massive rush of adrenaline."

"Any Porsche driver will feel instantly at home in the Turbo R, as the cabin is pure 911. The pedals are perfectly located for heel-and-toe shifting, and the transmission is silky smooth. With 490 bhp, the Ruf Turbo R offers a massive rush of adrenaline. In addition, it's superbly balanced while the all-wheel drive system and traction control overcome the tail-happy excesses of a stock 911. Perhaps the most surprising aspect of the Turbo R is how docile it feels in traffic."

As expected, the cockpit is very businesslike, although leather seats are offered.

Milestones

1977 Alois Ruf makes his first car: a modified Porsche 911 Turbo.

1981 Ruf becomes one of just a few companies to gain German Manufacturers' Certification.

Ruf also modified Porsche 930s, turning them into street terrors.

1987 A Ruf CTR breaks the world speed record for production cars at 211 mph.

1993 Porsche launches the new 993-series 911, with its more rounded shape and uprated 3.6-liter engine, including a turbo version; Ruf also offers a twin-turbocharged model.

Carrera 4s (on which many Rufs are based) are most able to cope with severe increases in power.

1997 Although the all-new Porsche 911 is launched, Ruf continues to offer its Turbo R conversion for the 993-series car.

UNDER THE SKIN

Better still

The Turbo R is based on one of the world's best sports cars, the 993-series Porsche 911. To cope with the extra power, Ruf lowers the suspension 1.5 inches and fits stiffer springs, Bilstein shocks, stiffer anti-roll bars front and rear and a front strut brace for extra rigidity. The wheels are also unique to Ruf. Power is applied via Porsche's permanent four-wheel-drive system, using a central differential with viscous coupling and a traction control system to keep wheelspin at bay.

Four-wheel drive with central viscous coupling

Lowered suspension

Larger front and rear anti-roll bars

Twin-turbo flat six

THE POWER PACK

Custom ground camshafts

Recalibrated Bosch Motronic fuel management system

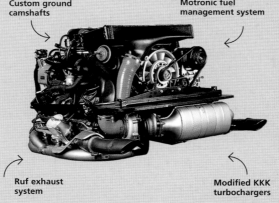

Ruf exhaust system

Modified KKK turbochargers

Modified 3.6 liter

Ruf's Turbo R upgrades to the stock 3.6-liter engine include different pistons, modified cylinder heads, and aggressive camshafts. In doing these modifications, Ruf retains the stock displacement and 8.0:1 compression ratio. Special KKK turbos modified with integral wastegates replace the stock turbocharger system. In addition, the stock exhaust is replaced with custom Ruf pipes, while a remapped fuel management system permits the boxer engine to produce a respectable 490 bhp.

Docile demon

Unlike most ultra high performance cars, the Ruf Turbo R is surprisingly docile on a daily basis and is well suited to ordinary roads. However, when the accelerator meets the floorboard, the Turbo R reminds you what its true intentions are.

Turbo Rs operate with ease in normal driving as well as racing situations.

Porsche **911 RUF**

For most people, a stock 911 Turbo is fast enough, yet others demand still more. Ruf satisfies their needs by building a tweaked 911 that is among the fastest supercars in the world.

Unique alloy wheels

Ruf designed the unique 18 x 8.5-inch front and 18 x 10-inch rear five-spoke alloy wheels which are shod in Bridgestone Potenza S-02 tires.

Deep front spoiler

Downforce at the front end is enhanced by the addition of a chin spoiler. This, coupled with the 'whale tail' rear spoiler, glues the car to the road at high speeds.

Optional uprated interior

Although a stock 911 interior is fitted to most Turbo Rs, RUF offers an upgrade including a Ruf sports steering wheel and leather seats with the company's logo. A roll cage and race harness are available for customers who plan to race their Ruf-modified Porsches.

Twin KKK turbochargers

Special KKK twin turbochargers with integral wastegates allow the engine to build more boost and make nearly 500 bhp. 3.8-second 0-60 mph sprints and a near 200 mph top speed are the result of this obscene amount of power.

No clutch pedal

A six-speed manual transmission is standard, but RUF also offers a special electronic clutch system that allows gear shifts just like an ordinary manual transmission with a fingertip control. There is no need for a conventional clutch pedal.

All-wheel drive

Traction is a great concern when you have nearly 500 bhp sitting behind you. With Porsche's sophisticated permanent all-wheel drive system, using a central differential and a traction control system, wheelspin and tail slides rarely occur.

Specifications

1997 Porsche 911 Ruf Turbo R

ENGINE

Type: Horizontally opposed six-cylinder

Construction: Aluminum block and heads

Valve gear: Two valves per cylinder operated by a chain-driven overhead cam

Bore and stroke: 3.94 in. x 3.01 in.

Displacement: 3,600 cc

Compression ratio: 8.0:1

Induction system: Remapped Bosch Motronic fuel injection

Maximum power: 490 bhp at 5,500 rpm

Maximum torque: 480 lb-ft at 4,800 rpm

Top speed: 192 mph

0–60 mph: 3.8 sec.

TRANSMISSION

Six-speed manual with electronic clutch option

BODY/CHASSIS

Unitary monocoque construction with steel two-door coupe body

SPECIAL FEATURES

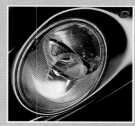

993s can be distinguished by their deeper-set high-intensity headlights.

Massive twin intercoolers are required to produce 490 bhp.

RUNNING GEAR

Steering: Rack-and-pinion

Front suspension: Struts with lower wishbones, coil springs, telescopic shock absorbers and anti-roll bar

Rear suspension: Multi-link axle with coil springs, shock absorbers and anti-roll bar

Brakes: Discs (front and rear)

Wheels: Alloy, 18-in. dia.

Tires: 225/40ZR 18 (front), 285/30 ZR 18 (rear)

DIMENSIONS

Length: 167.0 in.   **Width:** 70.7 in.

Height: 50.5 in.   **Wheelbase:** 89.4 in.

Track: 55.5 in. (front), 59.0 in. (rear)

Weight: 3,090 lbs.

Porsche 935

One of the world's most successful sports racing cars, the Porsche 935 stayed competitive for an incredible nine years, winning five world championships as well as the Le Mans and Daytona.

"...ultimate 911 development."

"In its day, the 935 looked like the ultimate 911 development—those looks did not lie. Luckily, with almost 600 bhp to play with, the 935 has a wider rear track than any 911 as well as huge tires. It's more forgiving than early 911 Turbos once you get used to its clutch, the even heavier steering, and the incredible noise made by the flat-six just behind you. Like all racing cars, it only makes sense at speed when the steering lightens and the tires and brakes have warmed up."

Spartan interior features a large tachometer, boost gauge to the right, oil and engine temperature to the left.

Milestones

1976 The first 935 appears in the new Group 5 category in the World Championship for Makes. It is based on the 911 Turbo but with a smaller engine to fit within the new rules. Despite having to change the intercooler layout after the authorities complain, the 935 still wins the Championship.

The 935 K3 that won Le Mans in 1979 averaged 108 mph.

1977 Now using twin turbochargers and with an extra 40 bhp, the 935 again wins the Championship.

1978 Changes see the new water-cooled four-valve heads, more power, and revised bodywork, but these special 'Moby Dick' cars only raced twice, winning at Silverstone, coming in eighth at Le Mans.

1979 Although private 935s race on for years, the best 935 performance comes in this year: the Kremer 935 K3 of Klaus Ludwig and the Whittington brothers wins Le Mans with 935s also placing in second and third place.

The Cooper/Woods 935 was fourth at Le Mans in 1981.

UNDER THE SKIN

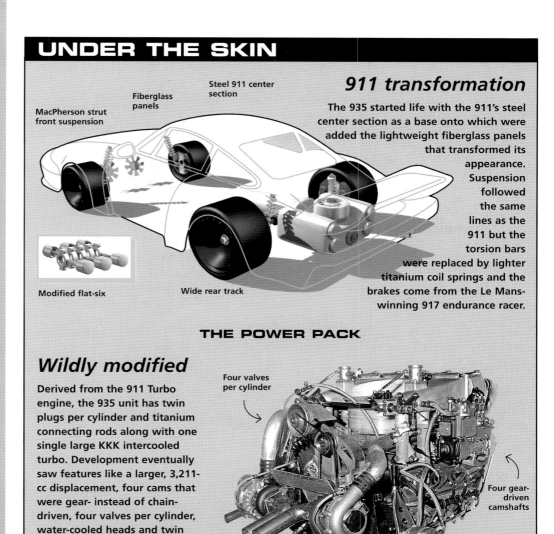

Steel 911 center section

Fiberglass panels

MacPherson strut front suspension

Modified flat-six

Wide rear track

911 transformation

The 935 started life with the 911's steel center section as a base onto which were added the lightweight fiberglass panels that transformed its appearance. Suspension followed the same lines as the 911 but the torsion bars were replaced by lighter titanium coil springs and the brakes come from the Le Mans-winning 917 endurance racer.

THE POWER PACK

Wildly modified

Derived from the 911 Turbo engine, the 935 unit has twin plugs per cylinder and titanium connecting rods along with one single large KKK intercooled turbo. Development eventually saw features like a larger, 3,211-cc displacement, four cams that were gear- instead of chain-driven, four valves per cylinder, water-cooled heads and twin turbos. Ultimately, as much as 800 bhp can be extracted from this wildly modified flat-six.

Four valves per cylinder

Four gear-driven camshafts

Twin turbochargers

Water-cooled cylinder heads

'Moby Dick'

Last and fastest of the 935 line is known as 'Moby Dick.' This has dual-cam cylinder heads and 800 bhp in high boost form. New regulations had allowed the car to be lower and the long aerodynamic nose and tail helped high speed: 'Moby Dick' could exceed 225 mph. It won on its Silverstone debut.

The Stommelen/Schurti 'Moby Dick' at Le Mans in 1978.

Porsche 935

The 935 was used by a host of private teams for very good reasons. It was fast, reliable, and extremely strong. With a 935 you could almost guarantee a finish.

Alloy roll cage
The alloy roll cage performs two functions—protecting the driver and making the whole structure stiffer.

Plexiglass windows
To keep weight down, Plexiglass is used for the side windows. Porsche actually made the 935 lighter than the regulations allowed so they could put weight back in the form of ballast where it is most needed—in the front.

Flat-six engine
Group 5 regulations stipulate that the engines used are based on those of a production car. To begin with the 935's was very similar, but was stronger, had slightly smaller displacement, and later had four valves per cylinder.

Front MacPherson struts
Because the regulations required that the same form of suspension was used in Group 5 cars as on the production cars, Porsche uses MacPherson struts. But at the rear, titanium springs are used.

Intercooler vents
After the intercooler in the tail was banned Porsche was forced to fit two smaller intercoolers, one on each side ahead of the rear wheels where air is fed to them through vents behind the doors.

Porsche 911 center section
The only significant part of the structure of the production 911 which is retained is the center section and floorpan.

Single turbo
Initially, the 935 used a single large KKK turbo mounted right at the tail of the car behind the engine, whose compression ratio was lowered to 6.5:1.

Fiberglass and polyurethane bodywork

The body contributes nothing to the 935's strength. Its detachable panels can be made in fiberglass or a lightweight polyurethane foam sandwich material.

Porsche 917 brakes

Brakes from the production 911 Turbo on which the 935 is loosely based would not have coped. The 935 uses the enormous vented discs and four-pot calipers used Porsche 917 racing cars.

Front oil cooler

With dry-sump racing engines, there's no oil pan for the oil to sit in. It's pumped around from a separate tank, in this case in the 935's nose. It's placed there, along with an oil cooler, to help weight distribution.

Specifications
1976 Porsche 935

ENGINE

Type: Flat-six

Construction: Alloy crankcase, cylinder barrels and heads

Valve gear: Two valves per cylinder operated by single chain-driven overhead cam per bank of cylinders

Bore and stroke: 3.66 in. x 2.75 in.

Displacement: 2,856 cc

Compression ratio: 6.5:1

Induction system: Bosch mechanical fuel injection with intercooled KKK turbocharger

Maximum power: 590 bhp at 7,900 rpm

Maximum torque: 434 lb-ft at 7,900 rpm

Top speed: 200 mph

0–60 mph: 3.1 sec.

TRANSMISSION

Four-speed manual

BODY/CHASSIS

Strengthened Porsche 911 floorpan with alloy roll cage and fiberglass/polyurethane foam body panels

SPECIAL FEATURES

The titanium coil springs are lighter than the 911's steel torsion bars, and easier to tune and change for racing.

Large rear spoiler helps increase the downforce of high-speed stability of this 190-plus mph car.

RUNNING GEAR

Steering: Rack-and-pinion

Front suspension: MacPherson struts with lower wishbones and anti-roll bar

Rear suspension: Semi-trailing arms, coil springs, telescopic shocks and anti-roll bar

Brakes: Vented discs, 11.8 in. dia.

Wheels: Alloy, 11 in. x 16 in. (front), 15 in. x 19 in. (rear)

Tires: Dunlop racing

DIMENSIONS

Length: 183.3 in.   **Width:** 78.7 in.

Height: 50 in.   **Wheelbase:** 89.4 in.

Track: 59.1 in. (front), 61.4 in. (rear)

Weight: 2,139 lbs.

Porsche 993 TURBO

Porsche's 993 was the last of the 911 Turbo line to have the famous air-cooled flat-six engine. In this case it was a 3.6-liter producing more than 400 bhp, enough to give 180-mph performance. Roadholding was staggering, too.

"...fantastic grip."

"Twin turbos give simply awesome performance. Row through the six gears and the 993 can hit 100 mph in 9.3 seconds—its passing power is breathtaking. Porsche decided it wanted a car with the greatest possible roadholding so the four-wheel drive gives fantastic grip through wide tires. It feels impossible to drift the car; no matter how fast you corner, your bravery runs out long before the car loses grip."

The fascia of the 993 has a clean and solid look to it.

Milestones

1975 The first 911

Turbo is released. The 930 has a single large KKK turbo and produces 245 bhp from 3 liters, to give a top speed of 150 mph with 0-60 in 6.1 seconds.

The Group B racing 959 was the first four-wheel drive Porsche.

1991 After a two-

year gap in production, the second-generation Turbo appears, with a larger turbocharger giving 315 bhp. As well as the two-wheel drive car, the four-wheel drive Carrera 4 is available.

The 993 has smoother lines than the preceding 911s.

1995 The third

generation Turbo is launched. It has a double-wishbone rear suspension and four-wheel drive. Power climbs to 400 bhp thanks to the use of two intercooled turbochargers.

UNDER THE SKIN

Four-wheel drive

Like the rest of the 911 family, the 993 Turbo has its engine mounted at the rear, beyond the rear-axle line. It has a refined four-wheel drive variable-split system with center viscous coupling. Rear suspension is a double-wishbone setup and the front has a modified MacPherson strut system, introduced on the first Carrera 4 in 1989. There is power-assisted rack-and-pinion steering, and the brakes are enormous vented discs.

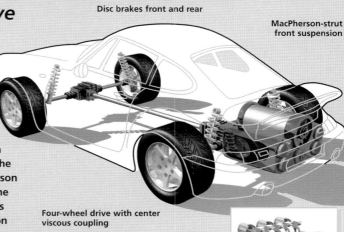

Disc brakes front and rear

MacPherson-strut front suspension

Four-wheel drive with center viscous coupling

Flat-six engine

THE POWER PACK

Hard-hitting boxer

By the end of the 1980s, Porsche's famous flat-six boxer engine had been increased to 3.6 liters for the first Carrera 4. In order to do so, it needed a new block, which was to be carried over for use in the 1993 Turbo. It was very oversquare at 4.00 inches x 3.05 inches, with a very wide bore, but there were still only two large valves per cylinder opened by just one overhead camshaft per bank. The key to its power output was one intercooled KKK turbocharger per bank of cylinders. With simple modifications it could produce up to 450 bhp in a road spec car.

Turbo S

Beyond the standard 993 Turbo was the winged Turbo S, with big air intakes in the rear wheel arches. This has power boosted up to 424 bhp at 5,750 rpm, along with 400 lb-ft of torque. Sensational acceleration and 180 mph were easily attainable.

The Porsche 993 has refined road manners and staggering performance.

Porsche **993 TURBO**

Wide and low, with huge flared rear wheel arches and distinctive sloping headlamps, the 993 Turbo is still instantly recognizable as a descendant of the very first 911 from the early 1960s.

Twin turbos

The flat-six-engine design lent itself to having one turbocharger for each bank of cylinders. Porsche used small German-made KKK K-16 turbos. Each one could thus be placed as close as possible to an exhaust manifold, quickening its response time and virtually eliminating lag.

Integrated bumpers

At the same time that Porsche changed the front headlamp design, it merged the bodywork and bumpers together into one smooth shape.

Alloy wheels

Alloy wheels have long been fitted to Porsche Turbos—they just keep getting bigger and bigger. Turbo 993s have massive 18-inch diameter alloys. They are this large for a couple of reasons: to accommodate brake discs that are greater than a foot in diameter and to carry very wide low-profile tires.

Four-wheel drive

Porsche applied four-wheel drive to the Carrera 4 in 1989 and then modified it for the second-generation model, with a wider variable torque split. It was this system, with its center viscous coupling and rear limited-slip differential that is applied to the 993 Turbo. Drive would normally be automatically applied to the rear wheels until the car's sensors detect that torque needs to be fed to the front wheels as well.

Rear-heavy

Despite being four-wheel drive and having the additional weight of two front drive-shafts, extended propshaft and front differential, the weight distribution of the 993 Turbo is still heavily rear-biased, with 55 percent of the weight at the back.

Specifications

1997 Porsche 993 Turbo

ENGINE
Type: Flat six
Construction: Alloy block and heads
Valve gear: Two valves per cylinder operated by a single overhead cam per bank of cylinders
Bore and stroke: 4.0 in. x 3.05 in.
Displacement: 3,600 cc
Compression ratio: 8.0:1
Induction system: Bosch electronic fuel injection with twin KKK turbochargers
Maximum power: 400 bhp at 5,750 rpm
Max torque: 400 lb-ft at 4,500 rpm
Top speed: 180 mph
0–60 mph: 3.8 sec.

TRANSMISSION
Six-speed manual with permanent four-wheel drive

BODY/CHASSIS
Unitary monocoque construction with steel two-door coupe body

SPECIAL FEATURES

The large alloy wheels house the massive vented disc brakes.

The huge rear spoiler produces downforce and aids straight-line stability.

RUNNING GEAR
Steering: Rack-and-pinion
Front suspension: MacPherson struts with lower wishbones and anti-roll bar
Rear suspension: Double wishbones with coil springs, telescopic shock absorbers and anti-roll bar
Brakes: Vented discs, 12.7-in. dia. (front and rear)
Wheels: Cast alloy, 8 in. x 18 in. (front), 10 in. x 18 in. rear
Tires: 225/40 ZR18 (front), 285/30 ZR18 (rear)

DIMENSIONS
Length: 167.7 in.   **Width:** 70.7 in.
Height: 51.8 in.   **Wheelbase:** 89.4 in.
Track: 55.5 in. (front), 59.3 in. (rear)
Weight: 3,307 lbs.

Renault 5 **TURBO 2**

In 1980 Renault revealed its rallying ambitions in the form of the ferocious Renault 5 Turbo. A silhouette supercar with up to 300 bhp from just 1.4 liters, it won the Monte Carlo Rally in 1981. The road cars were fast, too.

"...glued to the ground."

"The Turbo's interior is nearly as extreme as the car's performance. Supportive and stylish bucket seats give ultimate support, and the wheel and pedals are ideally positioned. Being mid-engined, wide-tracked and with a short wheelbase, its handling is firm and the car stays glued to the ground. With a relatively tiny engine, the revs have to be kept up to keep the turbo on boost; little happens below 3,000 rpm."

Inside, the Turbo 2 is surprisingly like a run-of-the-mill Renault 5, but has more supportive seats.

Milestones

1978 Renault
introduces the prototype Renault 5 Turbo at the Paris Motor Show.

In 1980 Renault also released a smaller R5 Gordini Turbo.

1980 Production of
the R5 Turbo begins. Rally regulations require that 1,000 cars are built for homologation. In fact, 1,300 are built.

1981 Jean Ragnotti
drives a 300-bhp factory R5 Turbo to an outright win in the Monte Carlo Rally and is also victorious in the Tour de Corse.

A later, race-inspired hot hatchback was the Clio Williams.

1982 Renault
launches the Turbo 2. It is a simpler and cheaper to make clone with steel instead of fiberglass body panels. It lasts until 1986, with 5,000 produced.

UNDER THE SKIN

Mid-engined monster

Although it looks similar, the Turbo has little in common with the standard R5. The suspension is all new, with double wishbones and longitudinal torsion bars at the front. Double wishbones are also employed at the rear, but with coil springs rather than torsion bars. The pushrod engine is allied to the larger five-speed transmission from the Renault 30 executive sedan, as its extra strength is needed to cope with the far greater torque output.

Composite body panels

All-independent suspension

Mid-mounted engine

Small in-line four

THE POWER PACK

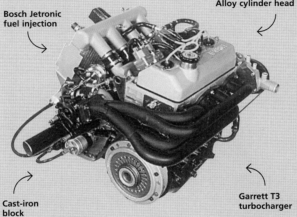

Bosch Jetronic fuel injection

Alloy cylinder head

Cast-iron block

Garrett T3 turbocharger

Small but powerful

The Turbo's powerplant is an unlikely one for a supercar. It is very small, with an iron block, pushrods, two valves per cylinder and wet cylinder liners. From here, though, it becomes interesting. The cylinder head is alloy and features hemispherical combustion chambers, and a Garrett T3 turbocharger, running 12.2 psi helps boost power to 160 bhp on road cars. Rally cars produce up to 300 bhp, but the ultimate R5 Turbo evolution—the Maxi—produces an amazing 550 bhp from a 1.5-liter unit.

Top scorer

In 1981, a Renault 5 Turbo driven by Jean Ragnotti won the prestigious Monte Carlo Rally. Bruno Saby drove one to win the French Rally Championship the same year. By 1984 Renault 5 turbos had racked up a total of 250 wins.

Turbos achieved outstanding success in Group B rallying.

Renault 5 TURBO 2

The mid-engined Renault 5 Turbo was designed to achieve two goals—to be a competitive World Championship rally car and to raise the profile of Renault's rather ordinary roadgoing models.

Turbocharged engine

Even the road cars have an excellent power output—160 bhp from just 1,397 cc—due to an intercooled Garrett turbocharger operating in conjunction with Bosch fuel injection.

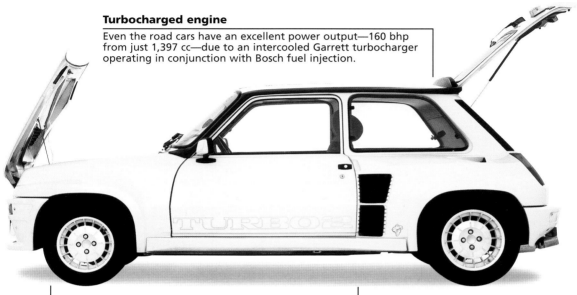

Front radiator

Although the engine is mounted behind the cabin, the radiator is at the front in the usual Renault 5 location; an electric fan assists cooling.

Intercooler vent

The vent on the left-hand side ahead of the rear wheel arch allows air to pass to the intercooler, which is mounted alongside the four-cylinder engine.

Rear-mounted transmission

In the standard Renault 5 the transmission is located ahead of the engine at the front of the car. In the mid-engined Turbo the whole package is rotated 180 degrees and moved back so that the transmission is toward the rear.

Wishbone rear suspension

The rear suspension is a double unequal-length wishbone system with long coil spring/shock absorber units mounted on top of spring-mounted turrets. These are connected by a bar in the engine bay to provide greater chassis stiffness.

Vented disc brakes

Braking on the Turbo is superb, as large vented discs are used all around. Both front and rear discs have a diameter of 10.2 inches.

Specifications

1984 Renault 5 Turbo 2

ENGINE

Type: In-line four-cylinder

Construction: Cast-iron block with wet cylinder liners and alloy cylinder head

Valve gear: Two valves per cylinder operated by pushrods and rockers

Bore and stroke: 3.0 in. x 3.03 in.

Displacement: 1,397 cc

Compression ratio: 7.0:1

Induction system: Bosch K-Jetronic fuel injection with single intercooled Garrett T3 turbocharger

Maximum power: 160 bhp at 6,000 rpm

Maximum torque: 158 lb-ft at 3,500 rpm

Top speed: 124 mph

0–60 mph: 7.7 sec.

TRANSMISSION

Five-speed manual

BODY/CHASSIS

Steel monocoque with fiberglass, alloy and steel two-door body

SPECIAL FEATURES

Huge vents behind the doors feed air into the twin intercoolers.

At 7.5 inches wide, the rear wheels are larger than those at the front.

RUNNING GEAR

Steering: Rack-and-pinion

Front suspension: Double wishbones with longitudinal torsion bars, telescopic shock absorbers and anti-roll bar

Rear suspension: Double wishbones with coil springs, telescopic shock absorbers and anti-roll bar

Brakes: Vented discs, 10.2-in. dia (front and rear)

Wheels: Cast-alloy, 5 x 13 in. (front), 7.5 x 13 in. (rear)

Tires: Michelin, 190/55 HR13 (front), 220/55 HR14 (rear)

DIMENSIONS

Length: 144.3 in.   **Width:** 69.0 in.

Height: 52.1 in.   **Wheelbase:** 95.7 in.

Track: 53.0 in. (front), 58.0 in. (rear)

Weight: 2,138 lbs.

Renault ALPINE A110

By combining small, light cars with powerful engines and Renault components, Alpine became a major force in world rallying during the late 1960s and early 1970s.

"...a true master of the road."

"Twisty roads beckon the A110; it feels lost on a big open highway. Once on a winding road it comes alive. Its responses are instant and the car darts into corners and exits them hard on the power. There may be a bit of tail-out oversteer, but that is all part of the technique and the fun. The A110 is also fast, reaching 60 mph in just over six seconds, and the speed feels so much greater in such a tiny machine."

Lightened for competition, this A110 features bucket seats, four-point harnesses, and very little in the way of luxury.

Milestones

1955 Jean Redelé
sets up Alpine in Dieppe. The first model is the A106.

A110s used many components from the Renault 8 Gordini.

1962 After building the 108, Redelé reveals the first A110.

1968 An A110 wins the
French Alpine Rally but fails to finish first at Monte Carlo.

Alpine also entered endurance racing with some success.

1971 Alpine takes
the World Rally Championship for the first time with four wins in the season.

1973 Alpine reclaims the World
Championship from Lancia, the 1972 winners.

1977 The last of the A110s is built in France,
alongside the late A310 at Dieppe.

UNDER THE SKIN

Utter simplicity

The chassis design of the A110 is simple. A single, large-diameter steel tube runs through the center line and acts as the main frame. It has welded supports attached to it for the wishbone front, and swing-axle rear suspension. The A110 features a rear-mounted Renault engine and transmission, and its handsome body is made from fiberglass to help keep overall weight to a minimum.

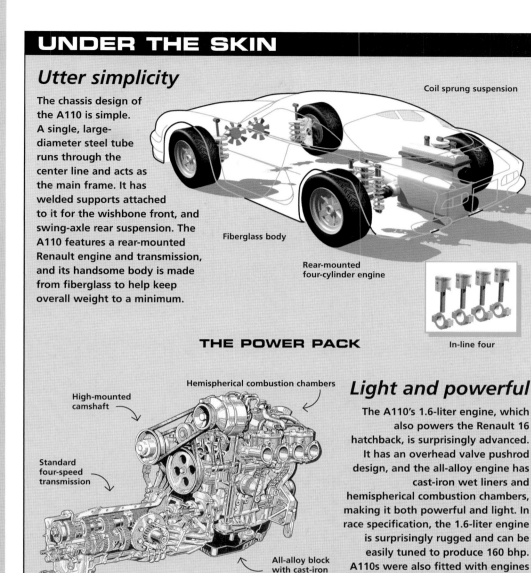

Coil sprung suspension

Fiberglass body

Rear-mounted four-cylinder engine

In-line four

THE POWER PACK

Hemispherical combustion chambers

High-mounted camshaft

Standard four-speed transmission

All-alloy block with cast-iron wet liners

Light and powerful

The A110's 1.6-liter engine, which also powers the Renault 16 hatchback, is surprisingly advanced. It has an overhead valve pushrod design, and the all-alloy engine has cast-iron wet liners and hemispherical combustion chambers, making it both powerful and light. In race specification, the 1.6-liter engine is surprisingly rugged and can be easily tuned to produce 160 bhp. A110s were also fitted with engines ranging from 1.1 to 1.5 liters.

Quicker still

The last of the A110s has a more powerful 1600-cc engine and also features revised rear suspension from the new A310. The double-wishbone rear end helps contain the oversteer that was so easily provoked on earlier cars.

The late-model Alpines had a more powerful 1600-cc engine.

Renault ALPINE A110

The A110 was an outstanding car. From the start of its production in 1963, steady improvements ensured that it remained competitive on the world rally stage for more than 10 years.

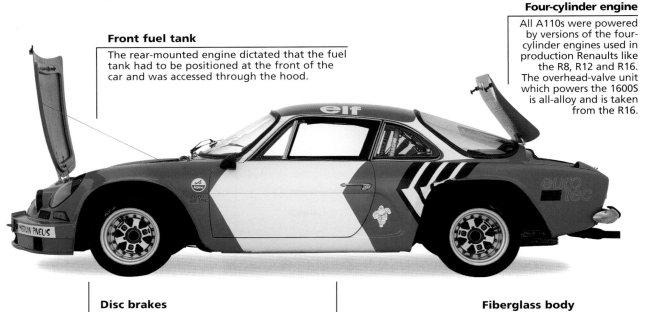

Front fuel tank

The rear-mounted engine dictated that the fuel tank had to be positioned at the front of the car and was accessed through the hood.

Four-cylinder engine

All A110s were powered by versions of the four-cylinder engines used in production Renaults like the R8, R12 and R16. The overhead-valve unit which powers the 1600S is all-alloy and is taken from the R16.

Disc brakes

With four-wheel disc brakes, the A110's stopping power was tremendous.

Fiberglass body

Because it was a limited production car and intended for competition, the body is constructed from fiberglass instead of steel.

Rear weight bias

With a rear-mounted engine and transmission, the A110 has a substantial rear weight bias that resulted in surprisingly light steering.

Wishbone front suspension

The front suspension was an effective system of upper and lower unequal-length wishbones with concentric coil spring/shock units and an anti-roll bar.

Dual shock absorbers

Whether fitted with swing axles or double wishbone rear suspension, there are two coil/shock units on each side.

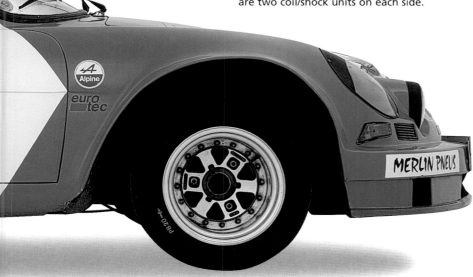

Specifications
1973 Alpine A110 1600S

ENGINE

Type: In-line four-cylinder Renault

Construction: Light alloy block and head with cast-iron wet liners

Valve gear: Two inclined valves per cylinder operated by a single block-mounted camshaft via pushrods and rockers

Bore and stroke: 3.07 in. x 3.30 in.

Displacement: 1,605 cc

Compression ratio: 10.25:1

Induction system: Two sidedraft Weber 45 DCOE carburetors

Maximum power: 138 bhp at 6,000 rpm

Maximum torque: 106 lb-ft at 5,000 rpm

Top speed: 127 mph

0–60 mph: 6.3 sec.

TRANSMISSION

Five-speed manual Renault

BODY/CHASSIS

Single tube backbone chassis with separate fiberglass two-door coupe body

SPECIAL FEATURES

The A110's single spine-type chassis is light and strong.

A front-mounted fuel tank doesn't leave too much space for luggage.

RUNNING GEAR

Steering: Rack-and-pinion

Front suspension: Double unequal-length wishbones, coil springs, telescopic shocks and anti-roll bar

Rear suspension: Swing axles with double coil springs/shock units per side

Brakes: Four-wheel discs, 10.2 in. dia.

Wheels: Alloy, 5.5 in. x 13 in.

Tires: Michelin or Dunlop radials, 185/70 VR13

DIMENSIONS

Length: 151.6 in.   **Width:** 59.8 in.

Height: 44.5 in.   **Wheelbase:** 82.7 in.

Track: 53.5 in. (front), 53.5 in. (rear)

Curb weight: 1,566 lbs.

Subaru **IMPREZA**

The Subaru Legacy made a competent rally car and certainly raised the company's profile. But its successor, the Impreza, was a true world-challenging rally car and has really helped the company's global image.

"...full-blooded performance."

"Although it's a stripped-out racer, there's a familiar and comfortable aura to the Impreza's cabin. This feeling, however, is misleading because once the key is turned all sensibilities are dropped in favor of full-blooded performance. With four-wheel drive, traction is superb, and the Subaru rockets off the line. With such a balanced chassis and nimble handling, the Impreza is probably the quickest rally racer in the world."

The rally Impreza is all business, with a substantial roll cage and rally bucket seats.

Milestones

1990 Subaru begins its first
serious assault on the World Rally Championship with the four-wheel drive turbocharged Legacy. Markku Alen, the most victorious rally driver in the world at the time, is hired to drive the car.

Rally wins have ensured good sales for the roadgoing Impreza.

1994 The release of the smaller
and more nimble Impreza leads Subaru and rally partner Prodrive to trade their Legacys for the new car.

Colin McRae and co-driver Derek Ringer won the championship in 1995.

1995 An epic struggle
between teammates Carlos Sainz and Colin McRae sees the world title decided in the final round. McRae is crowned Britain's and Subaru's first-ever world champion.

1998 A change in the regulations
from Group A to WRC sees the release of the two-door Impreza WRC.

UNDER THE SKIN

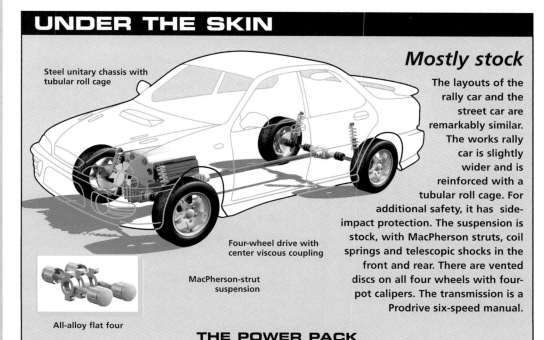

Steel unitary chassis with tubular roll cage

Four-wheel drive with center viscous coupling

MacPherson-strut suspension

All-alloy flat four

Mostly stock

The layouts of the rally car and the street car are remarkably similar. The works rally car is slightly wider and is reinforced with a tubular roll cage. For additional safety, it has side-impact protection. The suspension is stock, with MacPherson struts, coil springs and telescopic shocks in the front and rear. There are vented discs on all four wheels with four-pot calipers. The transmission is a Prodrive six-speed manual.

THE POWER PACK

Unbreakable boxer

One of the main reasons for Subaru's success in rallying is the strength of the four-cylinder 'boxer' engine. The 1,994-cc unit has an alloy block and heads with four valves per cylinder operated by twin overhead camshafts. In World Rally Championship specification, the transverse- mounted engine is protected by Subaru's own programmable electronic engine management chip. This controls the multipoint fuel injection as well as limiting the car to 300 bhp as dictated by FIA World Rally regulations. With adjustments to the chip and boost pressure, claims of up to 500 bhp are made from roadgoing Imprezas.

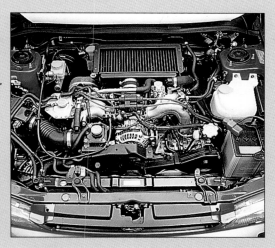

Giant killer

Before the Impreza, Subarus were regarded as subdued family cars. The 1995 championship win has irreversibly changed that view. Today, the roadgoing Impreza is viewed as a serious but less costly alternative to exotic supercars.

Rallying success has transformed Subaru's public image.

Subaru **IMPREZA**

The sensational performance of the Subaru Impreza has lifted the company from obscurity to the spotlight of international success. With every evolution, the Impreza seems to receive even more fans.

Flat-four engine

The turbocharged 16-valve 2.0-liter engine is a real powerhouse that is artificially limited to 300 bhp in order to comply with regulations.

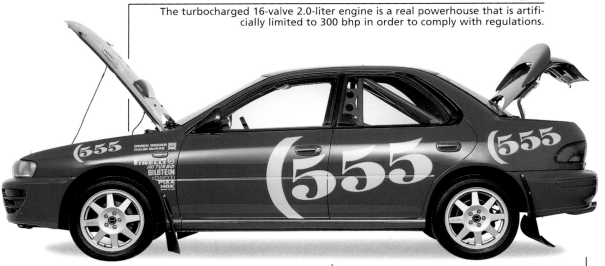

Green machine

Regulations state that the cars must conform to strict emissions testing, so the catalytic converter of the road car is retained. It is a three-way metallic catalyst.

Semi-automatic transmission

Prodrive does away with the stock five-speed manual and replaces it with its own six-speed sequential trans-mission.

Roll cage

To protect the driver and co-driver, a substantial roll cage is inside the car. The skeletal structure contains 25.5 meters of tubing, nearly six times the length of the car.

Specifications

1995 Subaru Impreza

ENGINE

Type: Horizontally opposed four-cylinder

Construction: Aluminum block and heads

Valve gear: Four valves per cylinder operated by twin overhead camshafts per bank of cylinders

Bore and stroke: 3.62 in. x 2.95 in.

Displacement: 1,994 cc

Compression ratio: Not quoted

Induction system: Multipoint fuel injection

Maximum power: 300 bhp at 5,500 rpm

Maximum torque: 348 lb-ft at 4,000 rpm

Top speed: 140 mph

0–60 mph: 3.2 sec.

TRANSMISSION

Six-speed semi-automatic

BODY/CHASSIS

Unitary monocoque construction with four-door sedan body

SPECIAL FEATURES

The large hood scoop feeds cool air to the intercooler.

This is Colin McRae's actual 1995 championship-winning car.

RUNNING GEAR

Steering: Rack-and-pinion

Front suspension: MacPherson struts with coil springs, shock absorbers and anti-roll bar

Rear suspension: MacPherson struts with multilink, coil springs, shock absorbers and anti-roll bar

Brakes: Vented discs (front and rear)

Wheels: Speedline (size depends on terrain)

Tires: Pirelli (size depends on terrain)

DIMENSIONS

Length: 170.9 in.   **Width:** 69.7 in.

Height: 54.7 in.   **Wheelbase:** 99.2 in.

Track: 58.8 in. (front and rear)

Weight: 2,711 lbs.

Four-wheel drive

Contemporary rallying demands four-wheel drive for success. Subaru has been producing 4x4 road cars since the 1970s and did not need to develop a system especially for the Impreza. There is a 50:50 front/rear torque split in the permanent system.

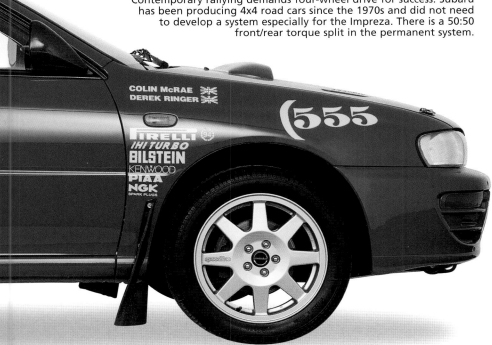

Sunbeam **TIGER**

Carroll Shelby didn't like to waste a good idea. Putting a Ford V8 into the AC Ace had produced the Cobra. Doing the same thing to the Sunbeam Alpine created the fierce Tiger.

"...absolutely effortless."

"The Tiger's straight-line speed is impressive and absolutely effortless thanks to the high gearing and unstressed engine, and it will power through long sweeping curves at great speed with perfect stability. Both clutch and gearshift are easy. On good roads, the Tiger is quite comfortable for a small car. However, fierce heat builds up under the hood in hot climates. Try to use all its performance and the axle will spin dramatically. On tight, twisty roads the car really shows the limitations of its chassis and suspension."

Tiger had a more luxurious interior than its four-cylinder stablemate, the Alpine.

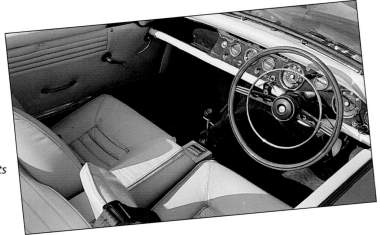

Milestones

1959 Sunbeam Alpine

is launched with a 1,494-cc four-cylinder engine.

Four-cylinder Alpine formed the basis of the V8 Tiger.

1964 First of the Tigers

is ready in time for the New York Show; the U.S. is intended as the major market for the car where it even becomes a successful rally car, appearing six months before going on sale in Europe.

1966 Although changes such as

larger, 14-inch, wheels are proposed, the MkII Tiger goes into production with only one major change: the bigger 4.7-liter V8 engine.

Extra power of Tiger meant it was a much more successful competition car than the Alpine.

1967 Production ends because

Chrysler has taken over Rootes and will not sell a Ford-engined car in the U.S.

UNDER THE SKIN

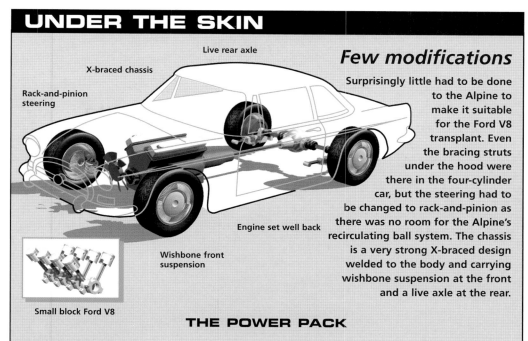

X-braced chassis

Live rear axle

Rack-and-pinion steering

Engine set well back

Wishbone front suspension

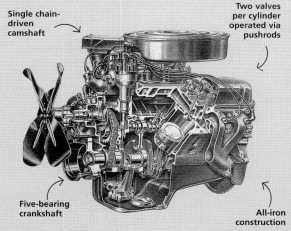

Small block Ford V8

Few modifications

Surprisingly little had to be done to the Alpine to make it suitable for the Ford V8 transplant. Even the bracing struts under the hood were there in the four-cylinder car, but the steering had to be changed to rack-and-pinion as there was no room for the Alpine's recirculating ball system. The chassis is a very strong X-braced design welded to the body and carrying wishbone suspension at the front and a live axle at the rear.

THE POWER PACK

Tiger torque

The Tiger started with the 260-cubic inch (4,261-cc) pushrod Ford V8 engine, as fitted to the early Cobra. Despite the far bigger capacity, clever design means it is not significantly heavier than the Alpine's four cylinder. It wasn't designed to rev very high, with maximum power coming in at only 4,400 rpm, because it relied on its great torque output for its power. Cramped under-hood conditions and the extra heat generated by the big engine means that overheating is not uncommon.

Single chain-driven camshaft

Two valves per cylinder operated via pushrods

Five-bearing crankshaft

All-iron construction

Top Tiger

The rarer and short-lived MkII Tiger is a better performer, with the larger, 4.7-liter, V8 giving 200 bhp and an extra 24 lb-ft of torque, dropping the 0-60 mph time down below eight seconds. Otherwise, there are few changes. It was axed shortly after launch due to the Chrysler take over.

MkII Tiger has larger 4.7-liter engine and an increase in power.

Sunbeam TIGER

At first glance, you couldn't tell a Tiger apart from an Alpine, but the difference became really obvious when the driver put his foot down and left you behind.

Rear battery

With the V8 engine taking up most of the space under the hood the battery was moved to the trunk, which also helped weight distribution.

Ford V8 engine

Ford agreed to supply V8 engines to a rival company because it knew the Tiger couldn't be built in enough volume to affect its own sporty Mustang.

Higher axle ratio

The more powerful, slow-revving, V8 meant that a new final drive ratio had to be fitted to the axle, and it was changed from 3.07:1 to 2.88:1 to provide the driver with relaxed high-speed touring.

Alpine brakes

Rootes had little money for development, so it retained the Alpine's 13-inch wheels, which meant there was no way of making the brakes bigger.

Ford transmission

Naturally, the Ford V8 engine is fitted along with the four-speed transmission used with it on American Fords.

Near equal weight distribution

Mounting the engine back in the chassis (so far that some spark plugs had to be removed from inside the car) gave the Tiger a 51/49 front-to-rear weight distribution.

Stiffer springs

The heavier and faster Tiger was fitted with stronger springs and revalved shocks.

Larger radiator

To cool the bigger Ford motor tightly squeezed into the Alpine engine bay, a larger crossflow radiator is used. However, cooling was still marginal.

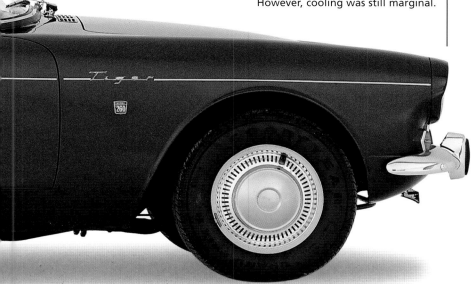

Specifications
1965 Sunbeam Tiger MkI

ENGINE

Type: Ford V8
Construction: Cast-iron block and heads
Valve gear: Two valves per cylinder operated by single block-mounted camshafts via pushrod and hydraulic lifters
Bore and stroke: 3.81 in. x 2.87 in.
Displacement: 4,261 cc
Compression ratio: 8.8:1
Induction system: Single Ford four-barrel carburetor
Maximum power: 164 bhp at 4,400 rpm
Maximum torque: 258 lb-ft at 2,200 rpm
Top speed: 117 mph
0–60 mph: 9.7 sec.

TRANSMISSION

Ford four-speed manual

BODY/CHASSIS

Unitary construction with welded-on X-braced chassis rails, two-door, two-seat convertible body

SPECIAL FEATURES

The Sunbeam Tiger MkI runs a highly tuned 4,261 cc engine. Like any light car with a big engine, the Tiger had lots of power and was very fun to drive.

Only the Tiger lettering on the side, the '260' badges and twin exhaust pipes showed the car was a Tiger.

RUNNING GEAR

Steering: Rack-and-pinion
Front suspension: Double wishbones, coil springs, telescopic shocks and anti-roll bar
Rear suspension: Live axle with semi-elliptic leaf springs, Panhard rod and telescopic shocks
Brakes: Discs 9.8 in. dia. (front), drums 9 in. dia. (rear)
Wheels: Steel disc, 4.5 in. x 13 in.
Tires: Dunlop RS5 5.9 x 13 in.

DIMENSIONS

Length: 158 in.   **Width:** 60.5 in.
Height: 51.5 in.   **Wheelbase:** 86 in.
Track: 51.8 in. (front), 86 in. (rear)
Weight: 2,644 lbs.

Toyota SUPRA TURBO

Toyota aimed this generation of the Supra at one market above all others—the U.S. It had to be big enough, bold enough and fully equipped to stand out from the mass of other similar coupes. It was, and in 232-bhp Turbo form, the Supra is also extremely fast.

"...you won't be disappointed."

"You won't be disappointed by the performance: the Turbo's enormous midrange torque rockets this heavyweight to 100 mph in just over 18 seconds. Drive it really hard, though, and the surprisingly precise steering and handling, and what initially feels like tenacious grip from the low-profile tires, start to struggle a little, suffering sudden and often dramatic oversteer. The ride is harsh and rigid for a luxury coupe, but the brakes are simply superb."

Standard equipment includes power everything, air conditioning and leather trim.

Milestones

1981 The Supra
name first appears as part of the Celica range. Unlike the four-cylinder Celicas, the Celica Supra has a 2.8-liter, straight-six, twin-cam engine with 168 bhp.

The Supra name arrived with the Celica Supra of 1981.

1986 A total restyle
makes the Supra far more rounded, and it looks bigger than it is. The engine is enlarged to 3.0 liters, and the cylinder head is changed to four valves per cylinder; power is now 200 bhp.

The 1993 incarnation of the Supra is a real supercar.

1989 The Supra gets
more spectacular performance when an intercooled turbo is added; power is up to 232 bhp.

1993 Toyota
introduces the next-generation Supra—a world-class supercar with a 324-bhp, 2.5-liter, twin-turbo, straight-six engine and far more style and performance.

UNDER THE SKIN

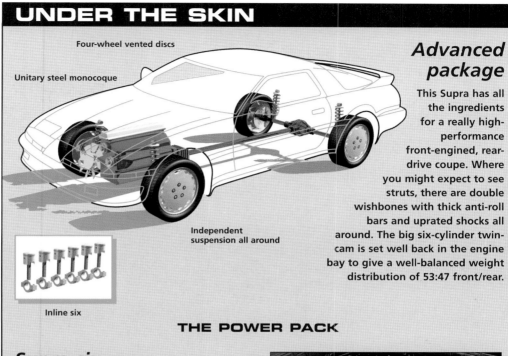

Four-wheel vented discs

Unitary steel monocoque

Independent suspension all around

Inline six

Advanced package

This Supra has all the ingredients for a really high-performance front-engined, rear-drive coupe. Where you might expect to see struts, there are double wishbones with thick anti-roll bars and uprated shocks all around. The big six-cylinder twin-cam is set well back in the engine bay to give a well-balanced weight distribution of 53:47 front/rear.

THE POWER PACK

Supra six

Powering the Supra is a development of the inline six-cylinder seen in the earlier Celica Supra but with a longer stroke and new cylinder head design. On top of the cast-iron block is an alloy, four-valve-per-cylinder head first seen in 1986, with twin, belt-driven, overhead camshafts. In normally aspirated form, it puts out 200 bhp. For the turbocharged version, compression was reduced to 8.4:1 and the ACIS (Acoustic Control Induction System) was dropped. An intercooler was added to increase air density and hence produce more power (232 bhp), resulting in truly formidable performance.

Super Supra

Adding a turbocharger to the straight-six Supra changed the car from a lazy grand tourer into a real luxury road rocket. Today there are very few cars that can offer this kind of punchy performance for so little money. It's a bargain secondhand buy.

The turbocharger gives a top speed of over 140 mph.

Toyota **SUPRA TURBO**

The Supra Turbo was powerful and fast, but it lacked the hard-edged distinctive look of the first Supra and is now totally overshadowed by the incredible twin-turbo genuine supercar that followed.

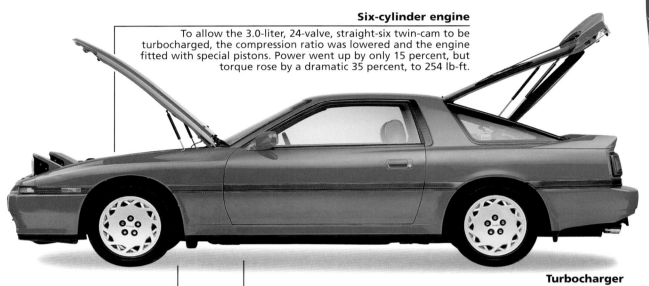

Six-cylinder engine

To allow the 3.0-liter, 24-valve, straight-six twin-cam to be turbocharged, the compression ratio was lowered and the engine fitted with special pistons. Power went up by only 15 percent, but torque rose by a dramatic 35 percent, to 254 lb-ft.

Five-speed transmission

The standard transmission is a five-speed manual, geared to give a relaxed 25.7 mph per 1,000 rpm in top. It is fitted with a stronger clutch to stand the extra power and torque. A four-speed automatic was an available option.

Turbocharger

Before the Supra Turbo, Toyota had experience with both supercharging and turbocharging and knew it was the ideal way to boost mid-range torque. The turbo was used along with an air-to-air intercooler to keep intake charge temperatures low. Maximum boost was a moderate 7.3 psi.

Rack-and-pinion steering

The Turbo's mechanical specification includes rack-and-pinion steering. Due to the size of the car and its intended market, power assistance is inevitably included, and there are 3.4 turns lock to lock.

Large vented discs
Large vented disc brakes are fitted to the front and rear, the fronts being 11.9 inches in diameter, with 11.5-inch rears. ABS is standard, and the whole package is extremely impressive and fade-free.

Double wishbones
Toyota followed the best practice for the suspension, using double wishbones front and rear. The Turbo has extra locating rods for the rear subframe, as well as thicker anti-roll bars and uprated shocks.

Specifications

1989 Toyota Supra Turbo

ENGINE
Type: In-line six-cylinder

Construction: Cast-iron block and alloy cylinder head

Valve gear: Four valves per cylinder operated by twin overhead camshafts

Bore and stroke: 3.27 in. x 3.58 in.

Displacement: 2,954 cc

Compression ratio: 8.4:1

Induction system: Electronic fuel injection with turbocharger

Maximum power: 232 bhp at 5,600 rpm

Maximum torque: 254 lb-ft at 4,000 rpm

Top speed: 144 mph

0–60 mph: 6.5 sec.

TRANSMISSION
Four-speed automatic

BODY/CHASSIS
Unitary monocoque construction with steel two-door four-seater body

SPECIAL FEATURES

Unlike the next-generation Supra, this one has pop-up headlights.

A discreet rear spoiler is neatly integrated into the rear-end styling.

RUNNING GEAR
Steering: Rack-and-pinion

Front suspension: Double wishbones with coil springs, telescopic shock absorbers and anti-roll bar

Rear suspension: Double wishbones with coil springs, telescopic shock absorbers and anti-roll bar

Brakes: Vented discs, 11.9-in. dia. (front), 11.5-in. dia. (rear)

Wheels: Alloy, 7 x 16 in.

Tires: 225/50 VR16

DIMENSIONS
Length: 181.9 in.   **Width:** 68.7 in.

Height: 51.6 in.   **Wheelbase:** 102.2 in.

Track: 58.5 in. (front and rear)

Weight: 3,535 lbs.

TVR **CHIMAERA**

Although milder than the fearsome Griffith, the Chimaera is still a seriously fast sports car, built using the same recipe that makes early Corvettes great: a separate chassis, fiberglass body and a big V8 driving the rear wheels.

"...made for skillful drivers."

"Chimaeras are made for skillful drivers. There's a lot of power for a car with such a short wheelbase (14 inches shorter than a Corvette), and it's set up to give instant response to the incredibly quick steering. It's easily steered on the throttle, too. The V8 sounds great, and is accompanied by flexible power that gives serious overtaking ability. What's more, the ride is nowhere near as hard as you'd expect and the TVR feels immensely solid."

Classy gauges and a chunky wheel hint at the Chimaera's potent performance.

Milestones

1993 TVR launches the Chimaera, which

fills a hole in its range between the popular 'S' convertible and the mighty 5.0-liter Griffith.

The Griffith was the first of the modern wave of TVRs.

1995 At the top of the Chimaera range

now is the 5.0-liter version with the bored and stroked Rover engine from the Griffith 500, giving 340 bhp.

The Cerbera currently tops the TVR range.

1997 TVR fills a gap between

the 240-bhp 4.0-liter and 340-bhp 5.0-liter with the 4.5-liter version. The new engine is a long-stroke version of the 4.0-liter and gives 285 bhp at 5,500 rpm and 310 lb-ft of torque at 4,250 rpm. It has the same improvements as the 5.0-liter car, so there are bigger brakes, and new wheels that carry the Bridgestone S-02 tires are now fitted to all TVRs.

UNDER THE SKIN

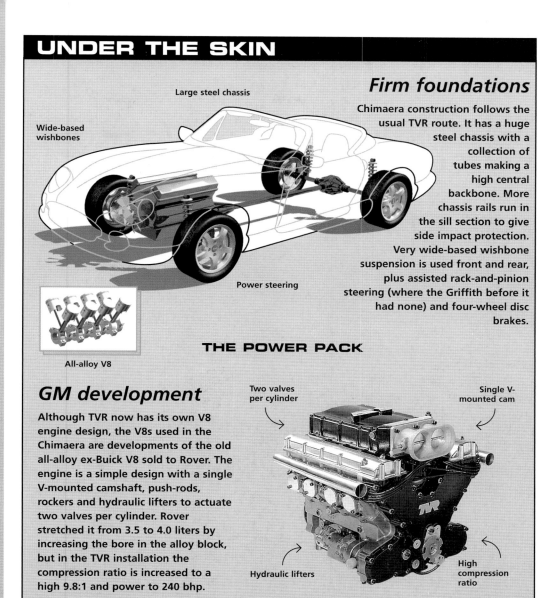

Large steel chassis

Wide-based wishbones

Power steering

All-alloy V8

Firm foundations

Chimaera construction follows the usual TVR route. It has a huge steel chassis with a collection of tubes making a high central backbone. More chassis rails run in the sill section to give side impact protection. Very wide-based wishbone suspension is used front and rear, plus assisted rack-and-pinion steering (where the Griffith before it had none) and four-wheel disc brakes.

THE POWER PACK

GM development

Although TVR now has its own V8 engine design, the V8s used in the Chimaera are developments of the old all-alloy ex-Buick V8 sold to Rover. The engine is a simple design with a single V-mounted camshaft, push-rods, rockers and hydraulic lifters to actuate two valves per cylinder. Rover stretched it from 3.5 to 4.0 liters by increasing the bore in the alloy block, but in the TVR installation the compression ratio is increased to a high 9.8:1 and power to 240 bhp.

Two valves per cylinder

Single V-mounted cam

Hydraulic lifters

High compression ratio

Top choice

The ultimate Chimaera is the 5.0-liter, which has the biggest stretch of the old Rover engine. It takes power up to 340 bhp and torque to 320 lb-ft. Naturally, performance rockets too, with a top speed of 165 mph and a 0-60 time of 4.1 seconds.

The 5.0-liter Chimaera is an exclusive beast that should be handled with care.

TVR **CHIMAERA**

Stunning looks as well as performance set the Chimaera apart. TVR styling is all carried out in-house in Blackpool, with traditional clay full-size models sculpted until the effect is just right.

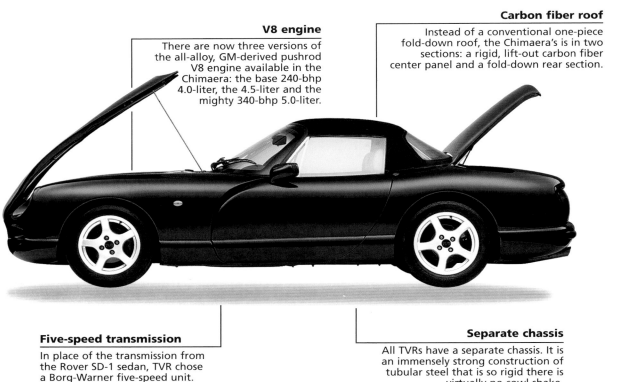

V8 engine
There are now three versions of the all-alloy, GM-derived pushrod V8 engine available in the Chimaera: the base 240-bhp 4.0-liter, the 4.5-liter and the mighty 340-bhp 5.0-liter.

Carbon fiber roof
Instead of a conventional one-piece fold-down roof, the Chimaera's is in two sections: a rigid, lift-out carbon fiber center panel and a fold-down rear section.

Five-speed transmission
In place of the transmission from the Rover SD-1 sedan, TVR chose a Borg-Warner five-speed unit. Its overdrive-fifth gives a relaxed 27.5 mph per 1,000 revs in top.

Separate chassis
All TVRs have a separate chassis. It is an immensely strong construction of tubular steel that is so rigid there is virtually no cowl shake.

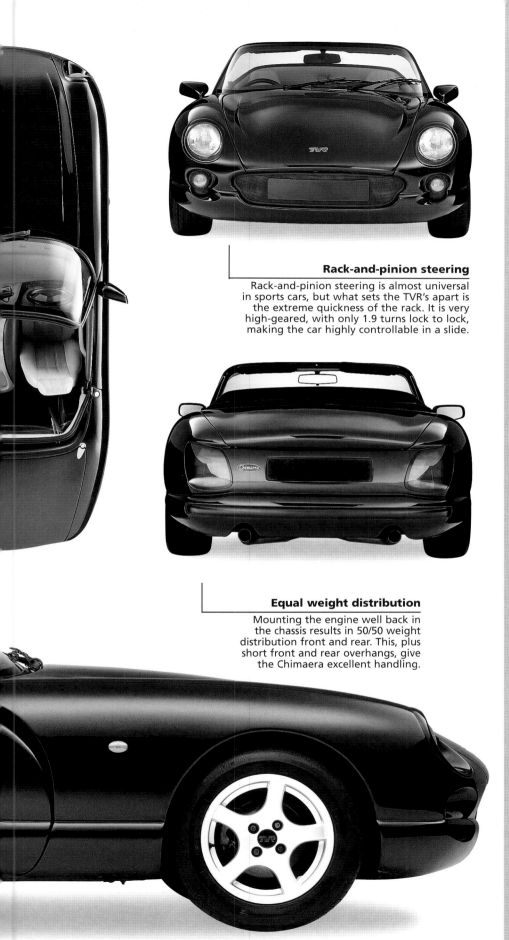

Rack-and-pinion steering

Rack-and-pinion steering is almost universal in sports cars, but what sets the TVR's apart is the extreme quickness of the rack. It is very high-geared, with only 1.9 turns lock to lock, making the car highly controllable in a slide.

Equal weight distribution

Mounting the engine well back in the chassis results in 50/50 weight distribution front and rear. This, plus short front and rear overhangs, give the Chimaera excellent handling.

Specifications

1998 TVR Chimaera

ENGINE

Type: V8

Construction: Alloy block and heads

Valve gear: Two valves per cylinder operated by a single camshaft with pushrods and rocker arms

Bore and stroke: 3.70 in. x 2.80 in.

Displacement: 3,950 cc

Compression ratio: 9.8:1

Induction system: Electronic fuel injection

Maximum power: 240 bhp at 5,250 rpm

Maximum torque: 270 lb-ft at 4,000 rpm

Top speed: 158 mph

0–60 mph: 5.2 sec.

TRANSMISSION

Five-speed manual

BODY/CHASSIS

Separate tubular-steel backbone chassis with fiberglass two-seater convertible body

SPECIAL FEATURES

The rear of the roof folds into the trunk, where the center section can be stored.

All TVRs are styled in-house at the company's Blackpool base.

RUNNING GEAR

Steering: Rack-and-pinion

Front suspension: Double wishbones with coil springs, telescopic shock absorbers and anti-roll bar

Rear suspension: Double wishbones with coil springs, telescopic shock absorbers and anti-roll bar

Brakes: Vented discs, 10.2-in. dia. (front), 10.7-in. dia. (rear)

Wheels: Cast-alloy, 7 x 15 in. (front), 7 x 16 in. (rear)

Tires: Bridgestone S-02, 205/60 ZR15 (front), 225/55 ZR16 (rear)

DIMENSIONS

Length: 179.1 in.   **Width:** 76.2 in.

Height: 50.2 in.   **Wheelbase:** 98.4 in.

Track: 57.5 in. (front and rear)

Weight: 2,260 lbs.

TVR **GRIFFITH**

The Griffith is a world away from TVR's kit-car origins. The quality is high, the design outstanding and the performance from its latest 5-liter V8 engine nothing short of staggering.

"...guarantees excitement."

"More than 300 bhp in a light car that has a short wheelbase guarantees excitement and the Griffith delivers a huge amount of it. Lurid power is only a touch of the throttle away, as the power overcomes the grip of the big rear tires despite the limited slip differential. Before the power-assisted steering became available, it took an acute combination of strength and finesse to control such behavior. You also need a firm hand for the gear shifter and a strong leg for the clutch, but the Griffith's breathtaking acceleration makes it all worth the effort."

Smart and stylish dashboard of the Griffith uses many recognizable switches and gauges.

Milestones

1963 The distant ancestor of the current Griffith has a Ford V8 and is named after U.S. Ford dealer Jack Griffith. It can reach 160 mph, but the car is very difficult to drive fast.

By the late 1980s, the wedge-shaped TVRs were beginning to look dated.

1990 TVR builds another Griffith, as a show car for the British Motor Show. Reaction is enthusiastic, so TVR decides to put the Griffith into production.

The Racing Tuscan showed TVR's potential.

1992 The production Griffith debuts. It is designed to use a variety of Rover V8 engines, from a 'basic' 240-bhp version, through a 250-bhp stage and up to the 280-bhp 4.3-liter version.

1993 An even more powerful Griffith appears. The engine is enlarged to 5 liters, to form the 340-bhp Griffith 500.

UNDER THE SKIN

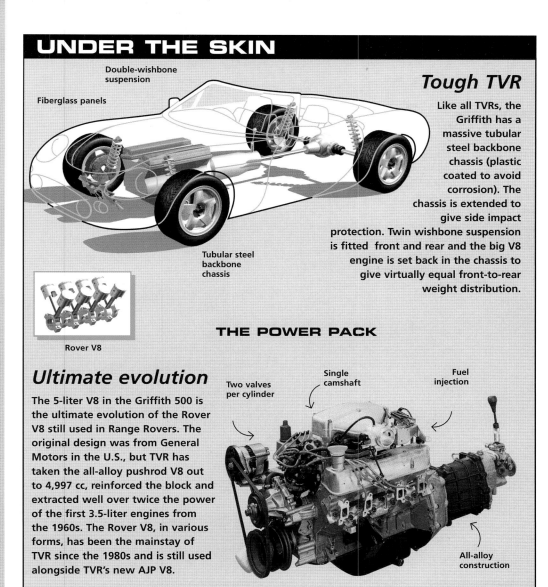

Double-wishbone suspension

Fiberglass panels

Tubular steel backbone chassis

Rover V8

Tough TVR

Like all TVRs, the Griffith has a massive tubular steel backbone chassis (plastic coated to avoid corrosion). The chassis is extended to give side impact protection. Twin wishbone suspension is fitted front and rear and the big V8 engine is set back in the chassis to give virtually equal front-to-rear weight distribution.

THE POWER PACK

Ultimate evolution

The 5-liter V8 in the Griffith 500 is the ultimate evolution of the Rover V8 still used in Range Rovers. The original design was from General Motors in the U.S., but TVR has taken the all-alloy pushrod V8 out to 4,997 cc, reinforced the block and extracted well over twice the power of the first 3.5-liter engines from the 1960s. The Rover V8, in various forms, has been the mainstay of TVR since the 1980s and is still used alongside TVR's new AJP V8.

Two valves per cylinder

Single camshaft

Fuel injection

All-alloy construction

Best of British

The Griffith's stunning looks don't come from an expensive Italian styling house or from computer-aided design, but from the eye of TVR boss Peter Wheeler and engineer John Ravenscroft. They sculpted a full-size foam model until they arrived at the Griffith's stunning shape.

Designed in-house, the Griffith looks spectacular from any angle.

TVR GRIFFITH

The Griffith is just like a modern-day AC Cobra, the concept being a very large powerful engine in a small convertible. Like the Cobra, there's very little to rival the Griffith.

Fiberglass bodywork

The fiberglass body is bolted to the tubular steel chassis to make a stronger, stiffer overall structure.

Flat-mounted radiator

The radiator is mounted at a very shallow angle and the air is drawn through it by twin electric fans. There was room to allow this because the engine is set so far back.

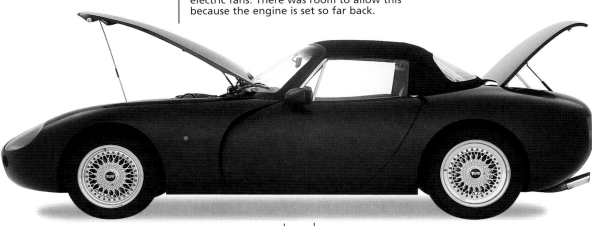

Rover transmission

Sensibly, the TVR use the same tough, five-speed transmission that Rover used in the fastest of its V8-engined cars, the Vitesse.

Tubular steel chassis

The tubular steel chassis is designed to give the Griffith an extremely strong central backbone, which is the way TVR has always designed its chassis.

Larger rear wheels

To cope with its huge power output, the Griffith has larger, 7.5 inch x 16 inch OZ Racing split-rim alloy rear wheels.

Optional leather trim

If you want your Griffith to be luxurious as well as very fast then leather seats and trim are an option.

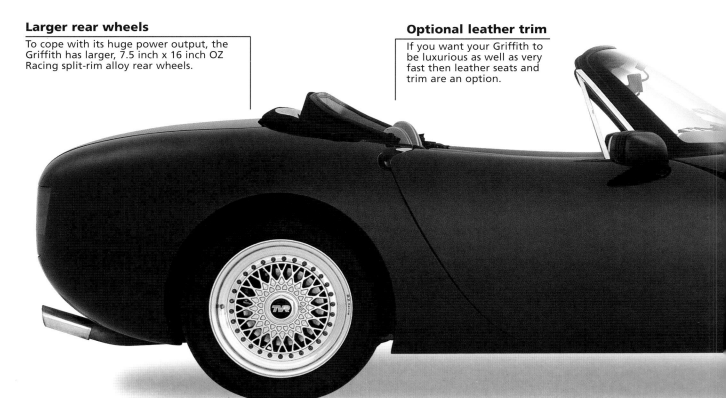

Equal weight distribution

With the engine set well back in the chassis, the heavy Rover transmission is near the center of the car: The weight distribution is almost ideal at 51 percent front, 49 percent rear.

Wishbone suspension

Twin wishbone suspension is used all around on the Griffith. The rear suspension is very similar to that found on the mighty TVR Tuscan racers.

Ford Sierra final drive

The final drive housing is actually a Ford Sierra part, but the gears inside are much stronger, with a Quaife limited slip differential to reduce wheelspin and help traction.

Specifications
1993 TVR Griffith 500

ENGINE
Type: V8, overhead valve
Construction: Alloy block and heads
Valve gear: Two valves per cylinder operated by single block-mounted camshaft via pushrods and rockers
Bore and stroke: 3.54 in. x 3.54 in.
Displacement: 4,997 cc
Compression ratio: 10:1
Induction system: Electronic fuel injection
Maximum power: 340 bhp at 5,500 rpm
Maximum torque: 351 lb-ft at 4,000 rpm
Top speed: 161 mph
0–60 mph: 4.3 sec.

TRANSMISSION
Five-speed manual

BODY/CHASSIS
Fiberglass two-door, two-seat convertible with tubular steel backbone chassis

SPECIAL FEATURES

The V8 has massive exhaust headers which have to be routed around the front of the engine.

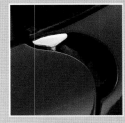

Small door handles are neatly recessed so the lines of the car are not spoiled.

RUNNING GEAR
Steering: Rack-and-pinion
Front suspension: Twin wishbones, coil springs, telescopic shocks and anti-roll bar
Rear suspension: Twin wishbones, coil springs and telescopic shocks
Brakes: Disc, vented 10.2 in. dia. (front), solid 10.7 in. dia. (rear)
Wheels: Alloy OZ, 7 in. x 15 in. (front), 7.5 in. x 16 in. (rear)
Tires: 215/50ZR15 (front), 225/50ZR16 (rear)

DIMENSIONS
Length: 156.1 in.   **Width:** 76.5 in.
Wheelbase: 58.4 in.   **Height:** 46.7 in.
Track: 58 in. (front), 58.4 in. (rear)
Weight: 2,304 lbs.

Vector **W8-M12**

The best way of describing the exotic Vector is that it's America's answer to Lamborghini. It boasts phenomenal power output and has the performance to make it a contender for the title of the fastest car on earth.

"...American exotica."

"If you have ever wondered what a fighter pilot must feel like, slide into the Vector and you'll have a good idea. Everything is designed for ultra-high speeds. Its controls resemble those of a jet fighter and the overall ride is the same. As for the acceleration, it's American exotica that can compete with Italian supercars. The Vector offers unearthly performance and is a pleasure to drive—especially in the three digit mph range."

The Vector is by no means your everyday car. Inside it is more like a Space Shuttle than a conventional car.

Milestones

1977 Gerald A. Wiegert's Vector W2 is presented in Los Angeles as "the fastest car in the world."

1990 After years of preparation, the W8 is launched using a Donovan small-block Chevy®-designed engine.

Originally, Vectors were built with domestic drivelines.

1992 A WX3 model has a new aerodynamic body, twin turbos and makes up to 1100 bhp.

1993 After a power struggle, Megatech eventually emerges as the new owner and the company moves to Florida. Since they also own Lamborghini, future plans include building the car with the Diablo's V12. By using the underpowered Italian engine, the Vector will no longer be a full-blooded and extremely powerful U.S. supercar.

On looks, the Vector is a match for any Lamborghini or Ferrari.

1995 With a Diablo 492 bhp V12 engine and a much cheaper price tag, the new M12 model is marketed.

UNDER THE SKIN

Like an aircraft

Based in a part of California well known for its advanced aerospace industry, Vector took full advantage of its location. Under the super-lightweight composite bodywork there is an aircraft-inspired aluminum chassis which is both light and very strong. The Vector's running gear may be state of the art, but it is also practical. The front end boasts independent double-wishbone suspension, while the rear end consists of a well-located de Dion tube and coil/shock units.

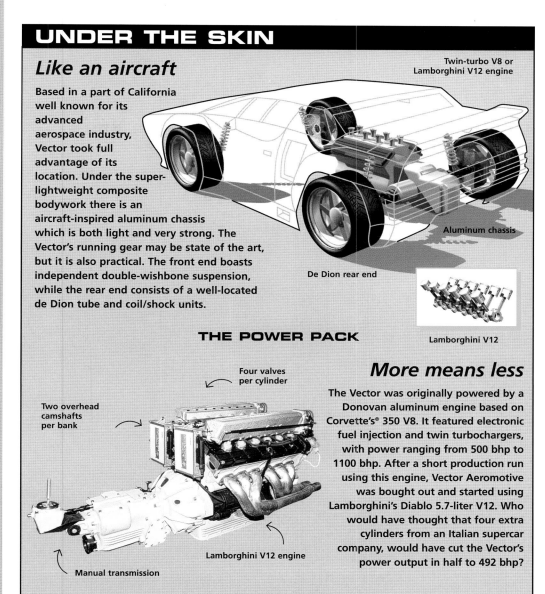

Twin-turbo V8 or Lamborghini V12 engine

Aluminum chassis

De Dion rear end

Lamborghini V12

THE POWER PACK

Four valves per cylinder

Two overhead camshafts per bank

Lamborghini V12 engine

Manual transmission

More means less

The Vector was originally powered by a Donovan aluminum engine based on Corvette's® 350 V8. It featured electronic fuel injection and twin turbochargers, with power ranging from 500 bhp to 1100 bhp. After a short production run using this engine, Vector Aeromotive was bought out and started using Lamborghini's Diablo 5.7-liter V12. Who would have thought that four extra cylinders from an Italian supercar company, would have cut the Vector's power output in half to 492 bhp?

Vector M12

When Megatech acquired Vector Aeromotive, it restyled its body and gave it an Italian supercar engine. While the new body panels bring the car into the 1990s, it should have kept the 1,100-bhp Chevy-designed V8. In comparison, the new V12 only makes 492 bhp.

The M12 uses Lamborghini's bigger but less powerful V-12 engine.

Vector W8-M12

Originally marketed as an all-American supercar using a Chevy-designed engine and a Toronado® transmission, the Vector W8 pulled the rug out from under both Lamborghini and Ferrari.

Aircraft-influenced design

As well as using aerospace materials and construction methods, the Vector's styling also recalls aircraft practice.

Advanced bodywork

Years before other manufacturers began using sophisticated composites in cars, the Vector's bodywork contained Kevlar, fiberglass and carbon fiber.

Honeycomb chassis

The advanced chassis is a semi-monocoque structure. Like an aircraft frame, it is constructed from tubular steel and bonded aluminum honeycomb, and is extremely light and incredibly strong.

Turbocharged Chevy V8

In a bid to make this an all-American supercar, the engine was derived from a Corvette V8 unit. To produce enough power to make this the fastest car in the world, Vector used twin intercooled Garrett H3 turbochargers.

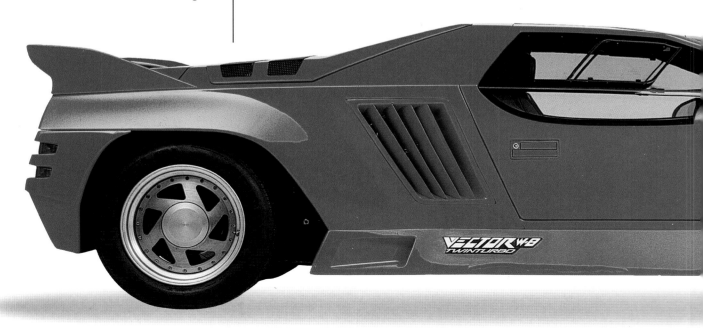

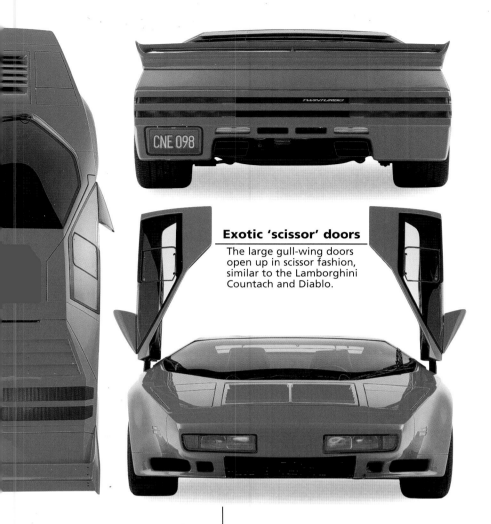

Exotic 'scissor' doors
The large gull-wing doors open up in scissor fashion, similar to the Lamborghini Countach and Diablo.

Oldsmobile® transmission
To transfer the immense power of the mid-mounted engine, Vector selected a suitably modified Toronado automatic transmission.

Powerful braking
With performance as breathtaking as the Vector's, brakes that can deal with speeds of up to 218 mph are required. The Vector has vented four-wheel discs measuring a massive 13 inches in diameter. Naturally, there is a sophisticated ABS system.

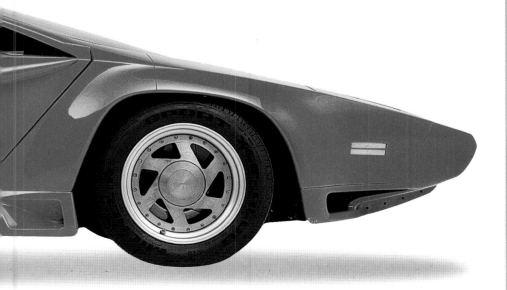

Specifications
1992 Vector W8

ENGINE
Type: V8
Construction: Cast-iron cylinder block and head
Valve gear: Two valves per cylinder operated by a single camshaft
Bore and stroke: 4.08 in. x 3.48 in.
Displacement: 5,973 cc
Compression ratio: 8.0:1
Induction system: Tuned port electronic fuel injection
Maximum power: 625 bhp at 5,700 rpm
Maximum torque: 630 lb-ft at 4,900 rpm
Top speed: 195 mph
0–60 mph: 4.1 sec.

TRANSMISSION
Three-speed automatic

BODY/CHASSIS
Semi-monocoque honeycomb chassis with two-door coupe body in composite materials

SPECIAL FEATURES

Twin Garrett turbochargers can boost power up to 1100 bhp, a figure the Diablo engine could never match.

The radiator is mounted horizontally in the nose of the car, leaving little space for luggage up front.

RUNNING GEAR
Steering: Rack-and-pinion
Front suspension: Double wishbones with coil springs and shocks
Rear suspension: De Dion axle with longitudinal and transverse arms and coil spring/shock units
Brakes: Four-wheel discs
Wheels: Alloy, 16-in. dia.
Tires: 255/45 ZR16 front, 315/40 ZR16 rear

DIMENSIONS
Length: 172 in.   **Width:** 76 in.
Height: 42.5 in.   **Wheelbase:** 103 in.
Track: 63 in. (front), 65 in. (rear)
Weight: 3,572 lbs.

Glossary of Technical Terms

A

A-pillar Angled roof supports each side of the front windscreen

ABS Anti-lock braking system

Acceleration Rate of change of velocity, usually expressed as a measure of time over a given distance such as a quarter of a mile, or from rest to a given speed, such as 0–60mph

Aerodynamic drag Wind resistance, expressed as a coefficient of drag (Cd); the more streamlined a vehicle, the lower the figure

Aftermarket Accessory fitted to a vehicle after purchase, not always offered by the manufacturer

Air-cooled engine Where ambient air is used to cool the engine, by passing directly over fins on the cylinders and cylinder head

Air dam Device at the front of a car to reduce air flow underneath the vehicle and thus reduce lift at high speeds

Aluminium block Engine cylinder block cast from aluminum, usually with cast iron sleeves or liners for the cylinder bores

Anti-roll bar Transverse rod between left and right suspension at front or rear to reduce body roll

B

B-pillar roof and door frame support behind the driver

bhp Brake horse power, 1 bhp = raising 550 foot-pounds per second; 1 bhp = torque x rpm/5252 with torque measured in foot-pounds

Blown engine or "blower" Engine fitted with a system of forced air induction such as a supercharger or turbocharger

Bucket seat Seat with added support in leg and shoulder area to secure the driver while cornering, used in rally sport

C

C-pillar Side pillar to the rear of the rear seats supporting the roof

Camshaft Engine component which controls the opening and closing of valves via lobes, either directly or indirectly

Carburetor Device for vaporizing fuel and mixing it with air in an exact ratio ready for combustion, via the inlet manifold

Chassis Component to which body, engine, gearbox and suspension are attached

Close ratio Gearbox with closely spaced ratios, used in competition

Clutch Device for controlling the transmission of power from the engine to the gearbox, usually by means of friction materials

Coil spring Helical steel alloy rod used for vehicle suspension

Column change Gearchange lever mounted on the steering column

Con rod Connecting rod that links the piston and the crankshaft, the little end connecting to the piston and the big end connecting to the crankshaft

Cylinder chamber in which piston travels, usually cylindrical in shape

Cylinder head Component which carries the sparkplugs, valves, and sometimes camshafts

D

Differential Arrangement of gears in the drive axle which allows the drive wheel on the outside of a bend to travel faster than the one on the inside

Disc brake System of braking by which friction pads are pressed against a flat, circular metal surface

Double wishbone Method of suspension where each wheel is supported by an upper and lower pivoting triangular framework

Downdraft carburettor Carburetor with a vertical barrel

Driveshaft Shaft that transmits drive from the differential to the wheel, especially on front wheel drive cars with independent rear suspension

Drivetrain Entire power transmission system from the engine's pistons to its tyres

Dry sump Where lubricating oil is contained in a separate reservoir rather than being held in the crankcase; often used in competition to prevent oil surge/starvation

E

Exhaust Device, usually of metal pipe construction, to conduct spent combustion gases away from the engine

F

Fascia A car's dashboard or instrument panel

Flathead Style of engine where the valves are mounted in the cylinder block, and the cylinder head has a flat surface

Flat twin/flat four Boxer engine configuration where cylinders are horizontally opposed to each other, such as in the VW Beetle

Floorpan Structural floor to a car, part of the chassis

Fluid clutch Clutch using a fluid coupling, flywheel, or torque converter

Forced induction Engine using a turbocharger or supercharger to pressurize the induction system to force air and hence more fuel, giving more power

Fuel injection Direct metered injection of fuel into the combustion cycle by mechanical or electro-mechanical means, first devised in 1902

G

Gearbox Component of the transmission system that houses a number of gears of different ratios that can be selected either automatically or manually by the driver. Different gears are selected to suit a variety of road speeds throughout the engine's rev range

Gear ratio The revolutions of a driving gear required to turn the driven gear through one revolution, calculated by the number of teeth on the driven gear divided by the number of teeth on the driving gear

Grand tourer Term originally used to describe an open-top luxury car, now typically a high performance coupé

Grill Metal or plastic protection for the radiator, often adopting a particular style or design of an individual manufacturer to make their car recognizable

GT Gran Turismo; Italian term used to describe a high performance luxury sports car or coupé

Gullwing Doors that open in a vertical arc, usually hinged along the centre of the roofline

H

H-pattern Conventional gear selection layout where first and third gear are furthest from the driver and second and fourth are nearest

Helical gears Gear wheel with its teeth set oblique to the gear axis which mates with another shaft with its teeth at the same angle

Hemi engine An engine with a hemispherical combustion chamber

Hydrolastic suspension System of suspension where compressible fluids act as springs, with intercon- nections between wheels to aid levelling

I

Independent suspension System of suspension where all wheels move up and down independently of each other, thus having no effect on the other wheels and aiding stability

Intercooler Device to cool supercharged or turbocharged air before it enters the engine to increase density and power

K

Kamm tail Type of rear body design developed by W. Kamm, where the rear end of the car tapers sharply over the rear window and is then cut vertically to improve aerodynamics

L

Ladder frame Tradition form of chassis with two constructional rails running front to rear with lateral members adding rigidity

Limited slip differential Device to control the difference in speed between left and right driveshafts so both wheels turn at similar speeds. Fitted to reduce the likelihood of wheelspinning on slippery surfaces

Live axle Axle assembly patented by Louis Renault in 1899. The axle contains shafts which drive the wheels

M

Manifold Pipe system used for gathering or dispersal of gas or liquids

Mid-engine Vehicle with its engine mounted just behind the driver and significantly ahead of the rear axle to provide even weight distribution, thus giving the car better handling characteristics

Monobloc An engine with all its cylinders cast in one piece

Monocoque Body design where the bodyshell carries the structural strength without conventional chassis rails (see "unitary construction")

O

Overdrive Additional higher ratio gear(s), usually on the third or fourth gear selected automatically by the driver

R

Rack and pinion System of gearing typically used in a steering box with a toothed rail driven laterally by a pinion on the end of the steering column

Radiator Device for dissipating heat, generally from the engine coolant

Rocker arms Pivoting arm translating rotational movement of the camshaft into linear movement of the valves

Roll bar Strong, usually curved bar either internally or eternally across a vehicle's roof then secured to the floor or chassis to provide protection in the event of the car turning over. Used on some open-top sportcars

Running gear General description of a vehicle's underbody mechanicals, including the suspension, steering, brakes, and drivetrain

S

Semi-elliptic spring Leaf spring suspension used on the rear axle of older cars in which the spring conforms to a specific mathematical shape

Semi-independent suspension System on a front-wheel drive car where the wheels are located by trailing links and a torsioned crossmember

Sequential gearbox Gear selection layout in which the selection is made by a linear movement rather than in the conventional H-pattern, used on some sportscars and rally cars

Servo assistance Servo powered by a vacuum, air, hydraulics, or electrically to aid the driver to give a powerful output from minimal input. Typically used on brakes, steering and clutch

Shock absorber Hydraulic device, part of the suspension system typically mounted between the wheel and the chassis to prevent unwanted movement, to increase safety and aid comfort. More correctly known as "damper"

Spark plug Device for igniting combustion gases via the arcing of current between two electrodes

"Split driveline" layout An extra set of epicyclic gears to provide a closer interval between the standard set of ratios, so an eight speed gearbox will actually have 16 gears

Spoiler Device fitted to the front of the car, low to the ground, to reduce air flow under the car and increase down-force, thus improving roadholding at higher speeds

Straight 6, 8 An engine with six or eight cylinders in a single row

Supercharger Mechanically-driven air pump used to force air into the combustion cycle, improving performance

Synchromesh Automatic synchronization using cone clutches to speed up or slow down the input shaft to smoothly engage gear, first introduced by Cadillac in 1928

T

Tachometer device for measuring rotational speed (revs per minute, rpm) of an engine

Torque The rotational twisting force exerted by the crankshaft

Traction control Electronic system of controlling the amount of power to a given wheel to reduce wheelspin

Transmission General term for the final drive, clutch and gearbox.

Transverse engine Engine type where the crankshaft lies parallel to the axle

Turbocharger Air pump for use in forced induction engines. Similar to a supercharger but driven at very high speed by exhaust gases, rather than mechanically to increase power output

U

Unibody Monocoque construction in which the floorpan, chassis and body are welded together to form one single structure

Unitary construction Monocoque bodyshell structurally rigid enough not to require a separate chassis

Unit construction Engine in which the powerplant and transmission are together as one, integrated unit

V

Venturi principle Basis upon which carburetors work: gas flowing through a narrow opening creates a partial vacuum

W

Wheelbase The measured distance between the front and rear wheel spindles

Index

88, Oldsmobile 158–61
88, Oldsmobile Super 162–5

American Graffiti 98–9
American Racing Torq-Thrust wheels
   Chevrolet Bel Air 28, 29
   Chevrolet Caprice 32, 33

A
A3 Lusso, Iso 137
A310, Renault 289
AC
   Ace 13, 296
   Cobra 289 12–15
   Cobra 427 310
   Cobra 427 Mk III 13
Ace, AC 13, 296
AJP V8, TVR 309
Alpine A110, Renault 288–91
Alpine, Sunbeam 297
ASC/McLaren, GNX 53
Aston Martin
   DB Mk III 19
   DB4 16–19
   DB5 17
   DB6 19
   Drophead Coupe 17

Virage 21
Zagato 20–3
Audi
RS2 24–7
S2 Avant 25
S4 Quattro 25

B
Bentley
   Mulsanne 29
   T1 29
   Turbo R 29
   Turbo R/T 28–31
Birdcage, Maserati 192–5
Bizzarrini GT Strada 32–5
BMW
   E36 41
   M Roadster 36–9, 44, 45
   M1 36–9
   M3 40–3
   M3 Evolution 43
   M635CSi 37
   Z3 M Coupe 44–7
   Z8 45
Bora, Maserati 196–9, 201
Bugatti, EB110 48–51
Buick
   GN 53, 54

GNX 52–5
GSX 52
Regal GNX 53, 55
T-Type 53, 54

C
C-Type, Jaguar 141, 146
C4 Corvette, Callaway 53, 57
C5 Corvette, Chevrolet 68
C43, Mercedes 221
Callaway
   C4 Corvette 53, 57
   Corvette Sledgehammer 56
   Corvette Speedster 56–9
Camaro, YSC 61, 73
Camaro ZL-1, Chevrolet 60–3
Celica, Toyota 301
Challenger T/A, Dodge 84–7
Chevrolet
   C5 Corvette 68
   Camaro ZL-1 60–3, 265
   Corvette GS 64–7, 217
   Corvette Roadster 69
   Corvette V8 136
   L88 Sting Ray 65
   Yenko Camaro 73
   Yenko Chevelle 72–5
   Yenko Corvair 73

ZR-1 65, 68–71
Chimaera, TVR 304–7
Cobra 289, AC 12–15
Cobra 427, AC 13, 310
Corvair, Yenko 73
Corvette GS, Chevrolet 64–7, 217
Corvette Roadster, Chevrolet 69
Corvette Sledgehammer, Callaway 56
Corvette Speedster, Callaway 56–9
Corvette V8, Chevrolet 136
Cosmo, Mazda 209
Cougar Eliminator, Mercury 224–7
Countach, Lamborghini 164–7, 168,
  169, 170
Cyclone, Mercury 225

D
D-Type, Jaguar 140–3, 145, 146, 149
Dart GTS 383, Dodge 85
Daytona, Ferrari 100–3, 202
DB Mk III, Aston Martin 19
DB4 GT, Aston Martin 16–19
DB5, Aston Martin 17
DB6, Aston Martin 19
De Tomaso
  Mangusta 76–9
  Pantera 77, 80–3, 196
  Vallelunga 77
Delta HF Turbo, Lancia 177
Delta Integrale, Lancia 176–9
Demon, Dodge 85
Diablo, Lamborghini 50, 165, 168–71
Diablo Roadster, Lamborghini 169
Dino 206GT, Ferrari 93
Dodge
  Challenger T/A 84–7
  Dart GTS 383 85
  Demon 85
  Hemi Daytona 117, 257
  RT/10 90
  Viper GTS-R 88–91

E
E-Type Lightweight, Jaguar 141,
  144–7, 156, 158
E36, BMW 41
E55 AMG, Mercedes 220–3
EB110, Bugatti 48–51
Espada, Lamborghini 137
Esprit S4, Lotus 189
Esprit V8, Lotus 188–91
Esprit V8 SE, Lotus 189
Evolution 2 Rally 037, Lancia 181

F
F1, McLaren 50, 212–15
F40, Ferrari 50, 104–7
F40 LM, Ferrari 105
F50, Ferrari 108–11
F355, Ferrari 93, 94
Fairlane Thunderbolt, Ford 128–31
Ferrari
  250 GTO 32, 33
  250 SWB Berlinetta 105
  275 GTB 101
  288 GTO 105, 109
  308 GT4 93
  360 Modena 92–5

365 GTB/4 101, 102
456 GT 97
512 M 98
512 TR 97
550 Maranello 96–9
Daytona 100–3, 202
Dino 206GT 93
F40 50, 104–7
F40 LM 105
F50 108–11
F355 93, 94
GTO 105
Spyder 101
Testarossa 24, 97
FF, Jensen 161
Firebird, Pontiac 265
500GT, Maserati 201
512 TR 97
512M, Ferrari 98
550 Maranello, Ferrari 96–9
Ford
  Fairlane Thunderbolt 128–31
  GT40 112–15
Mustang Boss 429 61, 116–19, 226
  Roush Mustang 120–3
  RS200 228
Shelby Mustang GT350 117, 124–7
  Shelby Mustang GT350R 125
  SVT Cobra 121
4-4-2 W30, Oldsmobile 248–51
400 GT, Lamborghini 173
456 GT, Ferrari 97
Frua, Maserati 205

G
Ghibli, Maserati 197, 200–3
Ghibli Spyder, Maserati 201
GN, Buick 53, 54
GNX, Buick 52–5
Griffith, TVR 304, 305, 308–11
Grifo, Iso 33, 136–9
GSX, Buick 52
GT, Lola 113
GT Strada, Bizzarrini 32–5
GT40, Ford 112–15
GT350, Shelby 117
GTO, Ferrari 105
GTO Judge, Pontiac 260–3

H
Hemi 'Cuda, Plymouth 61, 252–5
Hemi Daytona, Dodge 117, 257
Hemi Superbird, Plymouth 117,
  256–9
Honda
  NSX 134
  NSX-R 132–5

I
Impreza, Subaru 292–5
Integrale Evoluzione, Lancia 177
Interceptor, Jensen 160–3
Iso
  A3/C 137
  A3 Lusso 137
  Grifo 33, 136–9
  Lele 137

J
Jaguar
  C-Type 141, 146
  D-Type 140–3, 145, 146, 149
  E-Type Lightweight 141, 144–7,
    156, 158
  XJ13 148–51, 154
  XJ220 49, 152–5
  XK8 157
  XKR 156–9
  XKSS 141
Jensen
  FF 161
  Interceptor 160–3

L
L88 Sting Ray, Chevrolet 65
Lamborghini
  400 GT 173
  Countach 164–7, 168, 169, 170
  Diablo 50, 165, 168–71
  Diablo Roadster 169
  Espada 137
  LP400 165
  LP500S 165
  Miura 164, 172–5
  Miura S 173
  Miura SV 173
  Quattrovalvole 165
Lancer Evo V, Mitsubishi 236–9
Lancia
  Delta HF Turbo 177
  Delta Integrale 176–9
  Evolution 2 Rally 037 181
  Integrale Evoluzione 177
  Montecarlo 181
  Rally 037 180–3
  Stratos 184–7
Lele, Iso 137
Lola, GT 113
Lotus
  Esprit S4 189
  Esprit V8 188–91
  Esprit V8 SE 189
  S2 189
  Sport 300 189
LP400, Lamborghini 165
LP500S, Lamborghini 165

M
M Roadster, BMW 44, 45, 46
M1, BMW 36–9
M3, BMW 40–3
M3 Evolution, BMW 43
M635CSi, BMW 37
Mangusta, De Tomaso 76–9
Maserati
  500GT 201
  3500GT 204, 205
  Birdcage 192–5
  Bora 196–9, 201
  Frua 205
  Ghibli 197, 200–3
  Ghibli Spyder 201
  Merak 197
  Sebring 204–7
  Tipo 60 193
Mazda

Cosmo 209
RX-01 209
RX-7 208–11
McLaren
  F1 50, 212–15
  GNX 53
Merak, Maserati 197
Mercedes
  300SL 216–19
  C43 221
  E55 AMG 220–3
Mercury
  Cougar Eliminator 224–7
  Cyclone 225
Metro 6R4, MG 228–31
MG, Metro 6R4 228–31
Mitsubishi
  3000 GT 232–5
  Lancer Evo V 236–9
Miura, Lamborghini 164, 172–5
Miura S, Lamborghini 173
Miura SV, Lamborghini 173
Montecarlo, Lancia 181
Mulsanne, Bentley 29
Mustang Boss 429, Ford 61, 116–19,
  226

N
911 Carrera 2.7, Porsche 268–71
911 Carrera 4, Porsche 283
911 Carrera 4S, Porsche 273
911, Porsche 24, 26, 94, 269, 278,
  280, 281
911 RS 3.0, Porsche 269
911 Ruf, Porsche 272–5
917, Porsche 279
935 K3, Porsche 277
935, Porsche 276–9
993 Turbo, Porsche 280–3
Nissan
  240Z 241
  300ZX Turbo 240–3
  Skyline Turbo 244–7
NSX, Honda 134
NSX-R, Honda 132–5

O
Oldsmobile, 4-4-2 W30 248–51

P
Pantera, De Tomaso 77, 80–3, 196
Plymouth
  Hemi 'Cuda 61, 252–5
  Hemi Superbird 117, 256–9
Pontiac
  Firebird 265
  GTO Judge 260–3
  Ram Air IV 61
  Trans AM SD 264–7
Porsche
  356 269
  911 24, 26, 94, 269, 278, 280, 281
  911 Carrera 2.7 268–71
  911 Carrera 4 283
  911 Carrera 4S 273
  911 RS 3.0 269
  911 Ruf 272–5
  917 279

935 276–9
935 K3 277
993 Turbo 280–3

Q
Quattrovalvole, Lamborghini 165

R
R5 Turbo, Renault 285
Rally 037, Lancia 180–3
Ram Air IV, Pontiac 61
Regal GNX, Buick 53, 55
Renault
  5 Turbo 2 284–7
  16 289
  A310 289
  Alpine A110 288–91
R5 Turbo 285
Roush Mustang, Ford 120–3
Rover, Vitesse 310
RS2, Audi 24–7
RS200, Ford 228
RT/10, Dodge 90
RX-01, Mazda 209
RX-7, Mazda 208–11

S
S2 Avant, Audi 25
S2, Lotus 189
S4 Quattro, Audi 25
Sebring, Maserati 204–7
Shelby Mustang GT350, Ford 117,
  124–7
16, Renault 289
Skyline Turbo, Nissan 244–7
Sport 300, Lotus 189
Spyder, Ferrari 101
Stratos, Lancia 184–7
Subaru, Impreza 292–5
Sunbeam
  Alpine 297
  Tiger 296–9
Supra Turbo, Toyota 300–3
SVT Cobra, Ford 121

T
T-Type, Buick 53, 54
T1, Bentley 29
Testarossa, Ferrari 24, 97
300SL, Mercedes 216–19
300ZX Turbo, Nissan 240–3
308GT4, Ferrari 93
356, Porsche 269
360 Modena, Ferrari 92–5
365 GTB/4, Ferrari 101, 102
3000 GT, Mitsubishi 232–5
3500GT, Maserati 204, 205
Tiger, Sunbeam 296–9
Tipo 60, Maserati 193
Toyota
  Celica 301
  Supra Turbo 300–3
Trans AM SD, Pontiac 264–7
Turbo R, Bentley 29
Turbo R/T, Bentley 28–31
TVR
  AJP V8 309
  Chimaera 304–7

Griffith 304, 305, 308–11
240Z, Nissan 241
250 GTO, Ferrari 32, 33
250 SWB Berlinetta 105
275 GTB, Ferrari 101
288 GTO, Ferrari 105, 109

V
Vallelunga, De Tomaso 77
Vector
  W8-M12 312–15
  WX3 313
Viper GTS-R, Dodge 88–91
Virage, Aston Martin 21
Vitesse, Rover 310

W
W8-M12, Vector 312–15
WX3, Vector 313

X
XJ13, Jaguar 148–51, 154
XJ220, Jaguar 49, 152–5
XK8, Jaguar 157
XKR, Jaguar 156–9
XKSS, Jaguar 141

Y
Yenko Camaro, Chevrolet 61, 73
Yenko Chevelle, Chevrolet 72–5
Yenko Corvair, Chevrolet 73

Z
Z3 M Coupe, BMW 44–7
Z8, BMW 45
Zagato, Aston Martin 20–3
ZR-1, Chevrolet 65, 68–71